SUMMER WILDFLOWERS OF NEW MEXICO

Summer Wildflowers of New Mexico

William C. Martin
and Charles R. Hutchins

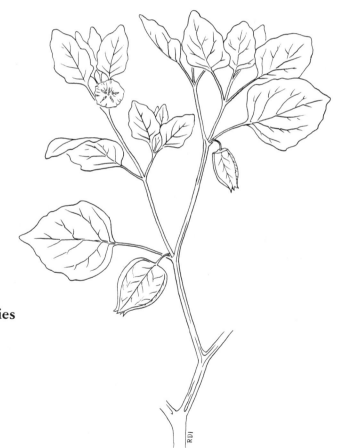

**The New Mexico
Natural History Series**

Barry S. Kues,
General Editor

University
of New Mexico Press

Albuquerque

Library of Congress Cataloging in Publication Data

Martin, William C., 1923–
  Summer wildflowers of New Mexico.

  (The New Mexico Natural History series)
  Includes index.
  1. Wild flowers—New Mexico—Identification.
I. Hutchins, Charles R., 1928–   II. Ivey, Robert
DeWitt.   III. Title.   Series.
QK176.M38   1986   582.13'09789   85-24629
ISBN 0-8263-0859-7
ISBN 0-8263-0860-0 (pbk.)

Color illustrations printed in Japan.

Contents

Introduction

Most people, even those with little or no formal training in botany, find flowering plants attractive and interesting and have developed a certain curosity about the identity and characteristics of the plants they encounter throughout our state.

New Mexico wildflowers are abundant in many habitats and in several life zones, ranging from desert areas in the southern part of the state to the alpine summits of the Sangre de Cristo range in the north-central part.

Of the more than four thousand species of plants growing wild in New Mexico, probably over a third of these can be designated as wildflowers, depending, of course, on one's definition of the term *wildflower*. By the usual definition, these plants are those whose flowers, by virtue of size, shape, or color, tend to attract attention. The dictionary definition would include in this category all plants growing without cultivation.

In this book, we have attempted to characterize and illustrate the major summer-blooming wildflowers of New Mexico. These plants are arranged according to family; for example, those belonging to the Lily family are grouped together because of associated characteristics. The same applies to those species belonging to other families.

Originally, we considered combining all plants having similar flower colors into groups, but we were reluctant to do so because a number of species may exhibit two or more color variants. We did not want to associate plants not necessarily closely related.

We have attempted to make the initial identification somewhat easier and more efficient by providing keys to identification to families and genera, using the common names for both family and generic categories. Final separation of species can be easily determined from the descriptions in the text.

Each wildflower in this book is described briefly, and pertinent data relating to general habitat, geographical distribution, and elevational range are presented. Each plant is designated by a number and by both common and scientific names. The number designating each species is the reference

1

number shown in both the index and the keys to identification and is not necessarily related to page numbers. In the text, descriptive material is presented on facing pages. The left page contains the description of three or four species; the right page presents drawings representative of these plants.

Note also, in the following section, a discussion pertaining to the use of the keys in the identification of families and genera. Of course, if one already has some idea about the identity of a particular plant, one can go the index and find the reference number, then compare the unknown plant with the descriptions and drawings.

This book is the second of a series of three books on the wildflowers of our state. The first volume dealt with the spring wildflowers; this second volume will concentrate on the summer wildflowers, and the third volume on the wildflowers that bloom in autumn. All books will be profusely illustrated.

Use of Keys To Identification

Most keys to identification are based on a series of alternative statements or couplets about the characteristics in question. Thus, identification, by use of a key, involves a simple process of elimination.

Note that major characteristics are designated in the keys by number and letter symbols, with pairs of alternatives following in succession. At the end of certain alternatives, instructions in parentheses direct the reader to another set of alternatives. This procedure continues, couplet by couplet, until one or more final categories are reached, beneath which a listing of one or more pertinent families and genera is provided. In some cases, the final category may direct the reader to additional keys to large groups, such as the Lily or Aster families.

For example, the first alternative, category 1a, is shown at the beginning of the key indicating "flower parts in 3s or 6s; leaf veins parallel." The alternative to this is the second part of the couplet or 1b which indicates "flower parts mostly in 4s or 5s, sometimes of 7 or more parts; leaf veins mostly branched." The next set of alternatives shown under 1a is that of ovary position, above or below the point of attachment of the petals and sepals. The choices lead directly to a listing of family and genus categories with an abbreviated list of characteristics, including flower color, noted for each one. Under alternative 1b, the next step is combination 3a and 3b, then successively 4a and 4b, 5a and 5b, 6a and 6b, and so on, until one or more families and genera are reached.

Let us consider an example to illustrate the use of this key. An analysis of flower parts of an unknown plant indicates that there are 5 petals present. The first alternative, category 1a, indicates parts in 3s or 6s, thus we select the characteristics for 1b; these describe the flower parts as being in 4s or 5s, or 7 or more. The instructions following 1b send us to alternatives 3a or 3b. Category 3a points out that flowers are arranged in headlike clusters, like those of daisies or dandelions. We decide that the flowers are not in headlike clusters, but in some other arrangement, thus category 3b is selected. Because there are 5 petals, we then proceed to alternative 4b.

Further examination of the flower shows that the petals are not all the same size or shape, thus the instructions at the end of 4a send us to 5a. Examination of the leaves shows the leaf arrangement is scattered or alternate; we proceed to 6a. Finally, because the flowers have a backward-pointing spur or spurs at the base, we choose alternative 9a. This final category leaves us with a comparatively simple choice between the Buttercup family, the Fumitory family, and the Violet family, based on some easily determined characters of flower and leaf morphology and flower color. If the stamens are numerous and leaves are palmately divided, our selection is the Buttercup family, more specifically the larkspurs. The numbers in parentheses following "Larkspur" refer to the numbers in the text of the three larkspurs in this category. A single choice can then easily be made, based on description and key characters. All unknowns can be keyed out in much the same way down to a few easily separated choices.

In order to assist the reader in better understanding the meaning of the relatively few technical terms used in this book, an illustrated glossary immediately follows on page 5. The terms are briefly described, this description often followed by a sketch illustrating the term. We have eliminated technical terms whenever possible but are aware that in some instances, the meaning of a particular term cannot be efficiently duplicated in everyday language.

Glossary

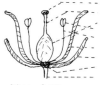

Typical Flower

stigma ⎫
style ⎬ *pistil*
ovary ⎭
anther ⎫ *stamen*
filament ⎭
petal—corolla ⎫ *perianth*
sepal—calyx ⎭
receptacle
pedicel

Achene. A dry one-seeded fruit that does not split open, common in the sunflower and buttercup families.

Acuminate. Tapering to a long point, as in the tip of a leaf.

Acute. Leaf tips or bases with margins that meet at an acute angle.

Alternate. Referring to parts of a plant (such as leaves or branches) that occur singly at a node.

Annual. A plant that germinates, develops, flowers, and fruits in a single growing season.

Anther. The saclike part of the stamen that contains the pollen.

Apex. The tip.

Apical. Occurring at the apex.

Armed. Bearing sharp-pointed projections.

Ascending. Angling upward, between growing straight up and spreading horizontally.

Axillary. Occurring in the axil between two connecting parts, such as where a leaf stalk joins the stem.

Banner. The upper petal of certain flowers such as pealike legume flowers.

Acuminate

Acute

Alternate

Ascending

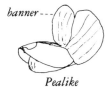

banner---

Pealike

5

Beak. A narrow projection on fruits or flower parts.

Berry. A fleshy fruit, not splitting open.

Bipinnate. Twice pinnate; as in one section of a pinnate leaf being again pinnate.

Blade. The expanded portion, especially of a leaf.

Bract. A modified leaf, usually subtending a flower or a group of flowers.

Bulb. An underground stem composed of fleshy scales and a very short axis.

Caespitose. Tufted or matted; occurring in tufts; many stems from the top of a single root.

Calyx. The outer whorl of perianth (flower) parts, referring to all the sepals.

Capitate. Headlike, often referring to a dense cluster.

Capsule. A dry, variously shaped fruit that splits open and has two or more compartments and usually several seeds.

Cordate. Heart-shaped.

Corm. A fleshy underground stem bearing inconspicuous, scalelike leaves.

Corolla. The inner whorl of perianth (flower) parts, referring to all the petals.

Corymb. A flat-topped or convex flower cluster with the lower pedicels longer than the upper ones, and the outer flowers maturing first.

Cyme. A flower cluster similar to a corymb with the central flowers maturing first.

Deciduous. Falling off.

Decumbent. Referring to stems with the base prostrate but with the terminal parts erect or ascending.

Deflexed. Bent or turned downward.

Dentate. Toothed, the teeth having approximately equal sides.

Digitate. With separate parts or lobes diverging from a common point of origin.

Entire. With an unbroken smooth margin.

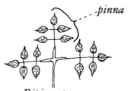

Bipinnate or
Twice-compound

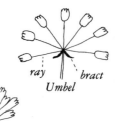

Umbel

Capitate

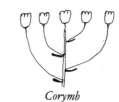

Corymb

Decumbent

Dentate

Palmate or Digitate

Entire

Epidermis. The outer layer of cells of the various plant parts.

Exserted. Projecting beyond, usually applying to flower parts such as stamens.

Fascicle. A cluster or bundle, as in a fascicle of leaves.

Filament. The stalk of an anther.

Free. With parts not united.

Fruit. A mature ovary; the seed-bearing structure of a plant.

Glabrous. Without hairs.

Globose. Spherical or rounded.

Hastate. Having divergent lobes at the base, as in leaves.

Head. A dense cluster of flowers subtended by bracts, the flowers sessile on a common receptacle.

Herb. A nonwoody plant.

Included. Not projecting beyond, as in stamens not protruding from a flower.

Involucre. A series of bracts subtending a cluster of flowers.

Irregular. Referring to a flower showing differences in size or shape of similar parts.

Lanceolate. Lance-shaped, broadest below the middle.

Lateral. Borne on the sides.

Leaflet. A division of a compound leaf.

Linear. Slender; having parallel sides, usually 8–10 times longer than wide.

Lobed. Having lobes (parts resulting from partial division).

Lyrate. Pinnatifid with small lower lobes and a large, rounded terminal lobe.

Oblanceolate. Lanceolate but attached at the narrow end and broadest above the middle.

Oblique. Slanted, with sides unequal.

Hastate

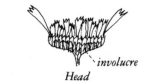

Head ‑ *involucre*

Irregular Flower

Linear

Lanceolate

Lobed

Lyrate

Oblanceolate

Oblique

Oblong. Elongate, with sides roughly parallel, usually less than eight times longer than wide.

Obovate. Ovate but attached at the narrow end and broadest above the middle.

Obtuse. Blunt, often referring to a leaf tip with the sides forming an obtuse angle.

Opposite. Referring to parts of a plant (such as leaves or branches) occurring in pairs on opposite sides of a node.

Ovate. Egg-shaped, broadest below the middle.

Palmate. With separate parts or lobes diverging from a common point of origin.

Panicle. Usually referring to any compound flower cluster.

Pealike. A corolla composed of a banner, wings, and keel, as in certain legume flowers.

Pedicel. The stalk of a single flower.

Perennial. A plant that lives for more than two years.

Petal. A single segment or unit of a corolla.

Petiole. The stalk of a leaf.

Pinna. A primary division of a pinnate or a pinnately compound leaf.

Pinnae. Plural of pinna.

Pinnate. Having leaflets arranged in two rows along a common axis.

Pinnatifid. Cleft, divided, or incised in a pinnate manner.

Pod. A dry fruit that splits open.

Prickle. A sharp projection from the epidermis of a plant.

Procumbent. Lying on the ground.

Prostrate. Lying flat on the ground.

Raceme. A cluster of flowers having an elongated axis with flowers borne on simple pedicels along the axis.

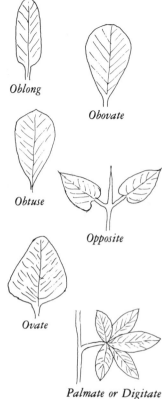

Oblong

Obovate

Obtuse

Opposite

Ovate

Palmate or Digitate

Panicle

Pealike

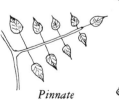

Pinnate

Raceme

Recurved. Curved downward or backward.

Reflexed. Bent sharply downward or backward.

Rhizome. A generally horizontal underground stem.

Sagittate. Shaped like an arrowhead, and with a V-shaped notch at the base.

Sagittate

Scarious. Thin, dry, and papery.

Sepal. A segment or unit of the calyx.

Sessile. Without a stalk, usually in reference to flowers or leaves.

Shrub. A woody plant, usually with several main stems and less than 15 ft. (4.5 m) tall.

Spatulate

Spatulate. Club-shaped, narrowed at the base, broader and rounded at the tip.

Spike. An elongated flower cluster bearing sessile flowers.

Spine. A leaf or part of a leaf modified into a sharp projection.

Spike

Spreading. Strongly diverging from the main axis, nearly horizontal, as applied to hairs, branches, fruiting pedicels, etc.

Spur. A hollow projection from a calyx or corolla.

Stipule. An appendage of a leaf, often attached where the petiole joins the stem.

stipule

Stipule

Stolon. A modified, horizontal, above-ground stem, usually developing roots at the nodes.

Tendril. A leaf modified into a slender, twining, holdfast structure.

Terminal. Of the end or apex.

Thorn. A modified branch, typically sharp-pointed at the tip.

Toothed. Having teeth, as in variously irregular leaf margins.

Trifoliolate

Trifoliolate. Having three leaflets.

Truncate. Having the end flattened or squared off.

Tuber. A thickened, fleshy, modified underground stem, usually a food-storage organ.

Truncate

Umbel. A flower cluster having flowers on pedicels or having rays of about equal length, these from the same point of origin at the apex of the flower stalk.

Unarmed. Not having prickles, spines, or thorns.

Undulate. Wavy on the margins.

Undulate

9

Vining. Referring to stems that trail or creep along the ground or along other supports.

Viscid. Sticky.

Whorled. Parts occurring in groups of three or more at one node, all at the same level, applied to branches or leaves.

Whorled

Key To Common Names of Families and Genera

1a. Flower parts in 3s or 6s; leaf veins parallel, not branched. (See 2a or 2b.)

1b. Flower parts mostly in 4s or 5s, sometimes of 7 or more parts; leaf veins mostly branched. (See 3a or 3b.)

2a. Ovary placed above the point of petal and sepal attachment.
Lily family. Sepals and petals usually similar; flowers rarely subtended by conspicuous bracts. See key to *Lily family* on page 31.
Spiderwort family. Sepals and petals unlike; flowers always subtended by conspicuous bracts.
   Dayflower (1). Petals unequal in size; staminal filaments without hairs. Flowers blue or white.
   Spiderwort (2). Petals equal in size; staminal filaments hairy. Flowers blue or white.

2b. Ovary placed below the point of petal and sepal attachment.
Amaryllis family. Stamens 6, pointing inward; sepals and petals similar.
   Century plant (19, 20). Leaves large and thickish, spine-tipped, in conspicuous basal rosettes. Flowers greenish yellow or yellow.
   Zephyr lily (21). Leaves grasslike. Flowers white, yellow, or pink.
Iris family. Leaves folded lengthwise and overlapping; 3 stamens; petals similar.
   Iris (24). Flowers more than 2 in. (50 mm) long. Flowers blue or white.
   Blue-eyed grass (22, 23). Flowers not more than 3/4 in. (20 mm) long. Flowers blue, white, or orange yellow.
Orchid family. Lower petal differing from the other petals in appearance. Lower petal conspicuous and saclike.
   Lady's slipper (25). Leaves at least 1 5/8 in. (4 cm) wide, scattered along the stem. Flowers yellow.

Fairy slipper (26). Leaves less than 1 ⁵/₈ in. (4 cm) wide, solitary at
the base of the stem. Flowers rose-colored with yellowish markings.
Lower petal usually not conspicuous and not saclike.
Leaves reduced to nongreen scales.
Spotted coralroot (27). Flowers brownish purple except for the
whitish, purple-spotted lower petal.
Leaves green, not reduced to scales.
Rattlesnake-plantain (28). Leaves basal, whitish along the veins.
Helleborine (29). Stems tall, leafy, with clasping, conspicuously
veined leaves. Flowers conspicuous.
Lady's tresses (30). Flowers small, whitish, in dense, usually
twisted racemes; lip petal irregularly toothed at the apex.
Bog orchid (31, 32, 33). Flowers small, purplish, greenish, or
whitish, in narrow racemes; lip petal with a slender spur at the
base.

3a. Flowers in headlike clusters resembling those of daisies or dandelions.
Aster family. See key to *Aster family* on page 39.

3b. Flowers not arranged in the above manner. (See 4a or 4b.)

4a. Petals or petallike parts 7 or more.
Buttercup family. Ovaries and stamens spirally arranged. Flowers white.
Marsh marigold; elk's lip (58). Leaves heart-shaped.
Baneberry (57). Leaves divided into 2 or 3 sets of 3 leaflets.
Cactus family. Stems jointed, somewhat fleshy; leaves reduced to spines.
Flowers conspicuous, with numerous parts. See key to *Cactus family* on
page 37.
Purslane family. Low-growing herbs with fleshy leaves.
Bitterroot (47). Nearly naked flowering stems. Flowers red or pink.
Loosestrife family. Plants with often angled stems and branches and
opposite or alternate leaves. Flowers white or purple.
Loosestrife (191). Leaves alternate, entire, lance-shaped to oblong.
Flowers pink or purple.
Loasa family. Herbage with barbed or stinging hairs.
Stickleaf (180, 181). Leaves and stems with short, barbed hairs; 20 or
more stamens. Flowers yellow.
Lizard's-tail family. Herbs of moist places; leaves oblong-ovate; flowers in
conical spikes.
Yerba mansa (34). Flower spikes subtended by several white, petallike
structures.

4b. Petals or petallike parts 4–6. (See 5a or 5b.)

5a. Petals or corolla lobes unequal in size and/or shape. (See 6a or 6b.)

5b. Petals or corolla lobes equal or nearly so in size and/or shape. (See 11a
or 11b.)

6a. Leaves opposite or whorled. (See 7a or 7b.)

6b. Leaves alternate or basal. (See 9a or 9b.)

7a. Shrubs or trees.

Catalpa family. Flowers mostly 1¼–2 in. (30–50 mm) long; 2 or 4 stamens.

> *Desert willow* (300). Leaves simple. Flowers white or pink.

Honeysuckle family. Flowers usually 2 or more per cluster, mostly less than 1 in. (25 mm) long.

> *Inkberry* (313). Shrubs with simple leaves and flower clusters subtended by conspicuous bracts. Flowers yellow.
>
> *Elderberry* (309, 310). Flowers regular; leaves pinnately compound. Flowers white to pale yellow.
>
> *Snowberry* (312). Flowers regular; leaves simple.

Vervain family. Stems often 4–angled. Flowers tending to be irregular.

> *Aloysia* (253). Aromatic shrubs with terminal spikes. Flowers white or blue.

Acanthus family. Plants with 4–angled stems and simple, opposite leaves.

> *Desert honeysuckle* (303). Shrubs with whitish, peeling bark. Flowers reddish to orange.

7b. Herbs, the stems not woody. (See 8a or 8b.)

8a. Stems 4–angled.

Mint family. Flowers strongly 2–lipped; plants aromatic.

> Fertile stamens 2.
>> *Horsemint* (260, 261). Calyx with 5 equal teeth. Flowers purplish, pink, or white.
>>
>> *False pennyroyal* (262). Calyx 2–lipped; upper lip of corolla flat. Flowers pink or purple.
>>
>> *Sage* (263, 264). Calyx 2–lipped; upper lip of corolla curved. Flowers red, blue, or purple.
>
> Fertile stamens 4.
>> Calyx with 10 teeth.
>>> *Horehound* (270). Stems densely whitish woolly; calyx 10–ribbed. Flowers white to purple.
>>
>> Calyx with 5 or fewer teeth.
>>> Calyx 15–nerved or -ribbed.
>>>> *Giant hyssop* (268). Leaves often triangular and coarsely toothed. Flowers whitish.
>>>
>>> Calyx 10– or fewer-nerved.
>>>> *Germander* (265). Calyx 5–toothed; upper corolla lobe much shorter than the lower. Flowers white, blue, or pink.
>>>>
>>>> *Woundwort* (266). Leaves sessile or nearly so, flattish or notched at the base.
>>>>
>>>> *Selfheal* (267). Leaves petioled; flowers in dense, terminal spikes. Flowers violet.

Mint (269). Flowers in clusters in the axils of the upper leaf pairs. Flowers pink to violet or white.

Vervain family. Leaves variously toothed or lobed; stems often square; 5 corolla lobes, slightly unequal; 4 stamens, in 2 groups.

Phyla (254). Flowers in dense axillary clusters on conspicuous stalks; fruits of 2 nutlets. Flowers bluish or whitish.

Vervain (255, 256, 257, 258, 259). Flowers in terminal spikes or headlike clusters; fruits of 4 nutlets. Flowers pinkish to purplish.

8b. Stems round.

Figwort family. Corolla usually strongly 2–lipped; 2 or 4 stamens.

Toadflax (282). Corolla tube with a slender spur at the base; leaves linear or oblong. Flowers yellow.

Beardtongue (284, 285, 286, 287, 288). Corolla strongly 2–lipped, the fifth stamen represented by a sterile, often hairy filament. Flowers red, blue, or purple.

Speedwell (289). Corolla slightly irregular, not obviously 2–lipped; 2 stamens. Flowers white or blue.

Monkeyflower (290). Lower side of corolla tube with a pair of longitudinal ridges; leaves not lobed, often ovate or rounded. Flowers yellow.

Milkwort family. Slender herbs with irregular flowers in terminal, spikelike racemes. Flowers white.

Milkwort (164). Flowers white with greenish center.

Vervain family. Leaves variously toothed or lobed; stems often square; 5 corolla lobes, slightly unequal; 4 stamens, in 2 groups.

Phyla (254). Flowers in dense axillary clusters on conspicuous stalks; fruits of 2 nutlets. Flowers bluish or whitish.

Vervain (255, 256, 257, 258, 259). Flowers in terminal spikes or headlike clusters; fruits of 4 nutlets. Flowers pinkish or purplish.

Unicorn-plant family. Low plants; leaves long-stalked, with sticky hairs.

Unicorn-plant (301). Leaves triangular-ovate. Flowers reddish purple or white.

Honeysuckle family. Flowers usually 2 or more per cluster, mostly less than 1 in. (25 mm) long.

Twinflower (311). Delicate herb with simple leaves. Flowers whitish or pinkish.

Valerian family. Stamens 1–4, fewer than and inserted on the corolla lobes.

Valerian (314). Tall stems with pinnatifid leaves. Corolla yellowish.

9a. Flowers with a backward-pointing spur at the base.

Buttercup family. Stamens numerous.

Larkspur (60, 61). Leaves palmately divided. Flowers bluish.

Fumatory family. Leaves repeatedly dissected into many small segments.

Corydalis (70). Leaves and stems smooth. Flowers whitish to purplish.

Violet family. Leaves heart-shaped or lance-shaped.

Violet (177, 178). Flowers violet or yellow.

9b. Flowers not spurred. (See 10a or 10b.)

10a. Stamens 2–5, occasionally 6.

Figwort family. Corolla usually strongly 2-lipped; 2 or 4, occasionally 5 stamens.

    Stamens 2 or 5.

        Mullein (281). Stems and leaves softly and densely hairy. Flowers yellow.

        Speedwell (289). Corolla slightly irregular, not obviously 2-lipped; 2 stamens. Flowers white or blue.

        Kittentails (291, 292). Leaves basal; stems with a terminal, conspicuously bracted spike. Flowers white to purple.

    Stamens 4.

        Toadflax (282). Corolla tube with a slender spur at the base; leaves linear or oblong. Flowers yellow.

        Vining snapdragon (283). Stems prostrate; leaves triangular. Flowers blue.

        Clubflower (293). Leaves divided into 3–5 filiform divisions. Flowers yellowish or purplish.

        Lousewort (294, 295). Leaves toothed to pinnatifid; flower clusters in terminal racemes; upper lobe of corolla arched or beaked. Flowers yellowish green or reddish purple.

        Paintbrush (296, 297, 298). Plants with conspicuous colorful floral bracts and inconspicuous flowers. Flowers usually some shade of red.

        Owlclover (299). Leafy annuals with leaves sessile or nearly so; inflorescence terminal and bracteate. Flowers yellow.

Broomrape family. Yellowish brown to purplish, nongreen stems; leaves scalelike. Flowers tubular, curved, yellowish brown to brownish purple.

    Broomrape; cancerroot (302). Parasitic. Flowers brownish purple.

Legume family. Leaves usually compound; 10 or more stamens.

    Ratany (118). Sepals unequal; upper 3 petals constricted at the base; lower 2 petals greatly reduced and greenish. Flowers reddish.

Unicorn-plant family. Low plants; leaves long-stalked, with sticky hairs.

    Unicorn-plant (301). Leaves triangular-ovate. Flowers reddish purple or white.

Catalpa family. Flowers mostly 1¼–2 in. (30–50 mm) long; 2 or 4 stamens.

    Desert willow (300). Leaves simple. Flowers white or pink.

Bluebell family. Flowers strongly irregular; staminal filament tube at least 15 mm long.

    Cardinal flower (318). Tall herb with toothed leaves. Flowers red.

10b. Stamens 7–10 or more.

Legume family. Leaves usually compound; 10 or more stamens. See key to *Legume family* on page 33.

Buttercup family. Ovaries and stamens spirally arranged; some members with irregular flowers.

Monkshood (59). Usually tall stems; leaves palmately cleft. Flowers purplish.

Milkwort family. Slender herbs with irregular flowers in terminal, spikelike racemes.

    Milkwort (164). Flowers white with greenish center.

11a. Stamens 8–many. (See 12a or 12b.)

11b. Stamens 2–7. (See 21a or 21b.)

12a. Leaves simple. (See 13a or 13b.)

12b. Leaves compound or appearing so. (See 17a or 17b.)

13a. Shrubs or trees, the stems woody and having bark. (See 14a or 14b.)

13b. Herbs, the stems not woody, devoid of bark. (See 15a or 15b.)

14a. Petals united to form a somewhat tubelike flower.

Heath family. Flowers urn-shaped; stems with many branches.

    Whortleberry (207). Low, spreading shrubs with often angled branches; leaves minutely toothed. Flowers white or pink, somewhat globe-shaped.

14b. Petals separate.

Rose family. Leaves alternate, often compound; stipules usually present.

    Western thimbleberry (101). Low, spreading shrub with simple, palmately lobed leaves. Flowers white.

    Apache plume (109). Leaves pinnately lobed; petals falling easily; styles conspicuously hairy. Flowers white.

    Cliffrose (110). Shrubs with glandular-dotted leaves. Flowers yellow.

Saxifrage family. Leaves simple, opposite or alternate, veined.

    Fenderella (95). Flowers in cymes; shrubs with small, opposite, often lanceolate leaves. Flowers white.

    Fendlerbush (96). Large shrubs with many branches; leaves lanceolate, often rolled under on the edges. Flowers white.

    Mock-orange (97). Large shrubs with many branches; leaves entire, mostly not more than ³/₄ in. (20 mm) long. Flowers white.

Tamarisk family. Small trees with drooping branchlets; leaves reduced to tiny scales.

    Tamarisk (176). Flowers pinkish or whitish.

Evening primrose family. Leaves alternate; 4 petals and sepals; 8 stamens.

    Calylophus (198). Subshrub with flowers in the axils of the upper leaves; stigmas unlobed. Flowers yellow.

15a. Stamens 15 or more. (See 16a or 16b.)

15b. Stamens 4–14.

Evening primrose family. Leaves alternate; 4 petals and sepals; 8 stamens. Petals ¹/₁₂–¹/₄ in. (2–6 mm) long.

    Gaura (192, 193). Flowers in narrow elongated clusters; petals not more than 6 mm long; stigmas with 4 slender lobes. Flowers white to pale pink.

Petals 1/4–1 1/2 in. (7–40 mm) long.

Fireweed (194). Tall perennial with large, lanceolate leaves. Flowers pink.

Evening primrose (195, 196, 197). Flowers in the axils of the upper leaves; petals mostly more than 3/8 in. (10 mm) long; stigmas with 4 conspicuous slender lobes. Flowers white, pink, or yellow.

Calylophus (198). Subshrub with flowers in the axils of the upper leaves; stigmas unlobed. Flowers yellow.

Geranium family. Leaves palmately or pinnately lobed; 5 petals and sepals; 5 or 10 stamens; fruit elongate and beaklike.

Geranium (156, 157). Stamens 10. Flowers white, pink, or purple.

Purslane family. Leaves fleshy; often 2 sepals.

Bitterroot (47). Sepals 2–8; petals 4–18. Flowers pinkish or reddish.

Flame flower. (48, 49). Sepals 2; petals 5; ovary completely superior. Flowers orange to pink, red, or purple.

Loosestrife family. Plants with often angled stems and branches and opposite or alternate leaves.

Loosestrife (191). Leaves alternate, entire, lanceolate to oblong. Flowers pink or purple.

Saxifrage family. Leaves simple, often with a rounded heart shape; 5, 8, or 10 stamens.

Alumroot (90, 91, 92). Leaves rounded, palmately veined; 5 stamens. Flowers red, pink, or greenish white.

Saxifrage (93, 94). Leaves ovate; petals sometimes notched at the tip; 10 stamens. Flowers white.

Heath family. Plants often evergreen; flowers urn-shaped or rotate.

Plants not green.

Pinedrops (208). Stems reddish purple or reddish brown; leaves scalelike, scattered. Flowers with united petals.

Pinesap (209). Stems reddish; leaves of reddish scales. Flowers with free petals.

Plants green.

Pipsissewa (210). Leaves thick, evergreen, lustrous, often whorled. Flowers nodding, white to pink or purple.

Sidebells (211). Leaves mostly basal; flowers in one-sided racemes. Flowers greenish white.

Wintergreen (212). Scapose, evergreen. Flowers nodding, greenish white.

Stonecrop family. Low perennials; leaves and stems fleshy.

Sedum (86, 87, 88). Flowers white, pink, or yellow.

Buckwheat family. Leaves usually with conspicuous stipules sheathing the stem.

Western dock (35). Leaves lanceolate; perianth of 6 parts.

Bistort (36). Leaves oblong to oblanceolate; perianth pinkish.

Caltrop family. Herbs and shrubs, often with compound leaves.

    Peganum (163). Glabrous perennial herb; leaves simple but variously pinnatifid. Flowers whitish to yellowish.

16a. Stems bearing spines, barbed bristles, or star-shaped hairs.

Cactus family. Stems jointed, somewhat fleshy; leaves reduced to spines. Flowers conspicuous, with numerous parts. See key to *Cactus family* on page 37.

Loasa family. Herbage with barbed or stinging hairs.

    Stickleaf (180, 181). Leaves and stems with short, barbed hairs; 20 or more stamens. Flowers yellow.

    Cevallia (179). Leaves and stems with slender, stinging hairs; 5 stamens. Flowers with whitish, plumelike petals and sepals.

Mallow family. Herbage with star-shaped hairs; stamens united into a column.

    Globemallow (171, 172, 173). Stamens appearing at the summit of the staminal tube; carpels splitting into segments resembling orange slices. Flowers orange, sometimes tinged with red.

    Prairie mallow (167). Leaves with rounded outline but palmately lobed. Flowers white.

    Mallow (168). Leaves rounded in outline, often slightly lobed, the margins with small, rounded teeth. Flowers white to pale blue.

    Wild hollyhock (170). Leaves large, stalked, 3- to 7-lobed. Flowers white to purple, constricted at the base.

    Poppy mallow (169). Leaves pedately cleft. Flowers white to purple, somewhat toothed at the tip.

    Scurfy mallow (174). Stamens appearing at the summit of the staminal tube; calyx without small bractlets immediately beneath it. Flowers yellowish.

Poppy family. Leaves and stems with milky juice.

    Prickly poppy (69). Leaves and stems usually conspicuously spiny. Flowers white with yellowish center.

16b. Stems without spines, short barbed bristles, or star-shaped hairs.

Buttercup family. Stamens and pistils in spiral arrangement.

    Buttercup; crowfoot (65, 66, 67). Leaves alternate; fruits of achenes. Flowers yellow or white.

    Marsh marigold; elk's lip (58). Leaves basal, somewhat heart-shaped; 6–12 petallike structures. Flowers white.

    Anemone (64). Leaves opposite or whorled; styles hairy but not feathery in appearance. Flowers white to pink.

Purslane family. Leaves fleshy; stamens often 2.

    Bitterroot (47). Leaves basal; flower stems nearly naked. Flowers pink or reddish.

    Flame flower (48, 49). Leaves alternate. Flowers orange to pink, red, or purplish.

Rose family. Leaves compound or strongly pinnatifid.

Agrimony (99). Leaves pinnate, with 5–9 toothed leaflets. Flowers yellow.

Yellow avens (107). Stems hairy, the upper leaves with 3 toothed leaflets. Flowers yellow.

Western thimbleberry (101). Low, spreading shrub with simple, palmately lobed leaves. Flowers white.

St. John's wort family. Leaves opposite, glandular-dotted.

St. John's wort (175). Flowers yellow, with numerous stamens.

17a. Leaves having 3 leaflets or 5 or more palmately arranged leaflets.

Caper family. Leaves compound, usually with 3 leaflets, 6–24 stamens.

Rocky Mountain bee-plant (83). Stamens 6. Flowers pinkish purple to white.

Clammyweed (84). Stamens 12–24. Flowers pinkish.

Jackass clover (85). Ill-scented annuals; fruits 2–lobed. Flowers yellow.

Rose family. Stamens and pistils usually numerous.

Agrimony (99). Leaves pinnate, with 5–9 toothed leaflets. Flowers yellow.

Strawberry (100). Leaflets 3, having doubly toothed margins. Flowers white.

Cinquefoil (105, 106). Styles not jointed to form 2 segments. Flowers yellow or red.

Yellow avens (107). Stems hairy, the upper leaves with 3 toothed leaflets. Flowers yellow.

Woodsorrel family. Leaves usually basal, with 3 leaflets, these often wedge-shaped.

Woodsorrel (158). Flowers yellow.

17b. Leaves pinnately compound with 5 or more leaflets, rarely with 2 leaflets. (See 18a or 18b.)

18a. Stamens 15 or more. (See 19a or 19b.)

18b. Stamens 8–12. (See 20a or 20 b.)

19a. Plants with whitish or yellowish sap; petals appearing fragile and crumpled.

Poppy family. Stamens numerous; fruit a capsule.

Prickly poppy (69). Stems and leaves prickly. Flowers white with yellow center.

19b. Plants without whitish or yellowish sap.

Buttercup family. Leaves divided twice or thrice into three segments.

Baneberry (57). Many flowers, in racemes. Flowers white.

Columbine (55, 56). Petals with conspicuous spurs. Flowers white, blue, yellow, or orange-red.

Clematis (62, 63). Vines with opposite leaves. Flowers white or purplish.

Legume family. Leaves mostly once or twice pinnately compound; stamens typically 10 or more. (See key to *Legume family* on page 33).

Rose family. Leaves once pinnately compound; stamens numerous.

Herbs.

Agrimony (99). Leaves pinnate, with 5–9 toothed leaflets. Flowers yellow.

Red raspberry (102). Leaves at least 2 in. (50 mm) long; ovaries exposed on a conical receptacle. Flowers white.

Cinquefoil (104, 106). Styles not jointed to form 2 segments. Flowers yellow or red.

Yellow avens (107). Stems hairy, the upper leaves with 3 toothed leaflets. Flowers yellow.

Shrubs.

Red raspberry (102). Leaves at least 2 in. (50 mm) long; ovaries exposed on a conical receptacle. Flowers white.

Wild rose (108). Leaves at least 2 in. (50 mm) long; ovaries enclosed in and hidden by the fleshy calyx tube. Flowers pink.

Apache plume (109). Leaves to ⁵/₈ in. (15 mm) long, the lobes narrowly oblong; petals fall off easily. Flowers white.

Cliffrose (110). Flowers yellow.

20a. Leaves opposite.

Caltrop family. Stamens in 2 whorls; 2–5 carpels, united.

Goathead (161). Prostrate annual; leaves with 6–14 leaflets. Flowers yellow.

Desert poppy (162). Low spreading annual; leaves with 8–16 leaflets. Flowers orange.

20b. Leaves alternate.

Caltrop family. Stamens in 2 whorls; 2–5 carpels, united.

Peganum (163). Leaves once or twice pinnatifid, the segments linear. Flowers white or yellow.

Rose family. Leaves once pinnately compound.

Cinquefoil (105). Flowers red.

21a. Shrubs or trees, the stems with bark. (See 22a or 22b.)

21b. Herbs. (See 24a or 24b.)

22a. Leaves opposite or whorled.

Honeysuckle family. Leaves opposite; 4 or 5 stamens.

Elderberry (309, 310). Leaves pinnately compound; flowers in large terminal clusters. Flowers white.

Honeysuckle (313). Leaves simple; flowers often in axillary pairs. Flowers whitish to yellowish or orange.

Snowberry (312). Leaves simple; flowers in small axillary clusters, funnel-shaped. Flowers pink.

Vervain family. Stems often 4–angled; flowers tending to be irregular.

Aloysia (253). Aromatic shrubs with terminal spikes. Flowers white or blue.

22b. Leaves alternate or basal. (See 23a or 23b.)

23a. Leaves compound.
Barberry family. Petals 6 or 9, in 2 or 3 rows; 6–18 stamens.
Barberry (68). Inner bark yellow; leaves hollylike; petals 6. Flowers yellow.
Sumac family. Petals usually 5, in a single row; 5 stamens.
Poison ivy (165). Leaves with 3 leaflets. Flowers greenish white.

23b. Leaves simple.
Olive family. Plants often woody, with 2 or 4 stamens.
Menodora (217). Stems to 1 ft. (30 cm) tall; leaves entire. Flowers yellow.
Buckthorn family. Petals 4 or 5; ovary surrounded by a fleshy, ringlike disk; 4 or 5 stamens.
Buckbrush (166). Leaves conspicuously 3-veined from the base of the blade; branches rigid, somewhat spinescent. Flowers white.
Heath family. Petals strongly united, the corolla somewhat urn-shaped; twice as many stamens as corolla lobes.
Whortleberry (207). Low shrub; branchlets often angled. Flowers white to pink, globular.
Saxifrage family. Stamens and petals attached to the rim of a floral cup; usually 5, 8, or 10 stamens, sometimes numerous.
Gooseberry currant (98). Stems with spiny nodes; leaves somewhat rounded in outline, 3- to 5-lobed. Flowers reddish or purplish.
Tamarisk family. Small tree with drooping branchlets; leaves reduced to tiny scales.
Tamarisk, salt-cedar (176). Flowers pinkish or whitish, small.
Loasa family. Herbage with barbed or stinging hairs.
Cevallia (179). Leaves and stems with slender, stinging hairs; 5 stamens. Flowers with whitish, plumelike petals and sepals.
Nightshade family. Flowers regular, the sepals and petals united, mostly 5-lobed; stamens attached to the corolla lobes.
Desert tobacco (272). Coarse herb with glandular hairs on the stems. Flowers narrowly funnelform, greenish white.
Honeysuckle family. Leaves opposite; 4 or 5 stamens.
Twinflower (311). Small herb with pairs of nodding pinkish flowers.

24a. Leaves opposite or whorled. (See 25a or 25b.)

24b. Leaves alternate or basal. (See 29a or 29b.)

25a. Leaves fleshy.
Purslane family. Low plants with usually fleshy leaves; often 2 sepals.
Bitterroot (47). Sepals 2–8; petals 4–18. Flowers pinkish or reddish.

Flame flower (48, 49). Sepals 2; petals 5; ovary completely superior. Flowers orange to pink, red, or purplish.

25b. Leaves not fleshy. (See 26a or 26b.)

26a. Leaves of a pair unequal in size.
Four-o'clock family. Flowers tubular, usually in small clusters subtended by greenish bracts; stamens usually projecting.
　　Flowers or clusters of flowers subtended by a series of united bracts.
　　　　Desert four-o'clock (37, 38, 39). Stems mostly erect, glabrous; leaves petioled. Flowers red, pink, or white.
　　　　Wild four-o'clock (40). Leaves ovate; flowers 6–8 per cluster. Flowers rose pink to purplish red.
　　Flowers or clusters of flowers subtended by a series of free bracts.
　　　　Stigmas linear; fruit winged.
　　　　　　Winged sand verbena (41). Wings of the fruit very conspicuous, translucent, conspicuously reticulately veined. Flowers white to pink.
　　　　　　Sand verbena (42). Stems often with sticky hairs; wings of the fruit not conspicuously veined. Flowers white or slightly pink.
　　　　Stigmas globular; fruits not winged.
　　　　　　Scarlet muskflower (43). Perianth funnelform. Flowers numerous, red, in capitate clusters.
　　　　　　Moonpod (44). Leaves ovate or rounded. Flowers greenish white, solitary or 2 in a cluster.
　　　　　　Angel trumpet (45). Stems elongate, spreading. Flowers white, tinged with purple or pink, the slender tube to 6 in. (15 cm) long.
　　　　　　Spiderling (46). Stems erect, smooth; flowers very small, less than 1/8 in. (2 mm) long. Flowers white to pinkish or purplish.

26b. Leaves of a pair or whorl equal in size. (See 27a or 27b.)

27a. Petals appearing separate.
Dogwood family. Flowers in open or dense clusters subtended by conspicuous corollalike bracts; 4 petals and stamens.
　　Dwarf cornel (206). Low herb; upper leaves in a crowded whorl.
Pink family. Leaves sessile, entire, usually narrow; petals often lobed or divided; 2–5 styles.
　　Campion (50, 51). Petals with a scalelike or fringed appendage at the base of the blade. Flowers crimson.
　　Starwort (52). Petals 2-cleft; 3 styles; 3–10 stamens. Flowers white.
　　Meadow chickweed (53). Stamens 10; styles 5. Flowers white.
　　Sandwort (54). Stamens 10; styles 3. Flowers white.
Milkweed family. Stems and leaves with milky juice; 5 petals, reflexed, the summit of the flower bearing 5 hoodlike structures.
　　Milkweed (224, 225, 226, 227). Leaves linear to broadly lanceolate. Flowers white to pink, purplish, or orange.

27b. Petals united to form a tube. (See 28a or 28b.)

28a. Ovary free from the calyx tube.

Gentian family. Glabrous herbs; leaves sessile, smooth-margined; as many stamens as corolla lobes and alternate with them.

Prairie gentian (218). Leaves sessile, thick, clasping at the base. Flowers blue to white or yellowish.

Deer's ears (219). Leaves in whorls of 3–7. Flowers greenish white, dotted with purple.

Gentian (220, 221). Leaves opposite, sessile. Flowers blue or purple, often fringed or appendaged between the lobes.

Phlox family. Variously hairy herbs, upright to matted; leaves with smooth or toothed margins; stamens at different levels in the corolla tube.

Phlox (238, 239). Leaves linear to lance-shaped or subulate, smooth-margined. Flowers white to lilac or pink.

Vervain family. Leaves variously toothed or lobed; stems often square; 5 corolla lobes, slightly unequal; 4 stamens, in 2 groups.

Phyla (254). Flowers in dense axillary clusters on conspicuous stalks; fruits of 2 nutlets. Flowers bluish or whitish.

Vervain (255, 256, 257, 258, 259). Flowers in terminal spikes or headlike clusters; fruits of 4 nutlets. Flowers pinkish to purplish.

Milkweed family. Stems and leaves with milky juice; 5 petals, reflexed, the summit of the flower bearing 5 hoodlike structures.

Milkweed (226, 227). Leaves narrowly lanceolate to broadly lanceolate. Flowers whitish to purplish.

Dogbane family. Stems and leaves usually with milky juice; leaves opposite or alternate.

Dogbane (222). Leaves opposite. Flowers whitish, often tinged with pink.

Amsonia (223). Leaves alternate, often crowded. Flowers blue.

28b. Ovary surrounded by and united to the calyx tube.

Madder family. Petals and stamens 4 or 5; anthers pointing inward.

Bedstraw (305, 306). Stems angled, minutely hispid; leaves in whorls of 4–8. Flowers greenish white.

Bluets (307, 308). Corolla lobes and stamens 4. Flowers white to pink or purple.

Valerian family. Stamens 1–4, fewer than and inserted on the corolla lobes.

Valerian (314). Leaves thickish, with conspicuous lateral veins; stem leaves typically pinnatifid. Flowers yellowish white.

29a. Leaf bases with large stipules sheathing the stem.

Buckwheat family. Herbs with usually alternate, mostly entire leaves.

Western dock (35). Flower parts 6; stamens 6; stigmas 3; fruits often 3-angled or 3-winged. Flowers inconspicuous.

Bistort (36). Basal leaves on slender petioles; stems terminating in a flowering spike. Flowers white or pink.

29b. Leaves without conspicuous sheathing stipules. (See 30a or 30b.)

30a. Leaves divided into usually numerous divisions; flowers in umbels; stems grooved, hollow.

Carrot family. Flower clusters often conspicuous but individual flowers small, each cluster usually composed of several spreading branches or rays; at the end of each ray are several pedicels subtending the flowers.

Individual flower clusters without small bracts at the base of the cluster of pedicels.

Cow parsnip (200). Plants stout; leaves compound, with large leaflets in 3s. Flowers white.

Mountain parsley (201). Branches of the umbel hairy. Flowers yellow to purple.

Individual flower clusters with small bracts at the base of the cluster of pedicels.

Osha (199). Smooth perennials with large, compound leaves. Flowers whitish to pinkish.

Poison hemlock (202). Poisonous perennials; leaves two or more times pinnate; stems smooth, with purple spots. Flowers white.

Fendler cowbane (203). Leaves simply pinnate or leaflets in 3s. Flowers white to purple.

Water parsnip (204). Leaves once pinnate; bracts of the inflorescence conspicuous. Flowers white.

Water hemlock (205). Smooth, poisonous perennials; leaves pinnately compound, the leaflets with small teeth. Flowers white.

30b. Leaves, flowers, and stems not fitting all of the above characters. (See 31a or 31b.)

31a. Petals separate. (See 32a or 32b.)

31b. Petals united. (See 33a or 33b.)

32a. Petals 4.

Mustard family. Stamens 6, usually 4 of them longer than the other 2.

Fruits not more than two and one-half times longer than wide.

Spectacle pod (79). Fruits flattish, 2-lobed, somewhat spectaclelike in appearance. Flowers white.

Peppergrass (80). Leaves entire or toothed; fruits small, flattish, ovate to oblong. Flowers mostly white.

Bladderpod (81). Low perennials; fruits small, usually rounded, inflated. Flowers yellow.

False flax (82). Leaves mostly entire, sagittate and clasping at the base; fruits obovate. Flowers yellowish.

Fruits more than three times longer than wide.

Leaves, at least the lower ones, pinnatifid.

Desert plume (73). Upper leaves often clasping the stem. Flowers creamy yellow to yellow.

Thelepodium (74). Basal leaves lyrate-pinnatifid; fruits linear, 1⅝–2¾ in. (4–8 cm) long. Flowers white to purple.

Watercress (78). Aquatic; leaf segments wavy. Flowers white.
Leaves entire to toothed.
Leaves ovate, heart-shaped, spatulate, or oblanceolate.
Bittercress (71). Leaves heart-shaped. Flowers white.
Whitlowgrass (72). Leaves spatulate or oblanceolate; mature fruits flattened, often twisted. Flowers yellow or white.
Leaves linear to narrowly lanceolate.
Wallflower (75, 76). Fruits very slender, erect, 2–4 in. (5–10 cm) long. Flowers yellow or orange.
Tansy mustard (77). Leaves twice pinnatifid. Flowers pale yellow or yellow.

Caper family. Stamens 6 or 8–24; leaves compound, usually with 3 leaflets.
Rocky Mountain bee-plant (83). Stamens 6. Flowers pinkish purple to white.
Clammyweed (84). Stamens 8–24. Flowers pinkish.
Jackass clover (85). Stamens 6; fruit a twin pod. Flowers yellow.

Purslane family. Leaves fleshy; often 2 sepals.
Bitterroot (47). Sepals 2–8; petals 4–18. Flowers pinkish to reddish.
Flame flower (48, 49). Sepals 2; petals 5; ovary completely superior. Flowers orange to pink, red, or purplish.

Stonecrop family. Leaves and usually the stems fleshy and mostly glabrous; stamens usually 5 or 10; carpels 4 or 5, distinct or nearly so.
Sedum (86, 87, 88). Stems erect to spreading. Flowers white to pink or purple.

32b. Petals 5 or more.
Flax family. Leaves sessile; 5 stamens and styles.
Flax (159, 160). Leaves linear to narrowly lanceolate; petals falling easily. Flowers white, blue, or yellow.
Geranium family. Stamens 10, sometimes 5; styles 5, united into a slender column; leaves often palmately veined.
Geranium (156, 157). Stamens 10. Flowers white, pink, or purple.
Purslane family. Leaves fleshy; often 2 sepals.
Bitterroot (47). Sepals 2–8; petals 4–18. Flowers pinkish or reddish.
Flame flower (48, 49). Sepals 2; petals 5; ovary completely superior. Flowers orange to pink, red, or purplish.
Milkweed family. Stems and leaves usually with milky juice; petals 5, reflexed, the summit of the flower bearing 5 hoodlike structures.
Milkweed (224, 225, 226, 227). Leaves linear to lance-shaped or ovate; flowers in umbellike clusters. Flowers white to purplish or orange.
Lizard's-tail family. Herbs; flowers in dense, terminal spikes, sometimes subtended by a series of white, petallike bracts.
Yerba mansa (34). Sandy soil of river valleys; leaves somewhat oblong or

25

ovate. Individual flowers inconspicuous but the spike subtended by
large, white, petallike bracts.

Saxifrage family. Stamens and petals attached to the rim of a floral cup;
usually 5, 8, or 10 stamens, sometimes numerous.

Parnassia (89). Herbs with 5 groups of gland-tipped filaments opposite
the petals. Flowers white.

Alumroot (90, 91, 92). Leaves mostly basal, orbicular to broadly ovate
in outline. Flowers greenish white, pink, or red.

Rose family. Leaves often pinnately compound; stamens numerous.

Agrimony (99). Leaves with 5–7 leaflets, these alternately smaller and
larger. Flowers relatively small, yellow.

33a. Stems vining or creeping, usually elongate.

Figwort family. Flowers funnelform but the lobes irregular.

Vining snapdragon (283). Leaves triangular, broadly notched at the base.
Flowers bluish.

Melon family. Coarse, rough, herbaceous vines with tendrils; leaves
palmately veined.

Buffalo gourd (317). Leaves somewhat triangular, with shallow, angled
lobes. Flowers conspicuous, yellow.

Melon-loco (316). Leaves reniform, shallowly toothed or lobed, or
sometimes wavy on the margins; stamens 3. Flowers yellow.

Cutleaf globeberry (315). Leaves deeply 3- to 5-lobed; fruits globose, red.
Flowers white.

Morning glory family. Prostrate or climbing vines without tendrils; flowers
funnel-shaped.

Leafless parasites without chlorophyll.

Dodder (228). Slender, yellowish, leafless stems twining around host
plants. Flowers white.

Leafy plants with chlorophyll.

Evolvulus (229). Plants prostrate to erect. Flowers blue or white.

Bush morning glory (230). Somewhat shrublike with the ends of the
branches trailing; leaves narrow and elongate. Flowers pinkish.

Star glory (231). Stems twining; leaves somewhat heart-shaped.
Flowers bright scarlet.

Bindweed (232). Leaves somewhat oblong, notched at the base, often
with a pair of basal lobes. Flowers pinkish or white.

33b. Stems not vining or creeping, mostly spreading to upright. (See 34a
or 34b.)

34a. Flower clusters one-sided, often curled like a scorpion's tail.

Borage family. Plants usually with stiff, spreading or appressed hairs; ovary
2-celled, deeply 4-lobed.

Flowers yellow.

Puccoon (250). Leaves linear, without teeth. Flowers sometimes with
irregular petal margins.

26

Agoseris aurantiaca
Orange-flowered mountain dandelion

Allium cernuum
New Mexico nodding onion

Anisacanthus thurberi
Desert honeysuckle

Antennaria parvifolia
Pussytoes

Color illustrations printed in Japan.

Aquilegia elegantula
Red columbine

Argemone polyanthemos
Prickly poppy

Asclepias tuberosa ssp. terminalis
Butterflyweed

Baileya multiradiata var. pleniradiata
Desert marigold

Callirhoe involucrata
Poppy mallow

Caltha leptosepala
Elk's lip

Calypso bulbosa
Fairy slipper

Castilleja confusa
Colorado paintbrush

Centaurea americana
American basketflower

Cirsium neomexicanum
New Mexico thistle

Clematis ligusticifolia
Western virgin's bower

Cleome serrulata
Rocky Mountain bee-plant

Cowania stansburiana
Cliffrose

Datura meteloides
Jimsonweed

Desmanthus illinoensis
Prairie bundleflower

Dodecatheon pulchellum
Southern shooting star

Echinocereus triglochidiatus
Hedgehog cactus

Engelmannia pinnatifida
Engelmann daisy

Epipactis gigantea
Helleborine

Erigeron philadelphicus
Common fleabane

Erysimum inconspicuum
Wallflower

Fallugia paradoxa
Apache plume

Fendlera rupicola var. folcata
Fendlerbush

Gaillardia pulchella
Firewheel

Gentiana affinis
Pleated gentian

Geranium richardsonii
Richardson's geranium

Helianthus annuus
Annual sunflower

Hypericum formosum
Western St. John's-wort

Iris missouriensis
Rocky Mountain Iris

Ipomoea leptophylla
Bush morning glory

Kallstroemia grandiflora
Arizona poppy

Lesquerella gooddingii
Goodding bladderpod

Lewisia pygmaea nevadensis
Nevada bitterroot

Linum lewisii
Western blueflax

Lobelia cardinalis sp. graminea
Western cardinal flower

Malva neglecta
Common mallow

Mentzelia pumila multiflora
Common stickleaf

Mimulus guttatus
Spotted monkeyflower

Oxybaphus coccineus
Red umbrellawort

Petalostemum scariosum
Prostrate prairie clover

Phacelia integrifolia
Tooth-leaf scorpionweed

Phlox caespitosa
Cushion phlox

Potentilla thurberi var. atrorubens
Red cinquefoil

Primula rusbyi
Rusby primrose (purple blossoms)

Ratibida columnifera
Prairie coneflower

Pterospora andromedea
Pinedrops

Robinia
New Mexico locust

Rosa woodsii
Wild rose

Schrankia occidentalis
Western sensitive briar

Saxifraga rhomboidea
Saxifrage

Sedum cockerellii
Cockerell stonecrop

Silene acaulis ssp. acaulescens
Moss campion

Sisyrinchium demissum
Blue-eyed grass

Solanum douglasii
Arizona nightshade

Sphaeralcea fendleri var. fendleri
Fendler globe-mallow

Thermopsis pinetorum
Big golden-pea

Verbena ciliata ciliata
Creeping vervain

Viola canadensis
Canada violet

Yucca elata
Soaptree yucca; palmilla

Zinnia grandiflora
Rocky mountain zinnia

Gromwell (251). Coarse, with bristly hairy stems; leaves lanceolate, entire, coarsely veined. Flowers tubular, yellow or orange.

Cryptantha (252). Plants usually low, bristly, hairy; leaves usually narrow. Flowers mostly small, white to yellow.

Flowers white, blue, or purple.

Coldenia (244). Stems mostly not more than 8 in. (20 cm) long; styles 2. Flowers white to pink.

Heliotrope (245, 246). Corolla funnel-shaped, the lobes represented by 5 angles. Flowers white or tinged with blue.

Hound's tongue (247). Coarse herbs; leaves entire; fruits lobed, covered with short, barbed prickles. Flowers white to purple.

Stickseed (248). Leaves mostly linear to oblanceolate or oblong; fruits of 4 nutlets bearing barbed prickles on the margins. Flowers white or blue.

Bluebells (249). Leaves lance-shaped; corolla funnel-shaped. Flowers bluish.

Cryptantha (252). Plants usually low, bristly, hairy; leaves usually narrow. Flowers mostly small, white to yellow.

Waterleaf family. Flower clusters similar in appearance to borages; ovary 1-celled, not lobed; style terminal.

Scorpionweed (241, 242). Leaves mostly variously toothed or lobed; herbage frequently sticky and glandular. Flowers white to blue.

Western waterleaf (243). Leaves strongly pinnatifid, of 7–13 segments. Flowers white or pale blue.

34b. Flowers variously arranged but the clusters not as above. (See 35a or 35b.)

35a. Stamens 2–4; flowers irregular or sometimes regular.

Figwort family. Flowers usually strongly irregular and funnelform.

Leaves opposite.

Toadflax (282). Stems smooth, erect, leafy; leaves entire, sessile. Flowers yellow or blue, with a spur at the base.

Beardtongue (284, 285, 286, 287, 288). Leaves opposite, usually relatively narrow; fifth stamen represented by an often hairy filament. Flowers of various colors.

Speedwell (289). Plants often very small; leaves sometimes toothed; corolla often less than 1/8 in. (2–3 mm) long. Flowers white to blue.

Monkeyflower (290). Corolla with a pair of longitudinal ridges on the lower side of the throat.

Leaves alternate or basal.

Toadflax (282). Stems smooth, erect, leafy; leaves entire, sessile. Flowers yellow or blue, with a spur at the base.

Vining snapdragon (283). Leaves triangular, broadly notched at the base. Flowers bluish.

Kittentails (291, 292). Leaves basal, toothed; inflorescence a dense terminal spike. Flowers white to purplish.

Clubflower (293). Leaves mostly divided into 3–5 linear or filiform divisions. Flowers yellowish or purplish.

Lousewort (294, 295). Leaves often pinnatifid; upper lip of corolla arched or beaked. Flowers white to yellowish green or purple.

Paintbrush (296, 297, 298). Flowers inconspicuous, not colorful, subtended by colorful, often lobed, leaflike bracts. Bracts greenish to purplish or red.

Yellow owlclover (299). Leaves linear, sometimes divided into slender segments. Flowers yellow in this species.

Olive family. Flower parts usually in 4s. Leaves opposite or alternate.

Menodora (217). Plants low, often woody at the base; leaves alternate. Flowers bright yellow or white.

Plantain family. Leaves basal; flowers in spikes on naked scapes.

Plantain (304). Leaves simple, lanceolate to broadly ovate, strongly veined. Flowers whitish and membranous.

35b. Stamens 5; flowers regular. (See 36a or 36b.)

36a. Stamens attached opposite the corolla lobes.

Primrose family. Leaves all basal; style unbranched.

Shooting star (213). Plants of damp habitats. Flowers nodding, the perianth parts reflexed; stamens conspicuously projecting. Petals white to pink or violet.

Primrose (214, 215). Calyx often with a white mealy deposit. Flowers pinkish purple with a yellowish throat.

Milkweed family. Leaves mostly linear to lance-shaped or ovate; stems and leaves with milky juice; petals and sepals 5, reflexed, the summit of the flower bearing 5 hoodlike structures.

Milkweed (224, 225). Leaves linear to lance-shaped; fruits of conspicuous follicles or pods. Flowers white to pink or orange.

Plumbago family. Stems sometimes woody at the base; leaves often basal.

Sea lavender (216). Plants scapose; leaves fleshy, basal; flowers small, violet, clustered at the ends of the branches.

36b. Stamens alternate with the corolla lobes.

Bluebell family. Calyx tube united with the ovary; style single but with 2–5 lobes; corolla often bell-shaped.

Harebell (319). Flowers nodding, bell-shaped, blue.

Nightshade family. Flowers usually folded lengthwise before opening; style single; stigma unlobed or 2-lobed.

Fruit a capsule.

Jimsonweed (271). Ill-scented; leaves large, often rhomboid. Flowers white to violet, large, usually very conspicuous.

Desert tobacco (272). Stems erect, with sticky hairs; stem leaves with earlike basal lobes. Flowers greenish white.

Fruit a berry.

Wolfberry (273). Shrubs with leaves broadest toward the tip and arranged in clusters; corolla narrowly funnel-shaped. Flowers white, often tinged with purple, or purple.

Groundcherry (274, 275). Calyx greatly inflated, papery, and ribbed at maturity; corolla somewhat bell-shaped. Flowers yellow with dark basal spots.

Nightshade (276, 277, 278, 279). Leaves simple and entire or pinnatifid, or compound; corolla rotate. Flowers white, yellow, or purple.

Scurfy groundcherry (280). Stems spreading or prostrate; leaves entire or pinnatifid. Flowers yellowish or purplish.

Phlox family. Stamens often at different levels; one style with 3 branches; flowers tubular, funnelform, or salverform, rolled lengthwise in the bud.

Ipomopsis (233, 234, 235). Leaves often with linear lobes; upper leaves not much reduced; calyx green. Flowers white to pink or purple.

Gilia (236). Leaves usually with slender lobes; upper leaves much reduced; calyx membranaceous. Flowers white to purple with yellow center.

Jacob's ladder (237). Leaves pinnate, the segments oblong or oval; plants aromatic. Flowers white to blue or yellow.

Collomia (240). Leaves linear to lance-shaped, the margins smooth; flower clusters with conspicuous bracts. Flowers white or pink.

Phlox (238, 239). Leaves entire, the corolla salverform. Flowers white to bluish or pinkish.

Dogbane family. Leaves opposite or alternate; carpels free at the base but fused at the summit.

Dogbane (222). Leaves opposite; fruit a pair of slender follicles or pods. Flowers white to pink.

Amsonia (223). Leaves alternate; fruits erect. Flowers pale blue.

Milkweed family. Stems and leaves with milky juice; petals and sepals reflexed, the summit of the flower bearing 5 hoodlike structures.

Milkweed (224, 225). Leaves linear to lance-shaped; fruits of conspicuous follicles or pods. Flowers white to pink or orange.

Morning glory family. Prostrate or climbing vines without tendrils; flowers funnel-shaped.

Evolvulus (229). Plants prostrate to erect. Flowers blue or white.

Figwort family. Flowers usually 2-lipped, occasionally nearly regular; stamens usually 4, occasionally 5; leaves variously arranged but simple.

Mullein (281). Leaves and stems softly woolly; stamens 5. Flowers nearly regular, yellow.

Borage family. Herbs with usually stiff, spreading or appressed hairs; ovary 2-celled, deeply 4-lobed.

Flowers yellow, orange, or occasionally white.

Puccoon (250). Leaves linear, without teeth. Flowers sometimes with irregular petal margins.

Gromwell (251). Coarse, bristly, hairy stems; leaves lanceolate, entire, prominently veined. Flowers tubular, yellow to orange.

Cryptantha (252). Plants usually low, bristly, hairy; leaves usually narrow. Flowers usually small, white to yellow.

Flowers white, blue, or purple.

Coldenia (244). Stems usually not more than 8 in. (20 cm) long; styles 2. Flowers white or pink.

Heliotrope (245, 246). Corolla funnel-shaped, the lobes represented by 5 angles. Flowers white or tinged with blue.

Hound's tongue (247). Coarse herbs; leaves entire; fruits lobed, covered with short, barbed prickles. Flowers white to purple.

Stickseed (248). Leaves mostly linear to oblanceolate or oblong; fruits of 4 nutlets bearing barbed prickles on the margins. Flowers white or blue.

Bluebells (249). Leaves lance-shaped; corolla funnel-shaped. Flowers bluish.

Cryptantha (252). Plants usually low, bristly, hairy; leaves usually narrow. Flowers usually small, white to yellow.

Key to the Common Names
of Genera of the Lily Family

1a. Leaves rigid and spine-tipped, in conspicuous basal rosettes. (See 2a or 2b.)

1b. Leaves neither rigid nor spine-tipped, not in conspicuous rosettes. (See 3a or 3b.)

2a. Leaves without teeth but usually with slender, spreading or curled filaments on the margins.
Yucca (3, 4). Inflorescence on a usually conspicuous bract-covered scape. Flowers white or greenish white.

2b. Leaves with curved, sharp, marginal prickles.
Sotol (5). Inflorescence of narrow panicles on conspicuous scapes. Flowers whitish or greenish white.

3a. Outer flower segments (sepals) green, narrower than the inner ones.
Mariposa lily (6). Each inner flower segment with a large, hairy gland near the base. Flowers white to purple, the sepals often with purple dots.

3b. Outer flower segments not green, essentially like those of the inner series. (See 4a or 4b.)

4a. Leaves linear, often grasslike.
Flowers arranged in umbellike clusters subtended by 1 or more conspicuous bracts.
Onion (11, 12, 13). Plants with an obvious onionlike odor; stamens separate at the base. Flowers white to pink or red.
Flowers in spikes, racemes, panicles, or solitary; bracts, when present, relatively small and inconspicuous.
Leaves basal or with 1 or 2 small leaves on the stem.
Crag lily (14). Flowers yellowish orange, without a conspicuous gland at the base of each segment.
Camas (8, 9). Flowers greenish white to yellowish white, with a conspicuous gland at the base of each segment.

31

Leaves scattered on the stem.

Alp lily (17). Leaves grasslike; stems to about 6 in. (15 cm) tall. Flowers yellowish white but pinkish-tinged or purple-veined on the outer surface.

Rocky Mountain lily (18). Leaves mostly alternate but whorled at the upper nodes. Flowers large, conspicuous, red to orange red, with purplish black spots near the base of the segments.

4b. Leaves lanceolate, ovate, or elliptic.

Styles separate.

Corn lily (10). Leaves very large, clasping, conspicuously veined. Flowers greenish white or white.

Styles united but stigmas often somewhat lobed.

Upper leaves whorled.

Rocky Mountain lily (18). Flowers red to orange red, with purplish black spots near the base of the segments.

Upper leaves not whorled.

Solomon's seal (7). Flower segments yellow, united to form a tube; flower stalks jointed near the flower.

Star flower (15). Flowers white, the segments separate.

Twisted stalk (16). Flowers greenish white, the segments separate, recurved at the tip.

Key to the Common Names
of the Genera of the Legume Family

1a. Corolla regular, with petals or lobes all alike; flowers in headlike or spikelike clusters; stamens usually conspicuously projecting from the flowers; leaves usually twice pinnate. (See 2a or 2b.)

1b. Corolla irregular, with petals or lobes unlike; flowers variously arranged; stamens usually not conspicuously projecting from the flower; leaves usually not twice pinnate. (See 3a or 3b.)

2a. Stamens 15 or more.
Fairy duster (111). Petals united to form a tube; staminal filaments united. Flowers reddish purple.
Acacia (112, 113). Petals and stamens separate. Flowers yellow or white.

2b. Stamens 5–12.
Plants with straight or slightly curved spines.
Honey mesquite (114). Shrubs or small trees. Flowers yellow or greenish yellow, in dense cylindrical spikes.
Plants with spines recurved or absent.
Sensitive briar (115). Stems creeping; leaves sensitive to the touch. Flowers pinkish, in globose heads.
Prairie bundleflower (116). Stems spreading to erect; leaves not sensitive to the touch. Flowers greenish white, in headlike clusters, the fruits strongly bent to one side.
Mimosa (117). Shrubs. Flowers pale pink or white, in spikes or headlike clusters; fruits often constricted between the seeds.

3a. Leaves simple.
Prostrate ratany (118). Low shrubs or herbs; leaves with silky hairs; stamens 3 or 4. Flowers reddish.

3b. Leaves pinnately compound. (See 4a or 4b.)

4a. Upper petal (banner) overlapped by the lateral petals, especially apparent just before the petals open out of the bud.

Senna (119). Leaves with an equal number of leaflets. Flowers yellow, solitary or in small clusters.

Poinciana (120). Leaves twice pinnately compound; staminal filaments reddish, conspicuously projecting from the flower. Flowers yellow.

Rushpea (121, 122). Leaves twice pinnately compound, the leaflets very small, often glandular-dotted; stamens 10, curved downward and forward. Flowers yellow, in racemes.

4b. Upper petal overlapping the lateral petals, especially apparent just before the petals open out of the bud. (See 5a or 5b.)

5a. Leaves with 3 leaflets or sometimes with 4 or more leaflets arranged in digitate fashion. (See 6a or 6b.)

5b. Leaves with 4 or more leaflets, these arranged in pinnate fashion. (See 10a or 10b.)

6a. Stamens separate; stipules conspicuous, leaflike.

Golden pea (123). Leaves with 3 leaflets. Flowers at least $^3/_8$ in. (10 mm) long, bright yellow, in racemes.

6b. Stamens united to form a tube. (See 7a or 7b.)

7a. Leaflets 5–15, digitately arranged.

Lupine (124, 125). Flowers blue, cream-colored, or purplish, the upper (banner) petal recurved on the margins.

7b. Leaflets typically 3. (See 8a or 8b.)

8a. Stems twining.

Wild bean (126). Leaflets linear, $1^1/_4$–2 in. (30–50 mm) long. Flowers purplish pink with a yellow, strongly curved keel petal.

8b. Stems not twining. (See 9a or 9b.)

9a. Leaves glandular-dotted.

Scurfpea (127). Lower leaves sometimes with 5 leaflets. Flowers blue or purple, about $^1/_4$ in. (6 mm) long.

9b. Leaves not glandular-dotted.

Leaflets toothed.

Clover (131, 132, 133). Flowers in heads or headlike clusters subtended by a series of bracts, mostly reddish to purple.

Alfalfa (134). Fruits coiled or curved. Flowers violet.

Sweet clover (135). Fruits straight. Flowers yellow, sometimes white.

Leaflets without teeth or the margins sometimes wavy.

Wright deervetch (136). Leaflets 3 or 5. Flowers yellow or orange.

10a. Leaflets glandular-dotted. (See 11a or 11b.)

10b. Leaflets not glandular-dotted. (See 12a or 12b.)

11a. Stamens 5.

Prairie clover (148, 149). Leaves odd-pinnate, mostly with 5–9 leaflets. Flowers white to pink.

11b. Stamens 9 or 10.

Indigobush (128, 129, 130). Leaves odd-pinnately compound, with 5–13 leaflets. Flowers rose pink, reddish purple, or yellow.

False indigobush (148, 149). Leaves odd-pinnately compound, with 5–9 leaflets. Flowers rose purple to white, pale yellow, or slightly pink.

Dune broom (152). Leaflets 9–19, very narrowly linear. Flowers yellowish.

12a. Leaves even-pinnately compound, with tendrils at the tip of the leaf rachis.

Peavine (143, 144). Style of the ovary hairy along the side opposite the banner petal. Flowers pink to purple, white, or yellow.

Vetch (145). Style of the ovary merely with a tuft of hairs just below the tip. Flowers bluish purple.

12b. Leaves odd-pinnately compound, without tendrils.

Flowers red, purple, or pink.

Sweet vetch (146). Leaflets 9–15. Flowers reddish or rose purple.

New Mexico locust (153). Leaflets 9–19. Flowers pink.

Red bladderpod (155). Leaflets 15–25. Flowers dull red.

Flowers blue or white.

Wild licorice (147). Pods prickly. Flowers blue or white.

Silvery locoweed (154). Plants with silvery hairs. Flowers white with a purple-tipped keel petal.

Key to the Common Names
of the Genera of the Cactus Family

1a. Stems obviously jointed; the point of attachment of spine clusters also containing very short barbed spines (glochidia). (See 2a or 2b.)

1b. Stems not obviously jointed; the point of attachment of spine clusters without short barbed spines (glochids). (See 3a or 3b.)

2a. Plants low, matted; joints club-shaped, marked with conspicuous projections (tubercles); spines strongly recurved.
Club cholla (182). Flowers yellow; fruit yellow.

2b. Plants clumped; joints obovate to orbicular, without conspicuous projections (tubercles).
Plains prickly pear (183). Flowers yellow, sometimes reddish; fruits reddish purple.

3a. Stems ribbed, the ribs formed from confluent tubercles. (See 4a or 4b.)

3b. Stems not ribbed, the tubercles distinct. (See 5a or 5b.)

4a. Flowers about ³/₄–1 in. (2–2.5 cm) long; spines mostly 12–19 per cluster.
Green pitaya (184). Flowers greenish or sometimes purplish red; fruit green.

4b. Flowers about 1¹/₄–3 in. (3–7.5 cm) long; spines mostly 3–12, sometimes as many as 16 per cluster.
Hedgehog cactus (185). Flowers red or scarlet; fruits red.
Fendler's hedgehog (186). Flowers reddish purple; fruits greenish at first, later becoming reddish.

5a. Spines, at least some of them, with transverse ridges. (See 6a or 6b.)

5b. Spines smooth or nearly so. (See 7a or 7b.)

6a. Point of spine attachment (areole) with long woolly hairs; spines sometimes curved but never hooked.

Turk's-head (187). Flowers pink; fruit red, densely covered with white woolly hairs.

6b. Point of spine attachment (areole) without long white hairs; at least one of the spines hooked.
Barrel cactus (188). Flowers yellow; fruit yellow, covered by rounded scales.

7a. Tubercles with a felt-lined groove from the tip to the middle or beyond.
Plains pincushion cactus (189). Flowers pink to purple; fruit green.

7b. Tubercles without a groove.
Simpson's pediocactus (190). Flowers pink to white or pale yellow; fruit green, tinged with red.

Key to the Common Names
of the Genera of the Aster Family

1a. Flower heads similar to those of dandelions, with all flowers having strap-shaped corollas. (See 2a or 2b.)

1b. Flower heads with flowers having corollas all 2-lipped, all tubular, or both tubular and rayflower-shaped. (See 3a or 3b.)

2a. Leaves alternate on the stem and often basal as well, the stem leaves frequently much smaller than the basal ones.
> Flowers pink or blue.
>> Leaves entire or toothed.
>>> *Wild lettuce* (323). Flowers blue.
>>> *Skeleton plant* (328). Flowers pink.
>> Leaves lobed.
>>> *Wire lettuce* (320). Flowers pink.
>>> *Chicory* (322). Flowers blue.
>>> *Wild lettuce* (323). Flowers blue.
> Flowers yellow or orange.
>> Fruits tapering to a slender beak at the top.
>>> *Meadow goatsbeard* (321). Leaves grasslike. Flowers yellow.
>>> *False dandelion* (324). Leaves not grasslike. Flowers yellow.
>> Fruits flattened or squarish at the top.
>>> *Fendler hawkweed* (327). Leaves without teeth or with minute teeth. Flowers yellow.
>>> *Dwarf dandelion* (329). Leaves without teeth or often lobed. Flowers yellow or orange.
>>> *Desert dandelion* (330). Leaves toothed or lobed. Flowers yellow.

2b. Leaves all basal.
> *Dandelion* (325). Leaves wavy or lobed. Flowers yellow.
> *Mountain dandelion* (326). Leaves without teeth or lobes. Flowers orange.

3a. Corollas of flowers all 2–lipped, the upper lip with 2 lobes or teeth, the lower lip with 3 teeth.

Brownfoot; perezia (331). Leaf bases clasping the stem, the margins with spiny teeth. Flowers rose purple or white.

3b. Corollas of flowers either all tube-shaped or having both tube-shaped central flowers and rayflower-shaped marginal flowers as in asters or sunflowers. (See 4a or 4b.)

4a. Flowers all tubular; heads never with rayflower-shaped flowers. (See 5a or 5b.)

4b. Flowers of two types; heads containing both tube-shaped central flowers and rayflower-shaped marginal flowers. (See 8a or 8b.)

5a. Leaves with teeth or lobes spine-tipped.
Thistle (332, 333, 334). Flower-head bracts spine-tipped. Flower heads relatively large. Flowers white to greenish white, pinkish purple, or purple.

5b. Leaves without spine-tipped teeth or lobes. (See 6a or 6b.)

6a. Flower-head bracts conspicuously fringed.
Star thistle (335). Flower heads conspicuous, the marginal flowers appearing somewhat rayflower-shaped but divided into slender lobes. Flowers purple to pink.

6b. Flower-head bracts not fringed. (See 7a or 7b.)

7a. Plants densely covered with conspicuous, white, woolly hairs; flowerhead bracts (phyllaries) mostly dry and papery and whitish to variously colored.
Pussytoes (336). Plants usually spreading, low growing, often matted. Flowers whitish.
Cottony everlasting (337). Plants erect, usually unbranched. Flowers whitish.

7b. Plants not bearing white, woolly hairs; flowerhead bracts (phyllaries) not dry and papery.
Leaves opposite.
Western throughwort (339). Leaves triangular, toothed but not lobed. Flowers white.
Arrowweed (367). Leaves narrowly triangular or arrowhead-shaped, with a pair of downward-pointing lobes at the base. Flowers yellow.
Leaves alternate.
Flowers purple to rose pink.
Ironweed (338). Leaves narrowly lanceolate to oblong, often toothed. Flowers purple to rose pink.
Palafoxia (368). Leaves lanceolate to oblong, not toothed but sometimes somewhat wavy on the margins. Flowers pink.
Flowers white, cream, or yellow.
Leaves dissected into linear or filiform lobes.

White ragweed (369). Flowers yellow.
Leaves not dissected but may be toothed.
  False boneset (340). Leaves tending to roll under somewhat on the edges. Flowers white or cream-colored.
  Gumweed (341). Leaves with edges flat; herbage of flowering heads often sticky. Flowers yellow.
  Bigelow butterweed (357). Upper leaves sessile, with earlike projections at the base. Flowers yellow.

8a. Leaves opposite. (See 9a or 9b.)

8b. Leaves alternate. (See 10a or 10b.)

9a. Corollas of ray flowers $1/12$–$1/5$ in. (2–5 mm) long.
Needleleaf dogweed (362). Leaves narrowly linear or needlelike. Ray flowers yellow.
Woodhouse bahia (373). Leaves parted into 3 linear segments. Ray flowers yellow.

9b. Corollas of ray flowers $1/4$–$1 1/4$ in. (7–30 mm) long.
Leaves divided into narrow segments.
  Threadleaf (380). Strap-shaped rays about $3/8$ in. (10 mm) long. Ray flowers yellow.
  Tickseed (381). Strap-shaped rays about $1/2$–$5/8$ in. (12–15 mm) long. Ray flowers yellow.
Leaves not lobed or divided but sometimes toothed.
  Strap-shaped rays about as wide as long.
    Rocky Mountain zinnia (379). Plants low-growing and somewhat spreading; leaves linear to narrowly lanceolate. Ray flowers bright yellow.
  Rays definitely longer than wide.
    Leafy arnica (356). Leaves lanceolate or oblanceolate; rays $1/2$–$3/4$ in. (12–18 mm) long, yellow.
    Plains blackfoot (374). Leaves linear to spatulate; rays $1/4$–$1/2$ in (7–12 mm) long, white with purple veins.
    Rough ox-eye daisy (378). Leaves lanceolate to triangular-ovate; rays $5/8$–$1 1/4$ in. (15–30 mm) long, yellow.
    Toothleaf goldeneye (390). Leaves ovate, toothed; rays $1/4$–$5/8$ in. (7–15 mm) long, yellow.

10a. Corollas of ray flowers pink, blue, purple, or white. (See 11a or 11b.)

10b. Corollas of ray flowers yellow. (See 12a or 12b.)

11a. Rays to about $3/8$ in. (9 mm) long.
Leaves lobed or divided.
  Lazy daisy (347). Leaves spatulate to oblong or obovate; rays 20–40, white, often pinkish or violet on the back.
  Western yarrow (360). Leaves divided repeatedly into numerous short segments; rays about 5–12, white, rarely pink.

Lyrate rubberbush (375). Leaves lyrate-pinnatifid; rays only about $^1/_{25}$ in. (1 mm) long, white.

Leaves unlobed or undivided, sometimes toothed.

Rays 75–150 or more per head.

Naked-headed fleabane (350). Rays mostly 75–100, pinkish or whitish.

Common fleabane (351). Rays mostly 150–200, pinkish or whitish.

Rays mostly 15–40 per head.

Lazy daisy (347). Leaves spatulate to oblong or obovate; rays 20–40, white, often pinkish or violet on the back.

White aster (352). Leaves linear or awl-shaped; rays $^1/_5$ in. (5 mm) long, white.

Small-flowered aster (355). Leaves linear to spatulate; rays about $^1/_5$ in. (5 mm) long, white or blue.

11b. Rays mostly $^3/_8$–1 in. (10–25 mm) long.

Leaves divided or lobed.

Central part of flower head elongated and cylindrical or cone-shaped.

Prairie coneflower (382). Rays often both yellow and brownish purple or sometimes yellow throughout.

Central part of flower head not elongated.

Tahoka daisy (353). Leaf lobes spine-tipped; rays purple.

Ox-eye daisy (361). Leaves sometimes merely deeply toothed, rays white.

Newberry white ragweed (370). Rays $^3/_8$–$^5/_8$ in. (8–14 mm) wide, white.

Leaves undivided or unlobed, but often toothed.

Dwarf Townsend's aster (348). Low-growing with short, spreading stems; leaves linear to spatulate or oblong; rays white or tinged with pink.

Smooth Townsend's aster (349). Plants erect; leaves linear to spatulate; rays bluish purple or pinkish purple.

Streambank aster (354). Leaves lanceolate to oblanceolate, sparingly spiny toothed; rays purple.

12a. Leaves variously divided or lobed.(See 13a or 13b.)

12b. Leaves undivided or unlobed, but often toothed. (See 14a or 14b.)

13a. Rays $^3/_4$–2 in. (20–50 mm) long.

Pinque; hymenoxys (366). Leaves with 3–7 linear segments; rays about 3–20 mm long.

Prairie coneflower (382). Central part of the flower head elongated to form a cylindrical or cone-shaped structure; rays $^3/_4$–1 $^5/_8$ in. (20–40 mm) long, sometimes multicolored yellow and brownish purple.

Cutleaf coneflower (383). Leaves coarsely laciniately divided or toothed; rays $1^1/_4$–2 in. (30–50 mm) long.

13b. Rays $^1/_4$–$^5/_8$ in. (5–15 mm) long.

Plants woolly throughout.

Desert marigold (363). Leaves spatulate in outline; rays about 20–50, ³/₈–⁵/₈ in. (10–15 mm) long.

Plants various but not woolly.

Flowerhead bracts very large, broadly ovate to rounded.

Green eyes (377). Rays yellow with dark veins.

Flower-head bracts linear to lanceolate.

Spiny goldenweed (345). Leaves with bristly toothed lobes or segments; flowerhead bracts with green center; rays about ³/₈ in. (8–10 mm) long.

Groundsel (358). Leaves irregularly divided into linear to filiform lobes; rays ¹/₄–³/₈ in. (5–8 mm) long.

Pinque (366). Leaves divided into 3–7 linear segments; rays mostly ¹/₈–³/₄ in. (3–20 mm) long.

Engelmann daisy (376). Leaves deeply pinnatifid; rays 8–10, about ³/₈ in. (10 mm) long.

Littleleaf goldeneye (389). Leaves ovate, toothed, the lower often opposite, the upper alternate; rays about 10–12, ¹/₄–⁵/₈ in. (7–15 mm) long.

14a. Rays ¹/₂–2 in. (12–50 mm) long. (See 15a or 15b.)

14b. Rays ¹/₁₂–³/₈ in. (2–11 mm) long. (See 16a or 16b.)

15a. Leaves ovate, lanceolate, or heart-shaped.

Crownbeard (384). Leaves lanceolate to ovate or heart-shaped, toothed; rays deeply cleft into 3 lobes, ³/₄–1 in. (20–25 mm) long.

Common annual sunflower (387). Leaves ovate, toothed. Rays 1–2 in. (25–50 mm) long.

Prairie sunflower (388). Leaves lanceolate to ovate; rays ⁵/₈-1 in. (15–25 mm) long.

Toothed goldeneye (390). Leaves ovate, toothed; rays mostly ¹/₄–⁵/₈ in. (7–15 mm) long.

15b. Leaves linear to narrowly lanceolate to spatulate.

Leafy arnica (356). Leaves lanceolate to oblanceolate; rays pale yellow, ¹/₂–³/₄ in. (12–18 mm) long.

Orange sneezeweed (372). Leaves spatulate to oblanceolate, to 1 ft. (30 cm) long; rays yellow to orange, ⁵/₈–1¹/₄ in. (15–30 mm) long.

Rough mulesears (385). Leaves linear to linear-lanceolate, very rough to the touch; rays ³/₄–1³/₈ in. (20–35 mm) long.

Parry wood sunflower (386). Leaves lanceolate to spatulate; rays pale yellow, ¹/₂–³/₄ in. (12–18 mm) long.

16a. Rays ¹/₈–¹/₄ in. (2–5 mm) long.

Snakeweed (342). Leaves linear; heads very small.

Western goldenrod (343). Leaves linear-lanceolate to lanceolate, 3-nerved.

Dwarf alpine goldenrod (344). Plants very short; leaves spatulate to oblanceolate; rays ¹/₁₂–¹/₆ in. (2–4 mm) long.

Dogweed (362). Leaves narrowly linear, often needlelike; rays $^1/_{12}$–$^1/_6$ in. (2–4 mm) long.

16b. Rays $^1/_4$–$^1/_2$ in. (6–11 mm) long.

Leaves with spiny teeth.

Spiny goldenweed (345). Leaves dissected or merely toothed, the teeth or lobes spine-tipped.

Leaves without spiny teeth or lobes.

Leaves ovate.

Toothleaf goldeneye (390). Leaves toothed; rays 10–12, $^1/_4$–$^5/_8$ in. (7–15 mm) long.

Leaves linear-lanceolate to oblanceolate or spatulate.

Parry goldenweed (346). Leaves oblanceolate to spatulate; rays $^1/_4$–$^3/_8$ in. (5–8 mm) long.

Wooton butterweed (359). Leaves oblanceolate to lanceolate; rays 6–10, about $^3/_8$ in. (8 mm) long.

Paper daisy (364). Leaves linear to spatulate; rays 3, $^1/_4$–$^3/_8$ in. (6–8 mm) long, persistent.

Silvery bitterweed (365). Plant with obvious silky hairs, the leaves with small dots; rays $^1/_4$–$^1/_2$ in. (6–12 mm) long.

Firewheel (371). Leaves entire to sinuately toothed; rays $^3/_8$–$^3/_4$ in. (10–20 mm) long, often multicolored yellow and brownish purple.

Descriptions and Illustrations
of Species

The 390 species of summer-blooming wildflowers characterized in this book are represented by both common and scientific names and the common name of the family to which each species belongs. These names are followed by a description of characteristics pertaining to the identification of each species, including size measurements where useful and flower color.

Additional remarks present a brief account of the maximum known range of distribution, the approximate distribution within New Mexico, the elevational range, and the kinds of habitats usually associated with this species.

Following the description and under the heading *Key Characters* is a listing of those features most useful in making a quick identification of the described plant. Where appropriate, additional remarks are included under the category of *Related Species*. These remarks deal with the identity of other closely related species which can be found occasionally as part of the summer flora.

Note also that each plant name is preceded by a number. This number refers only to the plant whose description follows and is used as a reference number in the keys to identification and in the index. These reference numbers are more useful than page numbers.

Each description is accompanied by a line drawing showing the major features. Many of these illustrations are further supplemented by color plates.

1. **Dayflower**   *Commelina erecta*   Spiderwort family

Perennial herb, the stems several, jointed, to about 16 in. (40 cm) long, erect to spreading. *Leaves* alternate, sheathing the stem at the base, linear to narrowly lanceolate, to 6 in. (15 cm) long and about 1/4–3/8 in. (5–10 mm) wide, with smooth margins. *Flowers* with two blue petals and a slightly larger white petal, all petals 3/8–5/8 in. (10--15 mm) long, the flower cluster arising from two long, tapered bracts. The delicate flowers of the dayflower (or widow's-tears) open about dawn and last until around noon.

Range and Habitat: New York to Colorado, southward to Florida, Louisiana, Texas, New Mexico, and Arizona. Usually found on dry hills and plains in fine or sandy soil, often in shady spots from north-central to southwestern New Mexico; 3,500–6,000 ft.

Key Characters: Dayflower is characterized by the long united bracts below the flower, and by the delicate petals, one whitish and the other two blue.

Related Species: Two other species of dayflower are similar but differ in having longer bracts and all petals blue.

2. **Western spiderwort**   *Tradescantia occidentalis*   Spiderwort family

Slender-stemmed herb from fascicled roots, the stems jointed, erect or nearly so, to about 2 ft. (60 cm) high. *Leaves* alternate, sheathing the stem at the base, narrowly lanceolate, to 20 in. (50 cm) long and 3/4 in. (2 cm) wide, with smooth margins. *Flowers* in umbellike clusters bearing gland tipped hairs, arising from 2 or 3 leaflike bracts, the three petals about the same size, blue, 3/8–5/8 in. (10–16 mm) long, usually only a few flowers of the cluster blooming at a time. The flowers of the spiderwort are showy, but last only a few hours, generally closing before noon. The tender shoots of this plant are sometimes used for food.

Range and Habitat: Wisconsin to Montana, southward to Texas, New Mexico, and Arizona. Usually found on dry hills and plains in somewhat sandy soils, sometimes in shady spots throughout New Mexico; 5,000–8,000 ft.

Key Characters: Spiderwort is characterized by the three similar blue petals and the flowers in an umbellike cluster.

Related Species: A variety of the Western spiderwort differs in being glabrous in and around the flower cluster.

3. **Hoary yucca; Schott yucca**   *Yucca schottii*   Lily family

Perennial with a treelike trunk to about 17 ft. (5 m) tall, often branching. *Leaves* clustered at the top of the stems or branches, 16–40 in. (40–100 cm) long, 5/8–1 5/8 in. (15–40 mm) wide, with few or no marginal fibers, these fine and brownish, if present. *Flowers* in clusters 12–32 in. (30–80 cm) long, at the ends of the stems or branches, these usually borne above the leaves on short, stout flower stalks. Flower segments 1–2 in. (25–50 mm) long, elliptic or broadest above the middle and tapering to the base. *Fruit* oblong, 2 3/4–5 1/8 in. (7–13 cm) long, becoming dark colored in age. The hoary yucca in bloom is truly a spectacular sight, especially in large stands.

Range and Habitat: New Mexico and Arizona to northern Mexico. Usually found on dry, rocky slopes and in canyons of southwestern New Mexico; 4,000–6,500 ft.

Key Characters: Hoary yucca is distinguished by the usually tall stems or trunks, and the relatively broad, smooth, bluish green leaves with fine, brownish, curling marginal fibers.

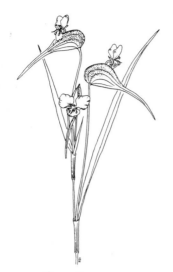

Commelina erecta

Yucca schottii

Tradescantia occidentalis

47

4. Soaptree yucca; palmilla   *Yucca elata*   Lily family

Perennial, often with a definite, usually branching trunk, the plant to about 18 ft. (6 m) tall. *Leaves* narrow, 10–30 in. (25–70 cm) long, 1 1/4–1 3/4 in. (6–12 mm) wide, with many fine fibers on the margins. *Flowers* in a large, much-branched, open cluster borne above the leaves on a long leafless stalk, the petals white, elliptic to lanceolate, 1/4–1 3/4 in. (3–4.5 cm) long. *Fruit* dry at maturity, 2–3 1/8 in. (5–8 cm) long, pale brown. The fruit, flowers, and young tender central leaves of this species are sometimes used for food, and the roots are used for making soap.

Range and Habitat: Southwestern Texas to Arizona and Mexico. Usually found on dry plains and hills in central and southern New Mexico; 3,500–5,500 ft.

Key Characters: Soaptree yucca is characterized by an obvious trunk in older specimens, and the narrow leaves.

Related Species: Soapweed yucca or amole is very similar but without a noticeable trunk, being leafy to the ground, and the flower cluster usually has fewer and shorter branches.

5. Sotol   *Dasylirion wheeleri*   Lily family

Perennial from woody underground crowns. *Leaves* numerous, in a cluster near the base of the plant, rigid, flat, to 3 ft. (90 cm) long and 5/8–1 in. (15–25 mm) wide, bearing numerous yellowish brown prickles on the margins. *Flowers* very numerous, unisexual, borne in a large narrow cluster (panicle) on a leafless stalk 10–12 ft. (3–4 m) tall, the flower segments less than 1/8 in. (2–3 mm) long. *Fruit* roundish, about 1/4 in. (6 mm) long. Sotol leaf fibers have been used for weaving, the young tender crowns for making mescal, and the young emerging flower stalks for food.

Range and Habitat: Western Texas to Arizona and northern Mexico. Found on dry hills in southern and west-central New Mexico; 3,500–6,500 ft.

Key Characters: Sotol may be easily recognized by the densely prickly leaf margins and the tall, narrow panicle of flowers.

Related Species: A similar species of sotol, *D. leiophyllum,* differs in having the leaf prickles curved toward the base of the leaf instead of toward the tip.

6. **Gunnison mariposa lily**   *Calochortus gunnisonii*   Lily family

Erect perennial herb, the stems to about 12 in. (30 cm) tall. *Leaves* alternate on the stem, linear, grasslike. *Flowers* 1 to 3 in a cluster at the end of a slender leafless stalk, bell-shaped, the petals white to purple, showy, about 1 1/4–1 3/4 in. (3–4.5 cm) long, each with a densely purple-bearded zone on the inner surface, the outer segments purple-spotted. Gunnison mariposa lily is a showy plant. This is one of our showiest wildflowers, sometimes used to make a thick tea to treat swellings.

Range and Habitat: South Dakota to Montana, southward to New Mexico and Arizona. Usually found in meadows and open ground in northern, central, and western New Mexico; 7,000–8,000 ft.

Key Characters: Gunnison mariposa lily is characterized by the densely purple-bearded zone on the inner surface of the petals, this zone wider than tall.

Yucca elata

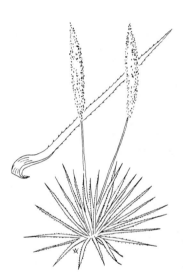

Dasylirion wheeleri

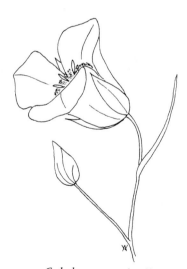

Calochortus gunnisonii

49

7. **Solomon's seal**   *Polygonatum commutatum*   Lily family

Perennial herb from jointed rhizomes, the stems stout, simple, 24–40 in. (60–100 cm) or more tall. *Leaves* alternate, the blades elliptic, usually 3–10 in. (8–25 cm) long and at least 1³/₈ in. (35 mm) wide, wrinkled on the margins, the nerves prominent. *Flowers* borne in clusters of 2–5, often on curved stalks, the 6 segments greenish yellow, ⁵/₈–³/₄ in. (17–20 mm) long. *Fruit* round, about ⁵/₁₆ in. (7–8 mm) in diameter, blue or black.

Range and Habitat: New England to Missouri, westward and southward to Georgia, Oklahoma, Colorado, and New Mexico. Found occasionally on shaded slopes in the mountains of northern New Mexico; 8,000–10,500 ft.

Key Characters: Solomon's seal may be recognized by the prominently veined, alternate leaves with wrinkled margins, and by the greenish white flowers on curved stalks.

8. **Death camas**   *Zygadenus elegans*   Lily family

Perennial herb from bulbs, the stems bluish green, without hairs, to 24 in. (60 cm) tall. *Leaves* few, keeled, ¹/₈–⁵/₈ in. (3–15 mm) wide. *Flowers* in clusters, on ascending pedicels, the subtending floral bracts ovate-lanceolate, the flower segments greenish white or tinged with yellow, ³/₁₆–³/₈ in. (5–10 mm) long, tapered toward the base, bearing greenish kidney-shaped glands toward the base. Death camas resembles wild onions, but is highly poisonous.

Range and Habitat: Saskatchewan to Alaska, southward to New Mexico and Arizona. Commonly found on wooded slopes in mountains throughout New Mexico; 7,000–12,000 ft.

Key Characters: Death camas is distinguished by the lack of an onionlike odor from the bulbs, the greenish glands at the base of the petals, and the flowers in branching clusters.

Related Species: Another death camas, *Z. gramineus*, differs in having narrower leaves; these not more than ⁵/₁₆ in. (8 mm) wide, and glands on the petals are oblong to nearly circular.

9. **Green death camas**   *Zygadenus virescens*   Lily family

Perennial herb from bulbs, the stems to about 20 in. (50 cm) tall, without hairs. *Leaves* few, linear, mostly near the base of the stem, grasslike. *Flowers* in branching clusters, the flower stalks usually spreading or curved downward, much longer than the subtending bract, the 6 flower segments tapering to the base, greenish white or faintly purple-tinged, to about ³/₁₆ in. (5 mm) long, bearing kidney-shaped glands near the base. This death camas is also highly poisonous.

Range and Habitat: New Mexico and Arizona to Central America. Usually found in coniferous forests from northern to south-central and western New Mexico; 8,000–11,000 ft.

Key Characters: This death camas may be distinguished by the bulbs without an onion-like odor, the widely branched flower clusters, and the flower segments tapering gradually to the base.

10. **Corn-lily**   *Veratrum californicum*   Lily family

Tall, coarse, perennial herb, the stems stout, densely clothed with matted hairs, to 7 ft. (2 m) tall. *Leaves* alternate on the stem, large, lance-shaped to oval, hairy beneath, 12–16 in. (30–40 cm) long, clasping at the base, with conspicuous veins. *Flowers* borne in branching, matted-hairy clusters to 20 in. (50 cm) long, the 6 segments white, oblong-ovate, about ¹/₂ in. (12 mm) long, bearing a Y-shaped greenish gland near the base. *Fruit* 1–1³/₈ in. (25–35 mm) long.

Range and Habitat: Montana to Washington, southward to New Mexico, Arizona, and California. Common in moist mountain meadows throughout New Mexico; 8,000–12,000 ft.

Key Characters: Corn-lily is distinguished by the large, conspicuously veined leaves, and by the long, hairy, branching clusters of white flowers.

Polygonatum commutatum

Zygadenus elegans

Zygadenus virescens

Veratrum californicum

11. Geyer onion   *Allium geyeri*   Lily family

Perennial herb 6–20 in. (15–50 cm) tall, from a strong-scented, fibrous-coated bulb. *Leaves* usually 3 per flowering stem, about ¹/₈ in. (2–3 mm) wide. *Flowers* borne in an erect umbel subtended by 2 or 3 single-nerved bracts, the flower segments white or pink, ¹/₄–³/₈ in. (6–10 mm) long. *Fruit* a capsule without obvious crests. Geyer onion has been used to flavor soups and gravy and is occasionally eaten raw.

Range and Habitat: Alberta to Washington, southward to Texas, New Mexico, and Arizona. Geyer onion is commonly found in meadows and on open slopes throughout New Mexico; 6,500–12,000 ft.

Key Characters: Geyer onion is characterized by the fibrous-coated, solitary bulb, the three leaves, and the single-nerved floral bracts.

Related Species: Large-petal onion (*A. macropetalum*) differs in usually having 2 leaves per stem and occurring on dry plains throughout New Mexico at elevations of 4,500–6,500 ft.

12. Red onion   *Allium rubrum*   Lily family

Perennial herb from a solitary bulb with an outer sheath of reticulate fibers, the flowering stems 8–16 in. (20–40 cm) tall. *Leaves* commonly 3 or 4 per scape, ³/₁₆–¹/₄ in. (4–6 mm) wide, flat or curved in cross-section. *Flowers* borne in an erect umbel, most of them sterile and replaced by small, spherical, reddish bulblets, the umbel arising from 2 or 3 single-nerved bracts, the flower segments, when present, pink, about ⁵/₁₆ in. (7 mm) long, often with a darker midnerve.

Range and Habitat: Alberta and British Columbia, southward to Oregon, Arizona, and New Mexico. Found occasionally on open slopes from northern to western and southwestern New Mexico; 7,000–9,500 ft.

Key Characters: Red onion is characterized by the fibrous-coated, usually solitary bulb, and by the flowers often being replaced by bulblets.

Related Species: Goodding's onion (*A. gooddingii*) differs in having few or no bulblets, the bulb scales with parallel fibers, and longer flower segments. It appears to be limited to moist, shaded canyons in southwestern New Mexico. Another wild onion, *A. brevistylum,* has a single bract subtending the umbel, deep rose-colored flowers, and occurs in south-central New Mexico at altitudes of 9,000–11,000 ft.

13. New Mexico nodding onion   *Allium cernuum*   Lily family

Perennial herb to about 20 in. (50 cm) tall, from clustered bulbs, the outer bulb scales only slightly fibrous. *Leaves* 4–6 per flowering stalk (scape), ¹/₈–³/₁₆ in. (3–7 mm) wide, nearly flat in cross-section. *Flowers* borne in nodding umbels from 2 subtending bracts, recurved at the tip, the 6 flower segments white to pink. The New Mexico nodding onion has been used as a food plant and is a small but attractive element of our mountain flora.

Range and Habitat: Western Texas to Arizona, southward to Mexico. Common on open slopes and in meadows throughout New Mexico; 6,500–9,000 ft.

Key Characters: New Mexico nodding onion is distinguished by the bulbs lacking fibrous outer scales, and by the nodding umbels.

Related Species: A variety, Rocky Mountain nodding onion, has leaves rounded on the back, and inner the scales of the bulb are pink to red instead of white.

Allium geyeri

Allium rubrum

Allium cernuum

53

| 14. | **Crag lily** | *Anthericum torreyi* | Lily family |

Perennial herb from clustered roots, the flowering stalk erect, leafless, 8–16 in. (20–40 cm) tall. *Leaves* borne at the base of the flowering stalks (scapes), linear, often longer than the scape. *Flowers* in narrow clusters (racemes) on jointed stalks, the 6 perianth segments yellowish orange, $5/16–1/2$ in. (9–12 mm) long, with a darker midvein. The crag lily is easily overlooked, but is a distinctive part of the New Mexico flora.
Range and Habitat: New Mexico to Arizona and Mexico. Found on gravelly or rocky slopes, often in open areas of pine woods, throughout New Mexico; 6,000–8,000 ft.
Key Characters: Crag lily may be identified by the 6 separate yellowish orange perianth segments, borne in narrow racemes, and the basal leaves.

| 15. | **Star flower** | *Smilacina stellata* | Lily family |

Perennial herb from creeping roots, the stem unbranched, erect to arching, devoid of hairs, 8–20 in. (20–50 cm) tall. *Leaves* alternate, lanceolate, prominently many-nerved, the petioles short or absent. *Flowers* in narrow clusters, the 6 segments white, $1/8–1/4$ in. (3–6 mm) long, separate. *Fruit* green with dark stripes at first, becoming nearly black.
Range and Habitat: Throughout much of temperate North America; also Europe. Usually found in damp woods or partially shaded slopes of mountains throughout New Mexico; 7,000–10,000 ft.
Key Characters: Star flower is easily recognized by the broad, prominently nerved, alternate leaves, the absence of bulbs, and by the narrow clusters of white flowers.
Related Species: False solomon's seal (*S. racemosa*) differs in having the flowers in wider, branching clusters, and the stamens longer than the flower segments.

| 16. | **Twisted-stalk** | *Streptopus amplexifolius* | Lily family |

Perennial herb from creeping rootstocks, the stems to 40 in. (1 m) tall, branched, limber, devoid of hairs. *Leaves* ovate, many-nerved, long-pointed at the apex, the base clasping the stem. *Flowers* solitary or 2 or 3 in a cluster, borne on stalks from the leaf axils, the 6 perianth segments greenish white, separate, $5/16–1/2$ in. (8–12 mm) long. *Fruit* a smooth, red berry.
Range and Habitat: Greenland to Alaska, southward to North Carolina, New Mexico, and California; Eurasia. Typically found in damp woods of northern New Mexico; 8,000–9,500 ft.
Key Characters: Twisted-stalk is easily recognized by the clasping leaves and the bell-shaped flowers on sharply bent stalks.

| 17. | **Alp lily** | *Lloydia serotina* | Lily family |

Low perennial herb from bulbous rootstocks, the stems leafy, 3–6 in. (7–15 cm) tall. *Leaves* linear, grasslike. *Flowers* solitary or 2 or 3 in a cluster, the 6 segments separate, yellowish white inside, pinkish and purple-veined on the outside, to about $3/8$ in. (10 mm) long. *Fruit* a capsule about $1/3$ in. (8 mm) long. The alp lily is often overlooked, partially hidden by the surrounding vegetation.
Range and Habitat: Alberta to Alaska, southward to Nevada, Colorado, and New Mexico. Found in high mountain meadows from northern to south-central New Mexico; 10,000–12,000 ft.
Key Characters: Alp lily is characterized by the low, leafy stems, the grasslike leaves, and the few purple-veined flowers.

Anthericum torreyi

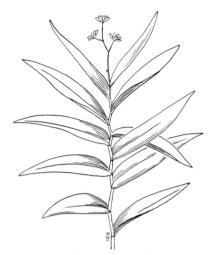

Smilacina stellata

Streptopus amplexifolius

Lloydia serotina

55

18.	Rocky Mountain lily	*Lilium umbellatum*	Lily family

Perennial herb from fleshy scaled bulbs, the stems leafy, 12–26 in. (30–65 cm) tall. *Leaves* alternate, except usually in whorls on the upper portion of the stem, hairless, linear to lance-shaped. *Flowers* borne singly or 2 or 3 in a cluster, the 6 segments red to orange red with purplish black spots near the base, spreading or recurved at the apex, 2–2³/₈ in. (5–6 cm) long. Rocky Mountain lily is a conspicuous, attractive flower but scarce and should be left undisturbed.

Range and Habitat: Ohio to Alberta, southward to Arkansas, New Mexico, and Arizona. Occasionally found in open woods from northern to south-central New Mexico; 7,000–8,000 ft.

Key Characters: Rocky Mountain lily may be recognized by the large orange to yellow petals with dark spots, and by the whorled upper leaves.

19.	Schott century plant	*Agave schottii*	Amaryllis family

Large, long-lived perennials without leafy stems. *Leaves* crowded in basal rosettes, linear, often curved, ¹/₄–³/₈ in. (7–10 mm) wide, green, tapering from the base to the tip, bearing fine, curved fibers on the margins, sometimes a few small teeth also present. *Flowers* borne in a dense, narrow, elongate cluster on stout flowering stalks to about 7 ft. (2 m) tall, the perianth segments yellow, 1¹/₄–2 in. (3–5 cm) long. *Fruit* a capsule about ¹/₂ in. (10–12 mm) long. Schott century plant in flower is a striking plant, sure to attract attention.

Range and Habitat: New Mexico to southern Arizona and northern Mexico. Found occasionally on dry, exposed, rocky slopes in extreme southwestern New Mexico; 5,000–7,000 ft.

Key Characters: Schott century plant is characterized by the basal rosette of narrow, tapering leaves usually without marginal spines, and by the dense, narrow, elongate cluster of flowers on a stout stalk.

20.	Mescal	*Agave parryi*	Amaryllis family

Long-lived perennial without leafy stems. *Leaves* in a basal rosette, numerous, bluish green, 2–4 in. (5–10 cm) wide, with backward-curved spines on the margins, concave in cross-section, tapering from about the middle to the spine-tipped apex. *Flowers* borne in open, branching clusters, on stalks 7–14 ft. (2–4 m) tall, the perianth segments yellow, tinged with red, about ¹/₄ in. (6 mm) long, the stamens exserted. *Fruit* a capsule about ¹/₂ in. (12 mm) long. Young mescal crowns have been used for food and for making a fermented drink; the leaves have been used for weaving.

Range and Habitat: New Mexico to southern Arizona and Mexico. Mescal may be found on rocky slopes of dry hills in southern New Mexico; 4,000–6,500 ft.

Key Characters: Mescal is distinguished by the bluish green leaves with spiny-toothed margins and by the broad panicle of conspicuous yellowish flowers.

Related Species: New Mexico agave (*A. neomexicana*) is similar but differs in having shorter, narrower leaves and smaller flowers, these yellow to orange and often reddish tinged. Another century plant (*A. palmeri*) has deep green leaves usually more than 16 in. (40 cm) long, and greenish yellow, often purple-tinged flowers.

Lilium umbellatum

Agave schottii

Agave parryi

21. **Zephyr lily**   *Zephyranthes longifolia*   Amaryllis family

Perennial herb from ovoid bulbs. *Leaves* linear, grasslike, 6–10 in. (15–25 cm) long. *Flowers* borne singly at the top of a leafless stalk to 14 in. (35 cm) tall, subtended by floral bracts ³/₄–1 in. (2–2.5 cm) long, the 6 similar perianth segments usually 1¹/₄–1¹/₂ in. (3–4 cm) long, bright yellow, the stamens not projecting from the flower. The conspicuous Zephyr lily usually appears about 10 days after a rain.

Range and Habitat: Western Texas to Arizona and Mexico. Usually found on dry hills and mesas in central and southern New Mexico; 3,000–7,500 ft.

Key Characters: Zephyr lily is characterized by the nearly spherical, deeply 3-lobed fruit, and by the yellow flowers with stamens not projecting beyond the perianth.

22. **Blue-eyed grass**   *Sisyrinchium demissum*   Iris family

Perennial herb, the stems erect, bluish green, mostly unbranched, often curved or twisted, 4–12 in. (10–30 cm) tall, somewhat winged on the angles. *Leaves* mostly basal, linear, grasslike, about ¹/₁₆ in. (2 mm) wide. *Flowers* in few-flowered clusters at the apex of the stems, arising from 2 sheathing bracts, these about equal in length, the petals blue violet, ¹/₄–³/₈ in. (7–10 mm) long. *Fruit* a capsule about ³/₁₆ in. (5 mm) long. Blue-eyed grass (not a true grass) is often overlooked, usually surrounded by dense stands of other vegetation.

Range and Habitat: Western Kansas to Colorado, Utah, and California, southward to Texas, New Mexico, and Arizona. Blue-eyed grass is frequently found in wet meadows or near springs or bogs in mountains throughout New Mexico; 6,000–9,000 ft.

Key Characters: Blue-eyed grass is easily recognized by the blue violet flowers, often with a yellow center, the grasslike leaves, and the spathlike bracts almost equal in length.

Related Species: Two other species of blue-eyed grass (*S. occidentale* and *S. montanum*) are similar, but the outer floral bract is much longer than the inner one.

23. **Arizona blue-eyed grass**   *Sisyrinchium arizonicum*   Iris family

Perennial herb, the stems erect, branching, 12–16 in. (30–40 cm) tall. *Leaves* linear, grasslike, conspicuously nerved, ³/₁₆–¹/₄ in. (5–7 mm) wide. *Flowers* few, in clusters at the apex of stems or branches, subtended by a pair of sheathing bracts, the petals similar, yellow or orange, ⁵/₈–³/₄ in. (15–20 mm) long. *Fruit* a capsule about ¹/₂ in. (12 mm) long. Arizona blue-eyed grass is neither a grass nor blue. Its large, yellow orange flowers are striking and attractive.

Range and Habitat: New Mexico to southern Arizona, probably ranging into northern Mexico. Occasionally found on wooded slopes in the mountains of southwestern New Mexico; 6,000–9,000 ft.

Key Characters: Arizona blue-eyed grass is easily recognizable by the large, yellowish orange flowers borne on branching, leafy stems.

Related Species: A less attractive plant, *S. elmeri,* has smaller flowers, usually not exceeding ¹/₂ in. (12 mm) long.

Zephyranthes lognifolia

Sisyrinchium demissum

Sisyrinchium arizonicum

24. **Rocky Mountain iris**   *Iris missouriensis*   Iris family

Perennial from rhizomes, to 28 in. (70 cm) tall. *Leaves* linear, glabrous, bluish green, 2-ranked and "V"-shaped in cross section at the base, $^{1}/_{4}$–$^{3}/_{8}$ in. (6–10 mm) wide. *Flowers* in terminal clusters, each subtended by 2 membranaceous bracts, the sepals about 2$^{1}/_{2}$ in. (6 cm) long, drooping, yellowish white at the constricted base, the expanded upper part mostly blue, sometimes with purple veins, the petals erect, white to purple. *Fruit* a capsule 1$^{1}/_{4}$–2 in. (3–5 cm) long. Wild iris is a conspicuous early summer plant of moist mountain meadows.
Range and Habitat: North Dakota to British Columbia, southward to New Mexico, Arizona, and California. Commonly found in open meadows in higher mountains throughout New Mexico; 7,500–10,500 ft.
Key Characters: Wild iris is easily recognized by its resemblance to the cultivated iris, though it is usually much smaller in size.

25. **Lady's slipper**   *Cypripedium calceolus*   Orchid family

Herbaceous perennial from thickened roots, the stems hairy, 10–20 in. (25–50 cm) tall. *Leaves* 4–6 per stem, large, 1$^{5}/_{8}$–4 in. (4–10 cm) wide, elliptic-lanceolate, several-nerved, with glandular hairs. *Flowers* showy, usually solitary at the tip of the stem, the sepals yellow, about 1$^{5}/_{8}$ in. (4 cm) long, the side petals yellow, longer than the sepals, the lower petal (lip) yellow with purple markings, about as long as the sepals, strongly inflated and moccasinlike. The lady's slipper orchid is relatively rare but is very showy. It does not transplant well, thus should be left undisturbed.
Range and Habitat: Newfoundland to British Columbia, southward to Georgia, New Mexico, and Arizona. Found occasionally in bogs, meadows, and damp woods in the higher mountains of New Mexico; 8,000–11,000 ft.
Key Characters: Lady's slipper is easily recognized by the large, orchid-shaped flowers marked with yellow and purple and with a conspicuously inflated lip petal, and by the large leaves.

26. **Fairy slipper**   *Calypso bulbosa*   Orchid family

Perennial herb from corms, the stems leafless, hairless, 4–6 in. (10–15 cm) tall. *Leaf* solitary, basal, 1$^{1}/_{4}$–2$^{1}/_{2}$ in. (3–6 cm) long, conspicuously veined, wavy on the margins. *Flowers* borne singly at the apex of the scape, nodding, the perianth rose-colored with yellow markings, about $^{1}/_{2}$ in. (10–15 mm) long, the lip or labellum larger, moccasinlike, hairy within. Fairy slipper is a small but most attractive plant of the mountains and, like Lady's slipper, does not transplant well and should be left undisturbed.
Range and Habitat: Labrador to Alaska, southward to New York, New Mexico, Arizona, and California. Found occasionally in woods in the mountains from northern to south-central New Mexico; 7,000–10,000 ft.
Key Characters: Fairy slipper may be recognized by the purple and yellow orchidlike flowers, and by the single leaf.

Iris missouriensis

Calypso bulbosa

Cypripedium calceolus

61

27. **Spotted coralroot**   *Corallorhiza maculata*   Orchid family

Perennial herb from rhizomes, the stems without green coloring, purplish to brownish or yellowish, 10–20 in. (25–50 cm) tall. *Leaves* scattered, reduced to scales, and devoid of chlorophyll. *Flowers* in narrow clusters at the summit of the stem, the sepals and lateral petals ³/₁₆–³/₈ in. (5–9 mm) long, mostly brownish purple, 3-nerved, the lip or labellum white, ³/₁₆–³/₈ in. (6–9 mm) long, spotted with reddish purple. Spotted coralroot is often overlooked in forests because it resembles a dry stick.

Range and Habitat: Nova Scotia to Alaska, southward to Florida, New Mexico, and California. Found frequently on shaded slopes in the mountains throughout New Mexico; 6,500–10,000 ft.

Key Characters: Spotted coralroot may be identified by the brownish yellow color, the absence of leaves, and the purplish spots on the corolla lip.

Related Species: Striped coralroot (*C. striata*) is very similar but differs in the lip being purple-striped instead of spotted.

28. **Dwarf rattlesnake plantain**   *Goodyera repens*   Orchid family

Perennial herb, the stems stout, with glandular hairs, leafless, twisted, from thick roots, 4–8 in. (1–2 dm) tall. *Leaves* in basal rosettes, ovate to oblong-ovate, dark green with white markings along the veins, ³/₈–1³/₁₆ in. (9–30 cm) long, on winged petioles. *Flowers* white or greenish white, borne in small, bracted, narrow, 1-sided clusters at the apex of the stems, the segments about ¹/₄ in. (6 mm) long, the lip without a spur. Dwarf rattlesnake plantain is a small, easily overlooked plant of deep forests.

Range and Habitat: Newfoundland to Alaska, southward to North Carolina, New Mexico, and Arizona; Eurasia. Found occasionally in deep, damp woods of mountains in northern and central New Mexico; 8,000–9,500 ft.

Key Characters: Dwarf rattlesnake plantain is characterized by the basal dark green leaves with conspicuous whitish markings, especially along the veins, and by the small orchid-type flowers.

Related Species: Giant rattlesnake plantain (*G. oblongifolia*) has much the same distribution in New Mexico but has larger leaves, these 1⁵/₈–2³/₈ in. (4–6 cm) long.

29. **Helleborine**   *Epipactis gigantea*   Orchid family

Perennial herb from creeping rhizomes, the stems leafy, to 32 in. (8 dm) tall. *Leaves* alternate, clasping the stem, ovate to lanceolate, to about 6 in. (15 cm) long, the veins conspicuous. *Flowers* few, to 1¹/₂ in. (30 mm) long, borne in a slender cluster, the sepals greenish and spreading, the petals greenish purple, shorter than the sepals, the lip or labellum about ⁵/₈ in. (15 mm) long, greenish with purple lines. Helleborine contains chlorophyll, thus it is neither parasitic nor saprophytic.

Range and Habitat: Montana to British Columbia, southward to western Texas, Arizona, and California. Found occasionally in damp woods, usually on seeping slopes, or in damp canyons from east-central to southern and western New Mexico; 7,000–8,500 ft.

Key Characters: Helleborine may be recognized by the often tall, leafy stems, and the flowers to 1¹/₂ in. (30 mm) long.

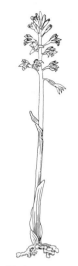

Corallorhiza maculata

Goodyera repens

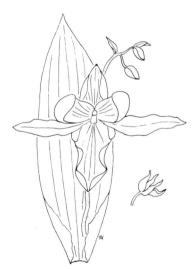

Epipactis gigantea

30. **Nodding Lady's tresses**   *Spiranthes cernua*   Orchid family

Perennial herb from thickened roots, the stems densely hairy in the upper part, to 20 in. (5 dm) tall. *Leaves* alternate on the stem, mostly near the base, linear-oblanceolate, long-pointed at the apex. *Flowers* small, white, in dense, hairy, spikelike clusters to 6 in. (15 cm) long, the sepals and lateral petals triangular-lanceolate, $^1/_8$–$^1/_2$ in. (3–12 mm) long, the lip or labellum about as long as the sepals. Lady's tresses is often hidden among grasses and sedges along streams.

Range and Habitat: Nova Scotia to South Dakota, southward to Florida, Texas, and New Mexico. Found occasionally in damp woods or along streams in northern New Mexico; 6,000–8,000 ft.

Key Characters: Nodding lady's tresses may be recognized by the flowers in 2 or 3 rows, and the densely hairy stems and leaves.

Related Species: Another species of lady's tresses, *S. vernalis,* has flowers in one row and linear leaflets. It should occur in eastern New Mexico.

31. **Bog orchid**   *Habenaria saccata*   Orchid family

Perennial herb from thick, fleshy roots, the stems glabrous, to 23 in. (58 cm) tall. *Leaves* glabrous, to 4 in. (10 cm) long, lanceolate or oblanceolate, acute at the apex. *Flowers* in narrow, elongate clusters (racemes), small, purple to greenish purple, about $^1/_2$ in. (12–14 mm) long, each flower subtended by a floral bract, the lateral petals about as long as the lip, the lip with a saclike spur, the sepals broader. Bog orchid is an inconspicuous plant, often hidden by the grasses and sedges with which it grows.

Range and Habitat: Alaska to British Columbia, Colorado, New Mexico, Arizona, and California. Often found along streams and in moist woods in the mountains from northern to south-central and western New Mexico; 8,000–11,000 ft.

Key Characters: Bog orchid may be identified by the leafy green stems, the narrow, spikelike raceme of purplish, typical orchid flowers, and the lip with a saclike spur.

32. **Few-flowered bog orchid**   *Habenaria sparsiflora*   Orchid family

Perennial herb from thickened roots, the stems glabrous, leafy, to 24 in. (60 cm) tall. *Leaves* glabrous, 4–8 in. (10–20 cm) long, the lower ones oblanceolate, obtuse at the apex, the upper ones lanceolate, acute at the tip, smaller. *Flowers* small, greenish white, borne in narrow, elongate clusters (racemes), the segments about $^3/_8$–$^1/_2$ in. (9–12 mm) long, ovate to lanceolate, the lip or labellum narrowly lanceolate, about $^5/_{16}$ in. (7–8 mm) long and with a slender spur.

Range and Habitat: Colorado to Washington, southward to New Mexico, Arizona, and California. Commonly found on moist wooded slopes or along streams in mountains throughout New Mexico; 7,500–9,000 ft.

Key Characters: The few-flowered bog orchid may be identified by the loosely flowered inflorescence, the greenish white flowers, and the large leaves.

Related Species: Two related bog orchids are less widely distributed. *H. limosa* differs in the length of the spur, this twice as long as the lip; *H. viridis* differs in having the floral bracts twice as long as the flowers.

Spiranthes cernua

Habenaria saccata

Habenaria sparsiflora

33. **Fringed orchid**   *Habenaria hyperborea*   Orchid family

Perennial herb from thickened roots, the stems erect, to 16 in. (40 cm) tall. *Leaves* usually all basal, sometimes some of them borne on the stem, linear or oblanceolate, the upper ones, if present, smaller. *Flowers* borne in narrow spikelike clusters (racemes) to $3^5/_8$ in. (9 cm) long, green or yellowish green, sometimes marked with brownish purple, the segments unlike in shape, ovate to lanceolate, the lip or labellum linear to lanceolate, $^1/_8$–$^5/_{16}$ in. (3–8 mm) long, the spur not as long as the lip.
Range and Habitat: Greenland and Newfoundland to Alaska, southward to New York, Nebraska, New Mexico, and California; also Asia and Iceland. Usually found in moist ground near lakes in the mountains from northern to south-central New Mexico; 7,500–9,500 ft.
Key Characters: Fringed orchid is characterized by the spur shorter than the greenish yellow lip, and the densely flowered inflorescence.
Related Species: White orchid (*H. dilatata*) differs in having the spur about as long as the lip and the flower segments white. It occupies about the same range and habitat as the fringed orchid.

34. **Yerba mansa**   *Anemopsis californica*   Lizard's-tail family

Succulent perennial herb from fleshy roots, the stems 4–20 in. (10–50 cm) tall. *Leaves* mostly basal, fleshy, elliptic-oblong, notched at the base, the blade and petiole each about 8 in. (20 cm) long, the few upper leaves scattered, ovate, clasping the stem, often with smaller leaves in their axils. *Flowers* inconspicuous, in dense terminal spikes with a series of white petallike bracts $^3/_8$–1 in. (10–25 mm) long at the base, each flower without sepals and petals but subtended by a single small white bract. Yerba mansa has long been used for various purposes as a folk medicine.
Range and Habitat: Western Texas to Utah, Arizona, and California. Usually found in open, moist areas, often in marshes or river valleys from central to western and southern New Mexico; 3,500–4,500 ft.
Key Characters: Yerba mansa may be recognized by the dense spikes of flowers subtended by conspicuous white, petallike bracts, and by the mostly basal, broad, fleshy leaves.

35. **Western dock**   *Rumex occidentalis*   Buckwheat family

Perennial herb, the stems coarse, 20–40 in. (5–10 dm) or more tall. *Leaves* alternate, each with a cylindric, usually membranaceous sheath surrounding the stem above the leaf base, the lower leaves lanceolate or ovate-lanceolate, 12–16 in. (30–40 cm) long, on long petioles, the margins wrinkled, the upper leaves smaller. *Flowers* in tight clusters, on jointed stalks, the perianth segments greenish, the 3 outer ones narrowly lanceolate, about $^1/_{12}$ in. (2 mm) long, the 3 inner ones (valves) about $^1/_4$ in. (5–6 mm) long and about as wide, net-veined, rounded. Western dock has been used for food, but care must be exercised in its preparation.
Range and Habitat: Labrador to British Columbia, southward to Texas, New Mexico, and California. Found usually in damp, often marshy ground in the mountains throughout New Mexico; 7,000–8,500 ft.
Key Characters: Western dock is characterized by the absence of grainlike swellings on the back of the smaller inner perianth segments, the lack of hairs on the stems and leaves, and the leaves mostly notched at the base.
Related Species: Pale dock (*R. altissimus*) is similar, but the lower leaves are smaller and one of the inner segments of the perianth has a swelling on the back. It occurs at lower elevations throughout New Mexico.

Habenaria hyperborea

Anemopsis californica

Rumex occidentalis

36. Bistort   *Polygonum bistortoides*   Buckwheat family

Perennial herb from large rhizomes, the stems erect, unbranched, usually swollen and jointed at the nodes, 10–32 in. (25–80 cm) tall. *Leaves* alternate, the basal ones stalked, oblong to oblanceolate, tapering at the base, the stem leaves smaller, lanceolate, sessile, each leaf base with a cylindrical sheath surrounding the stem. *Flowers* borne in a dense, terminal, spikelike cluster, the segments white to pink, about ¼ in. (4–6 mm) long. *Fruit* 3-angled. Bistort is conspicuous in moist mountain meadows.
Range and Habitat: Newfoundland to British Columbia and Alaska, southward to New Mexico, Arizona, and California. Found in moist meadows of higher mountains throughout New Mexico; 8,000–11,000 ft.
Key Characters: Bistort may be identified by the solitary, dense spike of white flowers on a jointed, unbranched stem bearing brownish sheaths at the nodes.

37. Desert four-o'clock   *Oxybaphus comatus*   Four-o'clock family

Perennial herb, the stems mostly erect, occasionally sparsely branched below the flower cluster, glabrous or nearly so. *Leaves* opposite, triangular-lanceolate to triangular-ovate, flattened to somewhat notched at the base, glabrous or nearly so, to 4 in. (10 cm) long, short-petioled. *Flowers* borne in open clusters, in calyxlike involucres with sticky hairs, these often blackish and jointed, the perianth tubular, 5-lobed, purplish red, sparsely hairy, about ⅜ in. (10 mm) long. *Fruit* about ³/₁₆ in. (3–5 mm) long, bearing short hairs. These delicate flowers usually open in late afternoon and close by mid-morning.
Range and Habitat: Western Texas to Arizona and Mexico. Common on dry hills and mountain slopes throughout New Mexico; 5,000–10,000 ft.
Key Characters: This desert four-o'clock is distinguished by involucres with few flowers and blackish jointed hairs, and by the night-flowering characteristic.
Related Species: White four-o'clock (*O. albidus*) differs in having sessile leaves, whitish stems, and white to pink flowers. It occurs in southern New Mexico. Another four-o'clock of south-central and western New Mexico, *O. pumilus,* differs mostly in having more spreading stems with sticky hairs.

38. Red umbrellawort   *Oxybaphus coccineus*   Four-o'clock family

Perennial herb, the stems erect, sometimes sparsely branched below the flower cluster, glabrous to somewhat hairy. *Leaves* opposite on the stem, linear, to 3¼ in. (8 cm) long and about ¼ in. (6 mm) wide, nearly sessile. *Flowers* borne in few-flowered, hairy, calyxlike involucres, these in loose, branching clusters, the perianth tubular, 5-lobed, deep red, ½–⅝ in. (12–15 mm) long. Red umbrellawort is a striking plant, opening from late afternoon to about mid-morning.
Range and Habitat: New Mexico to California and Mexico. Found usually in dry canyons and on dry slopes in south-central and southwestern New Mexico; 5,000–6,500 ft.
Key Characters: Red umbrellawort is distinguished by the large, deep red flowers, the night-blooming characteristic, and the long, narrow leaves.

Polygonum bistortoides

Oxybaphus comatus

Oxybaphus coccineus

69

39. **Desert four-o'clock**   *Oxybaphus glaber*   Four-o'clock family

Perennial herb, the stems mostly erect, glabrous or nearly so, sparsely if at all branched. *Leaves* opposite, linear to narrowly lanceolate, tapered at the base and apex, sessile or nearly so. *Flowers* borne in loose clusters of 1- or 2-flowered, glabrous involucres, the perianth tubular, 5-lobed, whitish to pale pink, about $^5/_{16}$ in. (7–8 mm) long.
Range and Habitat: Kansas to Colorado and Utah, southward to Mexico. Scattered on dry hills throughout New Mexico; 5,000–6,500 ft.
Key Characters: This desert four-o'clock may be identified by the narrow, tapered leaves, the white to pink flowers, and by the mostly glabrous involucres and fruit.
Related Species: Another desert four-o'clock, *O. nyctagineus,* has broader leaves borne on conspicuous petioles, the perianth pink and about $^3/_8$ in. (10 mm) long. It occurs in northwestern and central New Mexico at 4,000–6,500 ft.

40. **Wild four-o'clock**   *Mirabilis multiflora*   Four-o'clock family

Perennial herb, the stems mostly spreading, to 24 in. (60 cm) long. *Leaves* opposite ovate, rounded to notched at the base, somewhat fleshy, long-petioled, to about 2³/4 in. (7 cm) long. *Flowers* borne in calyxlike involucres in the leaf axils or in open, branched clusters, each involucre 5- to 8-flowered, the perianth tubular, 5-lobed, rose pink to purplish red, 1¹/4–2¹/2 in. (3–6 cm) long. *Fruit* oblong, glabrous. The wild four-o'clock is an attractive plant, growing in low, rounded mounds, and is usually covered with bright flowers from late afternoon to early morning.
Range and Habitat: Western Texas to Colorado, New Mexico, and Arizona. Commonly found on plains and hills throughout New Mexico; 4,000–7,500 ft.
Key Characters: Wild four-o'clock is distinguished by the spreading stems, the broad, petioled, somewhat fleshy leaves, and the large flowers borne in clusters of 5–8 in calyxlike involucres.
Related Species: *M. oxybaphoides* is similar but has much smaller perianth segments, each involucre bearing about 3 flowers, these purplish red and about ¹/4–⁵/16 in. (7–9 mm) long.

41. **Wooton sand verbena**   *Tripterocalyx wootonii*   Four-o'clock family

Annual herb, the stems much-branched, spreading to reclining. *Leaves* opposite, oval to elliptic, petioled, one of each pair larger than the other. *Flowers* borne in dense, headlike clusters at the apex of the branches, subtended by 4–6 involucral bracts about ³/8 in. (8–10 mm) long, the perianth white to reddish, with 5 short lobes and a narrow tube 1–1³/16 in. (25–30 mm) long. *Fruit* ⁵/8–³/4 in. (15–20 mm) long, with 4 broad wings. The fruit of this plant is probably more conspicuous than the flowers.
Range and Habitat: New Mexico to southwestern Colorado and northeastern Arizona. Usually found in deep sand of plains or low hills from northwestern to southwestern New Mexico; 5,000–6,000 ft.
Key Characters: This plant may be recognized by the dense, headlike clusters of verbenalike flowers, by the opposite, unequal leaves, and by the oblong fruit surrounded by 2–4 broad, translucent, conspicuously net-veined wings.
Related Species: *T. cyclopterus* is similar but the stems are more erect, the perianth is pink, and the fruit ³/4–1¹/8 in. (20–30 mm) long. It is found throughout New Mexico.

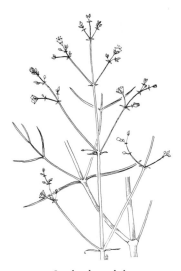

Oxybaphus glaber

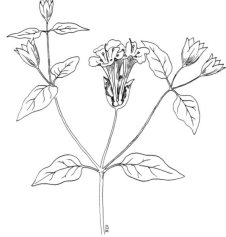

Mirabilis multiflora

Tripterocalyx wootonii

71

42. Sand verbena — *Abronia angustifolia* — Four-o'clock family

Annual herb, the stems prostrate to ascending, sticky, often also hairy, to 20 in. (50 cm) long. *Leaves* opposite on the stems, lanceolate to ovate, glabrous to sticky, slender-petioled, to 2 in. (5 cm) long. *Flowers* borne in headlike clusters on peduncles with sticky hairs, each cluster subtended by separate, lanceolate, slenderly pointed, greenish involucral bracts bearing sticky hairs, the perianth purplish red, with a tube ⁵/₈–³/₄ in. (15–20 mm) long. *Fruit* with wings partially surrounding the body, not conspicuously veined. This attractive plant shows some similarity to the true verbena, which belongs to another family.
Range and Habitat: Western Texas to Arizona and Mexico. Often found in sandy soil in southern New Mexico; 4,000–6,000 ft.
Key Characters: Sand verbena may be identified by the headlike cluster of purplish red flowers, and the wings only partially surrounding the fruit.
Related Species: Two other sand verbenas, *A. fragrans* and *A. elliptica,* differ in being perennials and in having white to rose pink flowers.

43. Scarlet muskflower — *Nyctaginea capitata* — Four-o'clock family

Perennial herb, the stems branched, spreading to erect, to 16 in. (40 cm) long. *Leaves* opposite, triangular-ovate to oval, not lobed or toothed, sticky-hairy, petioled, about 1¹/₂–3 in. (4–8 cm) long. *Flowers* numerous, borne in headlike clusters subtended by numerous linear to ovate involucral bracts, the perianth deep pink to red, the 5 lobes abruptly spreading above the long tube. *Fruit* about ¹/₅ in. (5 mm) long, not winged but often with 10 ribs. The scarlet muskflower, also known as the Devil's bouquet, is a strikingly handsome plant of southern slopes.
Range and Habitat: Western Texas and New Mexico. Occasionally found on dry, often shaded slopes of southern New Mexico; 3,000–4,000 ft.
Key Characters: Scarlet muskflower is characterized by the head of pink to red flowers subtended by numerous bracts, and by the fruits without wings.

44. Moonpod — *Selinocarpus diffusus* — Four-o'clock family

Perennial herb, the stems diffusely branched, bearing appressed hairs, to 12 in. (30 cm) long. *Leaves* opposite, thickish, mostly ovate, petioled, usually bearing short, stiff hairs, to 1 in. (25 mm) long. *Flowers* solitary or in pairs, subtended by very small involucral bracts, the perianth greenish white, tubular, about 1¹/₄–1¹/₂ in. (3–4 cm) long, the 5 stamens projecting slightly beyond the perianth. *Fruit* winged, about ¹/₄ in. (6 mm) long.
Range and Habitat: Western Texas to southern Nevada and California. Usually found on dry hills and in dry valleys from central to southern New Mexico; 4,000–5,500 ft.
Key Characters: Moonpod may be identified by the diffusely branched, low stems, the long greenish white flowers borne singly or in pairs, and the winged fruit.

45. Angel trumpet — *Acleisanthes longiflora* — Four-o'clock family

Perennial herb, the stems low and spreading, rough to the touch, to 40 in. (1 m) long. *Leaves* opposite, linear-lanceolate to triangular, thick, unequal in pairs, petioled, wavy to coarsely toothed on the margins, to 2 in. (5 cm) long. *Flowers* solitary in leaf axils or at the apex of the stem, sessile or nearly so, subtended by an involucre of 2 or 3 small, narrow, long-pointed bracts, the perianth white, tubular, with 5 abruptly spreading lobes, to about 6 in. (15 cm) long, tinged with purple or pink on the outside. *Fruit* 5-angled. Like other members of this family, angel trumpet is usually open from late afternoon to early morning.
Range and Habitat: Texas to California and northern Mexico. Found occasionally in dry, sandy, or rocky areas of southern New Mexico; 3,000–4,500 ft.
Key Characters: Angel trumpet is easily distinguished by the flowers borne singly, the long, slender, whitish to pinkish flower tube, and the 5-angled fruit.

Abronia angustifolia

Nyctaginea capitata

Selinocarpus diffusus

Acleisanthes longiflora

| 46. | Spiderling | *Boerhaavia coccinea* | Four-o'clock family |

Perennial herb, the stems branched, widely spreading to ascending, with glandular hairs, to 40 in. (1 m) long or sometimes longer. *Leaves* opposite, broadly ovate to nearly orbicular, usually without marginal teeth, unequal in pairs, petioled, to 2 about in. (5 cm) long. *Flowers* borne in open clusters on slender branches with glandular hairs, the perianth dark red, about ¹/₁₂ in. (2 mm) long. *Fruit* 5-ribbed.

Range and Habitat: Southern United States to tropical America. Found mostly on plains and along edges of cultivated fields in southwestern New Mexico; 4,000–6,000 ft.

Key Characters: This spiderling is characterized by the broad leaves, the glandular-hairy stems and leaves, and the deep red flowers borne in loose clusters.

Related Species: Another spiderling, *B. gracillima,* is similar, but the leaves and stems are glabrous, the flowers borne singly with the perianth about ¹/₆ in. (4 mm) long. It occurs in southern New Mexico at 3,500–4,500 ft.

| 47. | **Nevada bitterroot** | *Lewisia pygmaea* | Purslane family |

Perennial herb from thick fleshy roots, the stems very short, leafless except for a pair of membranous, bractlike leaves. *Leaves* basal, numerous, linear to narrowly oblanceolate, to 4 in. (10 cm) long and about ¹/₈ in. (2–3 mm) wide. *Flowers* usually borne singly at the apex of the stem, with 2–4 (usually 4) ovate sepals ¹/₄–³/₈ in. (7–10 mm) long, and with 5–9 pink to reddish petals ³/₈–⁵/₈ in. (10–15 mm) long. *Fruit* ovoid, ¹/₄–³/₈ in. (5–10 mm) long, with numerous seeds. This plant is easily overlooked because of its low stature.

Range and Habitat: Colorado to Washington, southward to New Mexico, Arizona, and California. Found occasionally on open slopes in the mountains from northern to south-central New Mexico; 7,500–9,000 ft.

Key Characters: Nevada bitterroot is usually characterized by 4 sepals, conspicuous flowers with several petals, essentially no stem, and by the thick, fleshy roots.

| 48. | **Flame flower** | *Talinum aurantiacum* | Purslane family |

Low, glabrous, perennial herb, the stems leafy, slender, woody at the base, to 16 in. (40 cm) tall. *Leaves* alternate on the stem, linear to narrowly elliptic, flattened, to 2³/₈ in. (6 cm) long. *Flowers* borne singly in the leaf axils, on slender stalks, these usually curving downward in fruit, the sepals 2, the 5 petals orange to scarlet, ³/₈–¹/₂ in. (10–12 mm) long. *Fruit* spherical, about ¹/₄ in. (6 mm) in diameter. The flame flower is a spectacular member of our flora.

Range and Habitat: Western Texas to southern Arizona and northern Mexico. Common on dry plains and rocky slopes of central and southern New Mexico; 3,500–6,500 ft.

Key Characters: This flame flower is easily recognized by the axillary, relatively large, bright orange to scarlet flowers, and the stems usually woody at the base.

Related Species: Another flame flower, *A. angustissimum,* is very similar, but the stem is not woody at the base, and the petals are yellow.

Boerhaavia coccinea

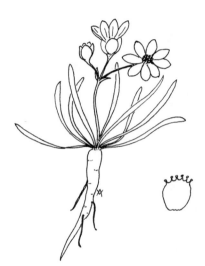

Lewisia pygmaea

Talinum aurantiacum

49. **Prairie flame flower**   *Talinum parviflorum*   Purslane family

Low, glabrous, perennial herb, the stems erect or nearly so, to 8 in. (20 cm) tall. *Leaves* alternate, slender, cylindrical in cross-section, fleshy, to 2 in. (5 cm) long and about ¹/₁₂ in. (2 mm) wide. *Flowers* borne in branching, open clusters that exceed the leaves, the 2 sepals green, ovate to elliptic, about ¹/₆ in. (3–4 mm) long, the 5 petals pink or purplish, about ¹/₆–¹/₄ in. (4–7 mm) long. *Fruit* spherical, about ¹/₆ in. (3–5 mm) in diameter. The prairie flame flower is an inconspicuous, easily overlooked plant.

Range and Habitat: Minnesota to North Dakota, southward to Arkansas, Texas, and Arizona. Usually found on brushy slopes or in pine woods throughout New Mexico; 4,500–7,500 ft.

Key Characters: Prairie flame flower is distinguished by the low, mostly erect habit, the slender, cylindrical leaves, and the loose cluster of pinkish red flowers exceeding the leaves.

Related Species: Showy flame flower (*T. pulchellum*) is somewhat similar but with axillary, solitary flowers, pink petals about ¹/₂–⁵/₈ in. (12–15 mm) long, and leaves ¹/₂–³/₄ in. (12–20 mm) long.

50. **Mexican campion**   *Silene laciniata*   Pink family

Perennial herb, the stems erect or nearly so, 8–24 in. (20–60 cm) tall. *Leaves* opposite, lanceolate, sessile, narrowed at the base, 1¹/₈–4 in. (3–10 cm) long. *Flowers* borne singly or in open, branching clusters, conspicuous, the 5 sepals united into a cylindrical tube, the 5 petals crimson, deeply cut into irregular lobes, bearing toothed appendages on the lower part. *Fruit* oblong. Mexican campion is a conspicuous and very attractive forest plant.

Range and Habitat: Western Texas to New Mexico and California. Common on wooded slopes throughout all but northeastern New Mexico; 6,500–10,000 ft.

Key Characters: Mexican campion is easily recognized by the relatively large, bright crimson flowers with each petal deeply cut into lobes.

51. **Moss campion**   *Silene acaulis*   Pink family

Perennial herb, the stems matted in mosslike cushions, less than 4 in. (10 cm) tall. *Leaves* linear, sessile, crowded, toothed and with a fringe of hairs on the margins, ³/₁₆–1³/₁₆ in. (5–30 mm) long. *Flowers* solitary, the calyx tubular, ¹/₄–³/₈ in. (6–10 mm) long, glabrous, the 5 petals pink to purplish pink, somewhat longer than the calyx. *Fruit* a cylindric capsule, about as long as the calyx.

Range and Habitat: Circumpolar in alpine habitats, extending southward along the Rocky Mountains to New Mexico and Arizona. Found in open meadows among rocks in the higher mountains of northern New Mexico; 11,000–12,500 ft.

Key Characters: Moss campion is characterized by the low, mosslike habit, the linear, crowded, sessile leaves, and the small flowers solitary on each stem.

Talinum parviflorum

Silene laciniata

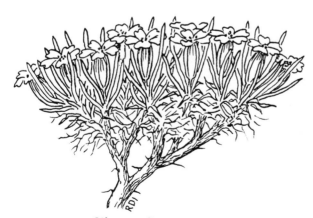

Silene acaulis

52. Chickweed *Stellaria longipes* Pink family

Perennial herb, the stems erect to ascending, angled, branched, 4–18 in. (10–45 cm) tall. *Leaves* opposite, sessile, linear to lanceolate, tapered at the base, acutely pointed at the apex, stiff, shiny. *Flowers* 1–3 in the leaf axils or in an open, terminal cluster, on erect or ascending stalks, the sepals 4 or 5, lanceolate to ovate, with whitish margins, 1/8–1/4 in. (3–5 mm) long, the petals white, 1/6–3/8 in. (4–8 mm) long. *Fruit* an ovoid capsule.

Range and Habitat: Greenland to Alaska, southward to New York, Indiana, New Mexico, and California; also Asia. Often found in moist ground throughout New Mexico; 7,000–12,500 ft.

Key Characters: This chickweed may be identified by the narrow, sessile leaves, the absence of glandular hairs, and the petals longer than the sepals.

Related Species: Another chickweed, *S. jamesiana,* has conspicuous glandular hairs and the petals are deeply 2-lobed.

53. Meadow chickweed *Cerastium arvense* Pink family

Perennial herb, the stems erect to ascending, roughly hairy, to 12 in. (30 cm) tall. *Leaves* opposite, linear to narrowly oblong or lanceolate, pointed at the apex, 3/8–13/8 in. (10–35 mm) long. *Flowers* few in loose clusters, on erect to nodding stalks, subtended by whitish-margined bracts, with 5 sepals 3/16–3/8 in. (5–8 mm) long, and 5 white petals, usually twice as long as the sepals. *Fruit* a straight, cylindric capsule, as long as or longer than the calyx.

Range and Habitat: North America. Commonly found in woods or on dry, open slopes or plains throughout New Mexico; 7,000–9,500 ft.

Key Characters: Meadow chickweed is characterized by having 5 styles and straight capsules splitting into 10 segments, with the petals at least twice as long as the sepals.

Related Species: Two similar mouse-eared chickweeds are *C. brachypodum,* an annual with weak stems and the fruit about twice as long as the calyx, occurring throughout New Mexico at 7,000–9,000 ft., and *C. beeringianum,* a perennial with matted stems and petals only 1/4–3/8 in. (6–9 mm) long, occurring in northern New Mexico at 10,000–12,000 ft.

54. Sandwort *Arenaria obtusiloba* Pink family

Caespitose perennial herb, the stems spreading to prostrate, glandular, to 20 in. (50 cm) long. *Leaves* densely crowded on the branches, linear, to 3/8 in. (8 mm) long. *Flowers* borne singly or 2 or 3 in a loose cluster, the 5 sepals about 1/6 in. (4–5 mm) long, hairy, the 5 petals separate, white, and 3 styles. *Fruit* a capsule 1/4–3/8 in. (6–10 mm) long.

Range and Habitat: Alberta and British Columbia to New Mexico, Arizona, and California. Found occasionally on rocky slopes of the higher mountains in northern to south-central New Mexico; 11,000–12,000 ft.

Key Characters: This sandwort is characterized by the petals much longer than the hairy sepals, the linear leaves, and its high mountain habitat.

Related Species: Two other sandworts, *A. aculeata* and *A. rubella,* are similar but not found as often. *A. rubella* is also a high mountain plant, but *A. aculeata* is found in sandy soil of northwestern New Mexico at 5,000–6,000 ft.

Stellaria longipes

Cerastium arvense

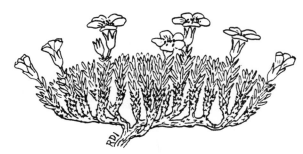

Arenaria obtusiloba

79

55. Rocky Mountain Columbine   *Aquilegia caerulea*   Buttercup family

Perennial herb, the stems glabrous or with glandular hairs above, to 32 in. (80 cm) tall. *Leaves* compound, divided into 2 or 3 leaflets, these 3-lobed, glabrous to sparsely hairy, 1¼– 3¼ in. (3–8 cm) long. *Flowers* large, showy, erect, 2–3¼ in. (5–8 cm) long and about as wide, with 5 petallike blue or white sepals ¾–1½ in. (2–4 cm) long and 5 white petals ⅝– 1 in. (15–25 mm) long, each petal extending into a blue (rarely white) spur 1⅛–2 in. (3–5 cm) long. *Fruit* of slender-tipped pods. Rocky Mountain columbine is one of our showiest flowers and is the state flower of Colorado.

Range and Habitat: Montana to Idaho, southward to New Mexico and Arizona. Usually found in woods and meadows in northern New Mexico; 7,000–12,000 ft.

Key Characters: Rocky Mountain columbine may be recognized by the elongated spurs, and by the large, showy, blue and white flowers. Occasionally pure white flowers are found.

56. Red columbine   *Aquilegia elegantula*   Buttercup family

Perennial herb, the stems usually glabrous, to about 32 in. (80 cm) tall. *Leaves* mostly glabrous and bluish white, 3-lobed, each lobe again 3-lobed. *Flowers* nodding, 1³⁄₁₆–1⅜ in. (30–35 mm) long, the sepals greenish, yellowish, or reddish, ¼–½ in. (7–11 mm) long, the petals yellow, about ¼–⅜ in. (6–8 mm) long, bearing red spurs ⅝–¾ in. (15–20 mm) long. Red columbine is an attractive plant, varieties of which are cultivated as ornamentals.

Range and Habitat: Colorado and Utah to northern Mexico. Commonly found in moist woods throughout all but eastern New Mexico; 7,000–10,000 ft.

Key Characters: Red columbine is easily recognized by its unique flower with 5 backward-extending red spurs and yellow petals, and by the twice 3-lobed leaves.

Related Species: Another red columbine, *A. triternata,* is similar but has shorter petals, longer sepals and spurs, and leaves that are thrice 3-lobed. Yellow columbine, *A. chrysantha,* has yellow petals, sepals, and spurs, all longer than those of the red columbine.

57. Baneberry; Cohosh   *Actaea arguta*   Buttercup family

Perennial herb, the stems glabrous or nearly so, to about 32 in. (80 cm) tall. *Leaves* compound, long-petioled, divided into 2 or 3 ovate leaflets, these bearing teeth or with 3–5 lobes. *Flowers* in a narrow cluster at the apex of the stem, with 4 or 5 early-falling sepals and 4–10 small white petals. *Fruit* of red or white berries ¼–⅜ in. (6–8 mm) long, on stalks ⅜–¾ in. (1–2 cm) long. Baneberry is easily confused with certain elderberries, but caution is urged as the baneberry is reputed to be very poisonous.

Range and Habitat: South Dakota to Alaska, southward to New Mexico, Arizona, and California. Commonly found in moist woods throughout New Mexico; 7,500–10,000 ft.

Key Characters: Baneberry may be recognized by the large, lobed leaves, and by the narrow cluster of white flowers or red or white berries at the apex of the stem.

Aquilegia caerulea

Aquilegia elegantula

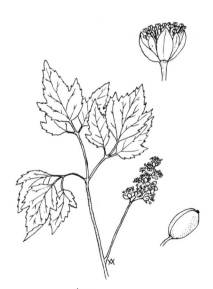

Actaea arguta

58. **Elk's lip** *Caltha leptosepala* Buttercup family

Perennial herb, the glabrous stems leafless or bearing a single bract, to about 8 in. (20 cm) tall. *Leaves* somewhat fleshy, mostly basal, glabrous, ovate to nearly orbicular and palmately veined, notched at the base, 1⁵/₈–3¹/₄ in. (4–8 cm) long,the margins bearing pointed or rounded teeth. *Flowers* 1 or 2 at the tip of each stem, conspicuous, white or yellow, the 6–12 sepals white and petallike, but true petals absent. *Fruit* of small pods about ¹/₂ in. (12 mm) long. Elk's lip is a low but conspicuous flower growing in patches in wet meadows.
Range and Habitat: Montana to Alaska and Washington, southward to New Mexico and Arizona. Normally found in wet meadows or often in boggy areas in mountains of northern New Mexico; 9,500–12,000 ft.
Key Characters: Elk's lip is characterized by the basal, long-petioled, somewhat heart-shaped leaves and by the leafless or nearly leafless flowering stem, this bearing 1 or 2 conspicuous white flowers.

59. **Monkshood** *Aconitum columbianum* Buttercup family

Stout perennial herb, the stems glabrous below, hairy in the upper part, to 80 in. (2 m) tall. *Leaves* petioled, 2–6 in. (5–15 cm) wide, deeply palmately cleft into 3 to 5 irregularly toothed divisions. *Flowers* showy, blue to creamy white, in loose, elongate, narrow clusters, the 5 sepals irregular in shape, the upper one larger than the others, helmet-shaped, forming a beaked hood ³/₈–⁵/₈ in. (10–15 mm) long, the upper 2 petals hooded but hidden under the upper sepal. Monkshood is a conspicuous, showy element of the summer flora, but is poisonous.
Range and Habitat: Montana to British Columbia, southward to New Mexico and California. Frequently found in moist ground, especially near springs or streams, throughout New Mexico; 7,500–11,000 ft.
Key Characters: Monkshood is easily recognized by the tall erect stems with an elongate, narrow inflorescence of hooded blue flowers.

60. **Larkspur** *Delphinium sapellonis* Buttercup family

Slender perennial herb, the stems erect, hollow, glabrous below, bearing glandular hairs among the flowers, 40–80 in. (1–2 m) tall. *Leaves* alternate, glabrous, mostly palmately divided, the divisions irregularly lobed or toothed. *Flowers* scattered, irregular, showy, subtended by threadlike bracts, the 5 sepals brownish or greenish and purple-veined, ovate, about ³/₈ in. (8–9 mm) long, the upper one projected into a spur ¹/₄–³/₈ in. (6–9 mm) long, the 4 petals inconspicuous. The larkspur is an attractive plant, but some are reputed to be poisonous.
Range and Habitat: Restricted to New Mexico. Found near streams from northern to central New Mexico; 7,000–10,500 ft.
Key Characters: This larkspur is characterized by the inflorescence bearing glandular hairs, the brownish sepals, the glabrous leaves, and by the tall stems.
Related Species: Two similar larkspurs include *D. robustum* from northern New Mexico, which has longer sepals, and *D. novomexicanum,* restricted to the Sacramento Mountains of south-central New Mexico, characterized by shorter stems and no glandular hairs in the inflorescence.

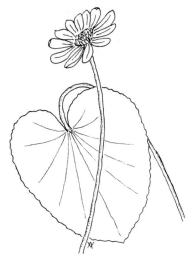

Caltha leptosepala

Aconitum columbianum

Delphinium sapellonis

83

61. Nelson's larkspur — *Delphinium nelsonii* — Buttercup family

Perennial herb, the stems erect, unbranched, leafy, glabrous or often with a dense covering of white hairs among the flowers, 12–24 in. (30–60 cm) tall. *Leaves* few, on petioles 1¼–3½ in. (3–9 cm) long, 1¼–2 in. (3–5 cm) wide, palmately divided into broad, wedge-shaped divisions, these cleft into 3 oblong, blunt segments. *Flowers* in narrow clusters at the summit of the stems, blue to bluish purple, the sepals ovate, ½–⅝ in. (12–15 mm) long, the upper one projecting into a spur about as long as the sepals. *Fruit* of slender pods ½–¾ in. (13–19 mm) long, usually hairy when young. Nelson's larkspur is reputed to be highly poisonous.

Range and Habitat: South Dakota and Idaho to Nevada, Colorado, Arizona, and New Mexico. Usually found on dry plains from northern to western New Mexico; 6,500–8,000 ft.

Key Characters: Nelson's larkspur is characterized by the leafy stems 12–24 in. (30–60 cm) tall, the usually somewhat hairy leaves not exceeding 2 in. (5 cm) wide, and the blue to bluish purple flowers.

Related Species: Another larkspur, *D. tenuisectum,* has leaves mostly 2¾–6½ in. (7–16 cm) wide, hairy leaves, and dark blue flowers. It occurs in meadows from central to southern and western New Mexico at 6,500–7,500 ft.

62. Bigelow leatherflower — *Clematis bigelovii* — Buttercup family

Perennial, the stems woody, at least at the base, erect, not vining, to about 20 in. (50 cm) tall. *Leaves* opposite, pinnately compound, the leaflets 2- to 5-lobed, glabrous. *Flowers* solitary on elongate stalks, nodding, the sepals thick, brownish purple or purple, hairy on the outside, ⅝–1 in. (15–25 mm) long, with matted hairs on the margins, no petals, the ovaries projecting into styles about 1¼ in. (3 cm) long, these feathery toward the apex.

Range and Habitat: New Mexico and Arizona. Frequently found on mountain slopes throughout New Mexico; 7,000–8,000 ft.

Key Characters: Bigelow leatherflower may be recognized by the thick, brownish purple, erect sepals, the pinnate leaves, and the styles feathery only toward the apex.

Related Species: Two similar leatherflowers, *C. hirsutissima,* with twice-pinnate leaves, and *C. pitcheri,* with strongly veined leaflets and nonfeathery styles, also occur in New Mexico.

63. Western virgin's bower — *Clematis ligusticifolia* — Buttercup family

Perennial herb, the stems trailing along the ground or climbing. *Leaves* opposite, pinnately compound, the 3–7 leaflets lanceolate, oblong, or ovate, pointed at the apex, with pointed, coarse teeth or lobes. *Flowers* usually several in loose clusters on long, hairy stalks, the sepals white, about ⅜ in. (10 mm) long, the petals absent, the ovaries projecting into narrowly featherlike styles, 1–2 in. (25–50 mm) long. The flowers are unisexual, with the staminate (male) flowers on one plant and the pistillate (female) flowers on another.

Range and Habitat: British Columbia to North Dakota, California, Texas, and Arizona. Commonly found on slopes and in canyons throughout New Mexico; 4,000–7,500 ft.

Key Characters: Western virgin's bower may be recognized by the densely vining habit, the white flowers, and the styles in fruit not exceeding 2 in. (5 cm) in length.

Related Species: Drummond clematis, *C. drummondii,* differs in having leaves densely covered with grayish hairs and the styles in fruit 2¼–4 in. (6–10 cm) long. It ranges from Texas to Arizona and Mexico at altitudes of 3,000–5,000 ft. and is usually found on slopes and in canyons of southern New Mexico. New Mexico clematis, *C. neomexicana,* differs from western virgin's bower primarily in having blunt rather than pointed leaf divisions. It ranges through New Mexico and Arizona at altitudes of 5,000–7,000 ft. and is often found in canyons in west-central to southwestern New Mexico.

Delphinium nelsonii

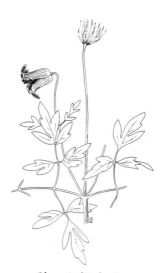

Clematis bigelovii

Clematis ligusticifolia

85

64. Meadow anemone   *Anemone canadensis*   Buttercup family

Perennial herb from slender rhizomes, the stems erect, 8–24 in. (20–60 cm) tall. *Leaves* of 2 types, the basal leaves long-petioled, deeply 3- to 7-parted into 3-cleft, strongly veined divisions, these hairy on the veins below, the stem leaves in 1–3 sets, similar but smaller and sessile. *Flowers* solitary at the apex of the stem, the sepals white, mostly 5, unequal, ³/₈–³/₄ in. (10–20 mm) long, petals absent, the fruiting heads globose. Anemones are beautiful and somewhat delicate but are reputed to be poisonous.

Range and Habitat: Labrador to Alberta, southward to Maryland, Colorado, and New Mexico. Usually found in woods or meadows, often along streams, from northern to south-central New Mexico; 7,000–8,500 ft.

Key Characters: Meadow anemone is characterized by the sessile involucral leaves, and the large, white sepals.

Related Species: Candle anemone, *A. cylindrica,* differs in having shorter, greenish white sepals and cylindric fruiting heads, and is widely distributed in New Mexico. Pacific windflower, *A. globosa,* differs in having several greenish yellow or purplish sepals and petiolate involucral leaves, and is found in northern New Mexico.

65. Desert crowfoot   *Ranunculus cymbalaria*   Buttercup family

Glabrous perennial herb from stolons, to 12 in. (30 cm) tall. *Leaves* mostly basal, notched and rounded at the base, with shallow, rounded lobes, long-petioled. *Flowers* solitary or in loose clusters at the summit of the stems, the 5 sepals glabrous, ¹/₈–⁵/₁₆ in. (3–8 mm) long, about as long as the 5 yellow petals, the fruiting heads cylindric, bearing 100 or more small achenes.

Range and Habitat: Alaska through western North America to Mexico. Common in wet ground throughout most of New Mexico except for the extreme eastern part; 5,000–8,000 ft.

Key Characters: Desert crowfoot may be identified by the presence of spreading or creeping runners, basal leaves with mostly rounded teeth, and small yellow flowers.

Related Species: The alpine *R. macauleyi* differs in having sepals with conspicuous black or brown hairs. It occurs in high mountain meadows from northern to south-central New Mexico at 12,000–13,000 ft., often at the edge of snow patches.

66. Crowfoot   *Ranunculus inamoenus*   Buttercup family

Perennial herb, nearly glabrous or with a scattering of stiff hairs, the stems leafy, not rooting at the nodes. *Leaves* of 2 kinds, the basal ones long-petioled, ovate to nearly orbicular, 3-lobed or with rounded teeth, the stem leaves sessile and deeply 3-lobed. *Flowers* solitary or in loose clusters, the 5 sepals spreading, hairy, nearly as long as the 5 yellow petals, these ¹/₈–¹/₃ in. (3–8 mm) long, the fruiting heads cylindric.

Range and Habitat: Alberta to New Mexico. Common in damp meadows throughout New Mexico; 7,000–10,000 ft.

Key Characters: This crowfoot is distinguished by having stems without runners, deeply lobed stem leaves, the fruits (achenes) with beaks less than ¹/₁₆ in. (1.0–1.5 mm) long, and yellow petals ¹/₈–¹/₃ in. (3–8 mm) long.

Related Species: *R. macounii* is similar, but the achene beak is more than ¹/₂₅ in. (1 mm) long and the fruiting heads are ovoid to globose. It occupies much the same range in New Mexico as *R. inamoenus.*

Anemone canadensis

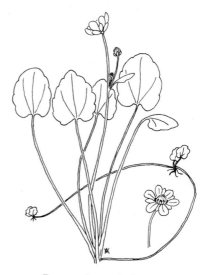

Ranunculus cymbalaria

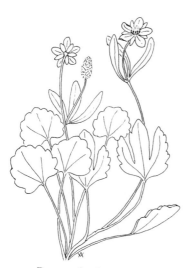

Ranunculus inamoenus

67. Heart-leaved buttercup   *Ranunculus cardiophyllus*   Buttercup family

Hairy, perennial herb, the stems erect, to 18 in. (45 cm) tall. *Leaves* of 2 types, the basal ones rounded, heart-shaped, coarsely lobed or parted, the stem leaves cleft or parted into narrow lobes. *Flowers* scattered, the 5 sepals hairy, tinged with red, the petals yellow, $^5/_{16}$–$^5/_8$ in. (8–15 mm) long, the fruiting head cylindric. *Fruit* of 50–100 hairy achenes per head.

Range and Habitat: Alberta to Washington, southward to New Mexico and Arizona. Often found in moist meadows and pine forests in mountains throughout all but eastern New Mexico; 7,000–9,000 ft.

Key Characters: This buttercup is characterized by the cordate leaves, the leafy stems, the large yellow petals, and the minute beak on the achenes.

Related Species: The very similar *R. eschscholtzii* may be found in high mountain meadows in northern New Mexico, and differs mostly in having glabrous stems.

68. Fremont barberry   *Berberis fremontii*   Barberry family

Shrubs, the stems rigid, stiffly erect or ascending, often clumped, not spiny, to 10 ft. (3 m) or more tall, the inner bark yellow. *Leaves* alternate, pinnately compound, to 3$^1/_4$ in. (8 cm) long, with 3–7, usually 5, ovate to oblong-ovate leaflets, these with wavy, coarsely spiny-toothed margins, the teeth 3 or 4 on each margin, the terminal leaflet not more than twice as long as wide. *Flowers* few, in loose racemes, with 6 separate sepals and 6 yellow petals. *Fruit* spherical to ovoid, yellow or reddish, $^3/_{16}$–$^5/_{16}$ in. (5–8 mm) in diameter. Barberry has been extensively used for food and medicine.

Range and Habitat: Colorado to Utah and California, southward to New Mexico and Arizona. Commonly found on dry slopes, usually with pinyon and juniper, in central and western New Mexico; 5,000–8,000 ft.

Key Characters: Fremont barberry is distinguished by the spineless stems, the leaves with 3–7, few-spined leaflets, the yellow or red fruits, and the terminal leaflets not more than twice as long as wide. The yellow inner bark is characteristic of all barberries.

69. Prickly poppy   *Argemone squarrosa*   Poppy family

Perennial herb, the stems erect, branched, spiny, to about 32 in. (80 cm) tall. *Leaves* deeply and irregularly pinnately cleft, oblong to oblong-ovate, spiny, especially on the veins beneath. *Flowers* conspicuous, white with a yellow center, the 2 or 3 sepals spiny, bearing a hornlike appendage ending in a sharp, stiff spine, the 6 petals $^3/_4$–2 in. (2–5 cm) long, thin and appearing somewhat crumpled. *Fruit* a spiny capsule $^3/_4$–2 in. (2–5 cm) long, spiny. Ancient Greeks believed the yellow sap of this plant was an effective cure for cataracts.

Range and Habitat: Colorado to New Mexico and possibly Arizona. Found on dry plains and slopes from northeastern to central and southeastern New Mexico; 3,000–6,500 ft.

Key Characters: This prickly poppy is distinguished by the spiny stems, the large white flowers with yellow centers, and capsules with green-based spines.

Related Species: Another prickly poppy, *A. polyanthemos,* differs in having brownish spines and is occasionally found in New Mexico at 4,000–7,000 ft.

Ranunculus cardiophyllus

Berberis fremontii

Argemone squarrosa

Stout perennial herb with watery juice, the stems erect, glabrous, to 40 in. (1 m) tall. *Leaves* alternate, 8–12 in. (20–30 cm) long, twice- or thrice-pinnately divided into ovate or lanceolate divisions ³/₄–1³/₈ in. (20–35 mm) long. *Flowers* in open clusters with 2 inconspicuous sepals and 4 white to pinkish or purplish petals about ³/₄ in. (2 cm) long, 1 of the outer petals with a spur as long or longer than the corolla, and 6 stamens. *Fruit* an oblong capsule ³/₈–³/₄ in. (1–2 cm) long. Corydalis is conspicuous when in flower.
Range and Habitat: Colorado and Utah to New Mexico. Found occasionally in damp canyons and on slopes in northern New Mexico; 8,000–9,500 ft.
Key Characters: This corydalis is characterized by the perennial habit, the white to purplish petals, and the spur ³/₈–⁵/₈ in. (10–15 mm) long.
Related Species: Scrambled eggs, *C. aurea,* is found on open slopes of mountains and valleys throughout New Mexico at 4,000–10,000 ft. It differs in having yellow petals, a shorter spur, and spreading stems, usually not exceeding 20 in. (50 cm).

71. **Heartleaf bittercress**   *Cardamine cordifolia*   Mustard family

Perennial herb, the stems glabrous to hairy, branched, to about 28 in. (70 cm) tall. *Leaves* alternate, petioled, heart-shaped, toothed on the margins, ³/₄–2³/₈ in. (2–6 cm) long. *Flowers* in narrow clusters, with 4 sepals and 4 white petals ³/₈–¹/₂ in. (8–12 mm) long, and 6 stamens. *Fruit* linear, erect, 1¹/₈–1¹/₂ in. (3–4 cm) long. Heartleaf bittercress usually grows along streams where the clusters of white flowers contrast with the dark green foliage.
Range and Habitat: Idaho to Wyoming, New Mexico, and Arizona. Commonly found in wet ground, usually along streams throughout New Mexico; 7,000–10,000 ft.
Key Characters: Heartleaf bittercress is characterized by the heart-shaped, dark green leaves and the clusters of small white flowers.

72. **Whitlowgrass**   *Draba aurea*   Mustard family

Perennial herb, the stems erect to sprawling, densely hairy with simple or branched hairs. *Leaves* of 2 types, the basal ones spatulate to oblanceolate, petioled, usually entire on the margins, the stem leaves oblanceolate to ovate, densely hairy. *Flowers* borne in loose clusters on erect or ascending pedicels, the 4 petals yellow, ¹/₆–¹/₄ in. (4–6 mm) long. *Fruit* an often twisted pod ⁵/₁₆–⁹/₁₆ in. (8–15 mm) long, hairy along the margins, the style persistent, about ¹/₂₅ in. (1 mm) long. Whitlowgrass (not a grass) is a colorful, often common plant of mountain slopes.
Range and Habitat: Alaska to New Mexico and Arizona. Commonly found on wooded and open slopes throughout New Mexico; 7,000–11,500 ft.
Key Characters: This whitlowgrass is characterized by the 4 yellow petals, the hairy fruits, and the branched hairs on the stalks.
Related Species: Another whitlowgrass, *D. streptocarpa,* differs in having basal leaves with long hairs on the margins and usually few or no branched hairs.

Corydalis caseana

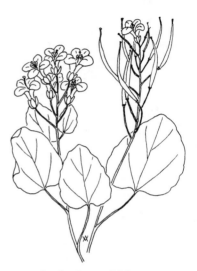

Cardamine cordifolia

Draba aurea

73. **Desert plume**   *Stanleya albescens*   Mustard family

Biennial herb, the stems erect, branching, glabrous. *Leaves* thick, petioled, the lower ones
pinnately lobed with the terminal lobe much larger than the others, the upper ones often
entire and with divergent basal lobes. *Flowers* in long clusters, the sepals greenish white, the
4 petals yellowish white, ³/₈–⁵/₈ in. (10–15 mm) long, about equaling the sepals, the blade
of the petal ¹/₆–³/₈ in. (4–10 mm) wide, but constricted and very narrow at the base. *Fruit* a
nearly cylindrical pod 1¹/₄–2¹/₂ in. (3–6 cm) long, on a conspicuous stalk, bending upward.
Range and Habitat: Colorado and Utah to New Mexico and Arizona. Usually found on
plains and in canyons of northwestern to west-central New Mexico; 5,000–6,000 ft.
Key Characters: This desert plume may be identified by the fruit on a conspicuous stalk,
and by the 4 yellowish white petals.
Related Species: Yellow desert plume, *S. pinnata,* differs in having yellow flowers.

74. **Wright thelypodium**   *Thelypodium wrightii*   Mustard family

Glabrous biennial herb, the stems erect, much-branched, 40 in. (1 m) or more tall. *Leaves*
simple, the basal ones pinnately lobed with a conspicuous terminal lobe, 4–6 in. (10–15 cm)
long, the stem leaves with smooth to toothed or pinnately lobed margins, narrowly
lanceolate, becoming smaller upward. *Flowers* in loose clusters, on widely spreading or
downward curving stalks, with 4 sepals about ¹/₄ in. (6 mm) long, the 4 white or pale purple
petals longer than the sepals. *Fruit* a slender, nearly erect pod 1⁵/₈–2³/₄ in. (4–7 cm) long, on
slender, spreading stalks. This plant is attractive even though it bears relatively small flowers.
Range and Habitat: Colorado to New Mexico, Arizona, and northern Mexico. Commonly
found on dry ground throughout New Mexico; 4,500–8,000 ft.
Key Characters: This plant may be recognized by the 4 white or purple petals, the glabrous
leaves and stems, and the toothed basal leaves.

75. **Western wallflower**   *Erysimum capitatum*   Mustard family

Coarse, hairy, biennial herb, the stems erect, to 32 in. (80 cm) tall. *Leaves* alternate, the basal
ones lanceolate, usually toothed, sometimes minutely so, pointed at the apex, 1⁵/₈–6 in. (4–
15 cm) long, ¹/₈–³/₈ in. (3–10 mm) wide, the stem leaves narrow, some usually with
branched hairs. *Flowers* in slender terminal clusters on stout stalks about ¹/₄ in. (4–6 mm)
long, with 4 sepals ¹/₃–¹/₂ in. (8–12 mm) long, and 4 yellow to orange or maroon petals ¹/₂–
³/₄ in. (12–20 mm) long. *Fruit* an erect to ascending, 4-angled pod 2–4 in. (5–10 cm) long,
and less than ¹/₈ in. (3 mm) wide. Western wallflower is one of our more conspicuous
wildflowers, thriving in a wide range of altitudes. The plant has been used for a variety of
medicinal purposes.
Range and Habitat: Saskatchewan to Washington, southward to New Mexico, Arizona, and
California. A common plant on open slopes throughout New Mexico; 7,000–11,500 ft.
Key Characters: Western wallflower may be recognized by the 4 large petals and the 4-
angled, erect, elongated fruit.
Related Species: The less common *E. asperum* differs in having widely spreading fruits. It is
also found throughout New Mexico on open plains or slopes at 5,000–8,000 ft.

Stanleya albescens

Thelypodium wrightii

Erysimum capitatum

93

76. **Wallflower**   *Erysimum inconspicuum*   Mustard family

Perennial herb, the stems stiff, erect, harshly hairy, to 24 in. (60 cm) tall. *Leaves* alternate, linear or lanceolate, ³/₄–2³/₄ in. (2–7 cm) long, the margins entire or toothed, the leaves mostly crowded near the base of the stem. *Flowers* borne in long, loose clusters at the apex of the stems, the sepals oblong, ¹/₄–¹/₃ in. (6–8 mm) long, the 4 petals pale yellow, about as long as the sepals. *Fruit* an erect, 4-angled, pod ³/₄–2 in. (2–5 cm) long. As the name implies, this wallflower is not one of our most conspicuous plants.

Range and Habitat: Nova Scotia to British Columbia, southward to New York, Missouri, Kansas, New Mexico, and Arizona. Found on plains and open slopes of eastern, northern, central, and south-central New Mexico; 4,500–7,500 ft.

Key Characters: This wallflower may be identified by the smaller petals, the erect fruits, and the often absent basal leaves.

Related Species: The related *E. repandum* (treacle mustard) is similar but the fruits are spreading and 2–3¹/₄ in. (5–8 cm) long. It is usually found in northern New Mexico.

77. **Linear-leaved tansy mustard**   *Sisymbrium linearifolium*   Mustard family

Perennial glabrous herb, the stems simple or branched, erect to spreading, to 40 in. (1 m) or more tall. *Leaves* simple, alternate, the basal ones lanceolate to spatulate, toothed on the margins, 2–4 in. (5–10 cm) long, the upper ones linear, entire. *Flowers* in loose clusters, with 4 sepals about ¹/₄ in. (5–6 mm) long, and 4 rose purple petals ¹/₂–³/₄ in. (12–20 mm) long. *Fruit* nearly erect, slender, 1⁵/₈–2³/₄ in. (4–7 cm) long, on slender, spreading stalks. This plant is moderately attractive but somewhat weedy.

Range and Habitat: Colorado to New Mexico, Arizona, and northern Mexico. Common on dry ground throughout New Mexico; 4,500–8,000 ft.

Key Characters: This plant may be recognized by the 4 rose purple petals, these tapering to the base, the glabrous stems and leaves, and the toothed basal leaves.

78. **Watercress**   *Rorippa nasturtium-aquaticum*   Mustard family

Glabrous, aquatic, perennial herb, the stems reclining except at the apex, rooting at the nodes, to 16 in. (40 cm) long. *Leaves* pinnately compound or pinnately lobed, the leaflets or segments wavy, the terminal lobe larger than the lateral ones. *Flowers* in short, dense clusters, the 4 white petals about twice as long as the sepals. *Fruit* sessile, linear, spreading, ³/₈–1³/₈ in. (1–3 cm) long. Watercress has long been used for salads and garnishing.

Range and Habitat: Introduced from Europe, now found throughout North America. Common in streams throughout New Mexico; 5,000–8,000 ft.

Key Characters: Watercress is easily recognized by its aquatic habitat, the pinnately divided leaves, and the 4 white petals.

Related Species: Yellow cress, *R. sinuata,* occurring in wet ground, usually near streams throughout New Mexico, differs in having yellow flowers and wavy-lobed lower leaves.

79. **Spectacle-pod**   *Dithyrea wislizenii*   Mustard family

Erect annual herb, the stems simple or sparsely branched, 8–20 in. (20–50 cm) tall. *Leaves* simple, alternate, lanceolate, wavy-toothed or nearly smooth, grayish to whitish. *Flowers* in elongate, slender, terminal clusters, the 4 petals white, ³/₁₆–⁵/₁₆ in. (5–8 mm) long. *Fruit* flattened, resembling a pair of spectacles, each of the 2 cells about ¹/₄ in. (5–6 mm) wide.

Range and Habitat: Colorado and Utah to Mexico. Common on dry hills, mesas, and streamsides, usually in sandy soil, throughout New Mexico; 3,500–6,500 ft.

Key Characters: Spectacle-pod is easily recognized by the 4 white petals, the grayish appearance of the plant, and by the unique, spectacle-shaped fruit.

Erysimum inconspicuum

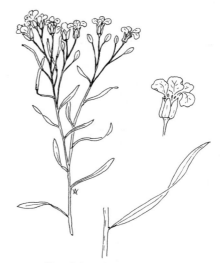

Sisymbrium linearifolium

Rorippa nasturtium-aquaticum

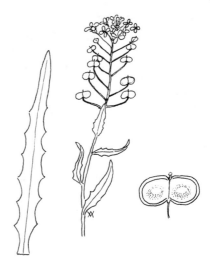

Dithyrea wislizenii

80. **Narrow-leaved peppergrass** *Lepidium montanum* Mustard family

Biennial or perennial herb, often woody at the base, the stems to 28 in. (70 cm) tall. *Leaves* of 2 kinds, the basal ones variously divided to pinnately lobed, sometimes nearly entire, to 6 in. (15 cm) long, the upper leaves linear, usually entire and reduced. *Flowers* borne in dense narrow clusters, the clusters becoming elongated in fruit, the 4 sepals oblanceolate to elliptic, the 4 petals white, much longer than the sepals. *Fruit* flattened, elliptic to ovate, the persistent style longer than the shallow notch at the apex, the seed solitary in each of the two cells. Peppergrass (not a grass) flowers throughout most of the spring and into the fall.
Range and Habitat: Wyoming to Oregon, southward to Texas, New Mexico, Arizona, and California. Commonly found on dry plains and slopes throughout New Mexico; 4,000–8,000 ft.
Key Characters: This peppergrass may be identified by the style exceeding the notch of the fruit, and by being biennial or perennial instead of annual. Four highly variable varieties occur in New Mexico.
Related Species: Another common peppergrass, *L. medium,* occurring throughout New Mexico at 4,000–7,000 ft. on dry plains and hills, differs in the style being shorter than the notch of the fruit or absent.

81. **Goodding bladderpod** *Lesquerella gooddingii* Mustard family

Perennial herb bearing star-shaped hairs throughout, the stems about 5–14 in. (12–35 cm) tall. *Leaves* of 2 types, the basal ones obovate to oblanceolate, petioled, entire or nearly so, $5/8$–1 in. (15–25 mm) long, $1/6$–$3/8$ in. (4–10 mm) wide, the upper ones oblanceolate to lanceolate, finely toothed. *Flowers* borne in loose, open clusters, the 4 petals yellow, about $1/4$ in. (6–7 mm) long, on stalks about $1/2$ in. (10–12 mm) long, these often S-shaped in fruit. *Fruit* a compressed, oblong-ellipsoid pod about $1/6$ in. (4 mm) long, bearing star-shaped hairs, the persistent style slightly shorter than the fruit. Bladderpod often occurs in dense patches, creating a blanket of yellow color on plains and hills.
Range and Habitat: New Mexico and Arizona. Found on rocky slopes and in ravines, often near streams in southwestern New Mexico; 6,000–6,500 ft.
Key Characters: This bladderpod may be distinguished by the compressed fruit rounded at the apex, bearing star-shaped hairs, and the yellow flowers.
Related Species: Two other bladderpods, *L. intermedia* and *L. pinetorum,* differ in having inflated fruits pointed at the apex.

82. **False flax** *Camelina sativa* Mustard family

Annual hairy herb, the stems erect, 12–32 in. (30–80 cm) tall. *Leaves* lanceolate, usually entire and clasping with earlike lobes at the base. *Flowers* borne in terminal, open clusters, the 4 petals mostly whitish. *Fruit* an ovoid, slightly flattened pod $1/4$–$3/8$ in. (6–9 mm) long, 3 to 4 times as long as the style. A robust plant, false flax is often found along roadsides.
Range and Habitat: Introduced from Europe, now widespread in the United States. Found occasionally in waste ground in northern to central New Mexico; 4,500–6,500 ft.
Key Characters: False flax may be recognized by the oblong fruit, the whitish flowers, and the seeds numerous in each of the two cells of the fruit.
Related Species: *C. microcarpa* is very similar, but the fruit is usually not more than $1/5$ in. (5 mm) long, about twice as long as the styles.

Lepidium montanum

Lesquerella gooddingii

Camelina sativa

97

83. **Rocky Mountain bee-plant**   *Cleome serrulata*   Caper family

Glabrous annual herb, the stems erect, branching, to 40 in. (1 m) or more tall. *Leaves* alternate, compound, usually petiolate, the 3 leaflets lanceolate to oblong-lanceolate, entire to toothed, usually 1³/₁₆–2³/₄ in. (3–7 cm) long. *Flowers* in crowded, terminal, bracted clusters, the 4 persistent sepals united at the base, the 4 petals constricted to a stalklike base, pinkish purple to white, ¹/₄–¹/₂ in. (8–12 mm) long, the stamens conspicuously projecting. *Fruit* a cylindrical pod 1–2 in. (25–50 mm) long, on a conspicuous stalk. Rocky Mountain bee-plant (often known as wild spinach) is a favorite food of natives and has been used in making a mordant for dyes.
Range and Habitat: Southern Canada to Missouri, Kansas, New Mexico, Colorado, and Arizona. Frequently found on plains and hills throughout much of New Mexico; 4,500–8,000 ft.
Key Characters: Rocky Mountain bee-plant is recognized by the conspicuously stalked fruit, the trifoliolate leaves, and the purplish white flowers with 4 petals and projecting stamens.
Related Species: Yellow bee-plant, *C. lutea,* is very similar but has yellow petals and occurs in northwestern New Mexico.

84. **Clammyweed**   *Polanisia trachysperma*   Caper family

Coarse, sticky, hairy herb, the stems erect, branched, 20–40 in. (5–10 dm) tall. *Leaves* alternate, with 3 oblanceolate to elliptic leaflets, these entire, blunt at the apex, ⁵/₈–1 in. (15–25 mm) long, petioled. *Flowers* in crowded, slender, bracted terminal clusters, the 4 petals white or yellowish white, ³/₈–¹/₂ in. (8–12 mm) long, the stamens exserted, purplish, ⁵/₈–³/₄ in. (15–20 mm) long. *Fruit* a pod 1¹/₈–2 in. (3–5 cm) long. Clammyweed in a conspicuous part of the summer flora but is unpleasant to the touch.
Range and Habitat: Canada to Missouri, Texas, New Mexico, and Arizona. Found on dry plains and hills, in gravelly or sandy stream beds, or along roadsides throughout New Mexicxo; 4,500–7,000 ft.
Key Characters: Clammyweed is distinguished by the compound leaves with 3 leaflets, the strongly sticky-hairy herbage, the white petals, and the purplish staminal filaments.
Related Species: Another clammyweed, *P. uniglandulosa,* has yellow petals and longer staminal filaments. It occurs mostly in dry ground in southern and southwestern New Mexico at altitudes of 4,000–6,500 ft.

85. **Jackass clover**   *Wislizenia refracta*   Caper family

Annual ill-scented herb, the stems erect, much-branched, to 40 in. (1 m) tall. *Leaves* alternate, compound, with 3 oblong to obovate, entire leaflets. *Flowers* small, numerous, borne in clusters, the 4 sepals about ¹/₁₆ in. (2 mm) long, the 4 yellow petals about ¹/₈ in. (3 mm) long. *Fruit* a pod divided into 2 distinct, single-seeded segments, on stalks ¹/₅–³/₈ in. (5–10 mm) long.
Range and Habitat: Western Texas to New Mexico, Arizona, and southern California. Found in valleys, usually in alkaline soils, of southern and western New Mexico; 4,000–5,000 ft.
Key Characters: Jackass clover is characterized by the compound leaves with 3 leaflets, the 2-parted, stalked fruits, and by the small yellow petals.

Cleome serrulata

Polanisia trachysperma

Wislizenia refracta

99

86. **Rose crown**   *Sedum rhodanthum*   Stonecrop family

Succulent, glabrous, perennial herb, the stems several, densely leafy, to 12 in. (30 cm) tall. *Leaves* alternate, linear-oblong to oblanceolate, entire to toothed, 5/8–1 1/4 in. (15–30 mm) long. *Flowers* in crowded axillary and terminal clusters subtended by leaflike bracts, the sepals separate, the petals about twice as long as the sepals, pink to white, about 3/8 in. (8–10 mm) long. *Fruit* 5-parted and with spreading tips. This stonecrop is one of the more attractive plants of high mountain meadows.

Range and Habitat: Montana to Utah, Colorado, New Mexico, and Arizona. Often found in rocky, open meadows in the mountains of central and northern New Mexico; 9,000–12,000 ft.

Key Characters: Rose crown is distinguished by having flowers in both narrow axillary and terminal clusters.

87. **King's crown**   *Sedum integrifolium*   Stonecrop family

Glabrous, perennial herb from thick, fleshy roots, the stems mostly erect, to 12 in. (30 cm) tall. *Leaves* alternate, succulent, oblong-ovate to obovate, sessile, entire to toothed, 3/8–3/4 in. (1–2 cm) long. *Flowers* unisexual or bisexual, in an open, terminal cluster, the sepals lanceolate, about 1/12 in. (2 mm) long, the petals oblong to oblanceolate, purplish or sometimes yellowish, about 1/6 in. (4–5 mm) long, the staminal filaments purplish and projecting from the flower. *Fruit* of 5 segments with each segment often spreading at the tip.

Range and Habitat: Alaska to Alberta, southward to Colorado, New Mexico, and California. Found in moist ground in the mountains of northern to south-central New Mexico; 7,500–12,000 ft.

Key Characters: King's crown is characterized by having the flowers in only terminal clusters, and the flowers are often unisexual.

88. **Cockerell stonecrop**   *Sedum cockerellii*   Stonecrop family

Perennial glabrous herb, the stems 4–8 in. (10–20 cm) tall. *Leaves* alternate, linear to spatulate, rounded at the apex. *Flowers* in terminal, bracted, open clusters, the sepals obtuse, about 1/4 in. (4–5 mm) long, the petals white or pink-tinged, longer than the sepals. *Fruit* 5-parted, erect or spreading at the tip. This is a very low-growing but attractive plant.

Range and Habitat: Colorado to New Mexico and Arizona. Found in rocky, often shaded places in the mountains throughout New Mexico; 7,000–11,500 ft.

Key Characters: This stonecrop is characterized by the open, branching clusters of flowers, the slender roots, the white to pink petals, and the flattened leaves.

Related Species: Yellow stonecrop, *S. stelliforme,* occurring in southwestern New Mexico, has cylindric leaves. Lanceleaf stonecrop, *S. lanceolatum,* occurs in northern New Mexico and has yellow petals.

Sedum rhodanthum

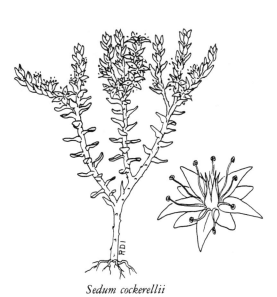

Sedum integrifolium

Sedum cockerellii

101

89.   **Parnassia**   *Parnassia parviflora*   Saxifrage family

Glabrous perennial herb, the scapes 6–12 in. (15–30 cm) tall, bearing a single, sessile,
bractlike, ovate, entire leaf below the middle. *Leaves* mostly basal, petioled, oval or ovate,
tapered to the base, ³/₈–³/₄ in. (1–2 cm) wide. *Flowers* solitary at the summit of the scapes,
the 5 sepals united at the base, the 5 petals elliptic to oval, white, ¹/₄–³/₈ in. (6–10 mm)
long. *Fruit* with many winged seeds. Parnassia may be easily mistaken for a grass when not in
flower.
Range and Habitat: Canada to Utah, Colorado, Arizona, and New Mexico. Occasionally
found in wet ground, especially seeps, throughout most of New Mexico; 7,000–9,000 ft.
Key Characters: This parnassia is distinguished by the mostly oval basal leaves tapering to
the base, and the solitary flowers with entire petals.
Related Species: *P. fimbriata,* found in wet ground of northern New Mexico, differs in having
the leaves notched at the base and the petals marginally fringed.

90.   **Pink alumroot**   *Heuchera rubescens*   Saxifrage family

Perennial herb, the stems leafless, 8–16 in. (20–40 cm) tall. *Leaves* usually basal, broadly
ovate to round, notched at the base, palmately veined, petioled. *Flowers* borne in open,
branching clusters with a 5-lobed calyx united to the base of the ovary and 5 pink petals
about twice as long as the sepals, the 5 stamens longer than the sepals. This alumroot is
easily overlooked.
Range and Habitat: New Mexico to Utah, Oregon, and California. Found in mountains
throughout most of New Mexico; 7,000–8,500 ft.
Key Characters: This alumroot is characterized by having a loose, open inflorescence, with
the stamens longer than the sepals.
Related Species: *H. pulchella,* found in canyons and on mountain slopes of northern and
central New Mexico, differs in having the flowers in dense, 1-sided clusters.

91.   **Coralbells**   *Heuchera sanguinea*   Saxifrage family

Perennial herb, the stems leafless, 8–16 in. (20–40 cm) tall. *Leaves* mostly basal, ovate to
nearly round, rounded and notched at the base, palmately veined, often bearing bristle-tipped
teeth and rounded lobes with long hairs on the margins. *Flowers* borne in open clusters, the
floral tube funnel-shaped to urn-shaped, the 4 sepals longer than the 5 deep pink or red
petals, the stamens shorter than the sepals. Coralbells is a conspicuous and attractive plant.
Range and Habitat: New Mexico to Arizona and northern Mexico. Found mostly in moist,
shaded, rocky niches in the mountains of southwestern New Mexico; 5,000–8,500 ft.
Key Characters: Coralbells may be distinguished by the deep pink or red flowers and the
stamens shorter than the sepals.
Related Species: *H. versicolor* is similar but the petals are pink, longer than the sepals, and
the stamens are longer than the sepals. It occurs in moist ground of most of New Mexico
except the eastern portion.

Parnassia parviflora

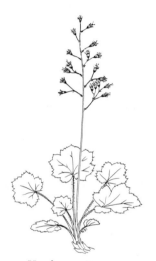

Heuchera rubescens

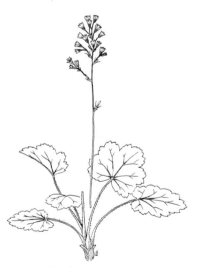

Heuchera sanguinea

92. **Rocky Mountain Alumroot**   *Heuchera parvifolia*   Saxifrage family

Perennial herb, the stems bunched, leafless, somewhat glandular, 4–16 in. (10–40 cm) tall. *Leaves* mostly basal, on mostly glabrous petioles, orbicular to broadly ovate, cordate at the base, with 7–9 lobes, the margins toothed and hairy. *Flowers* in loose terminal clusters, the 5 calyx lobes triangular and usually reflexed, the 5 petals greenish white, longer than the sepals, the floral tube greenish white to yellowish, the 5 stamens shorter than the sepals.
Range and Habitat: Alberta to British Columbia, southward to New Mexico and Arizona. Common in damp woods and rocky places in northern and central New Mexico; 7,000–10,500 ft.
Key Characters: This alumroot may be identified by the stamens shorter than the sepals, the glabrous or nearly glabrous petioles, and by the greenish white flowers.
Related Species: The endemic *H. wootonii* with greenish white flowers seems to be restricted to the Sacramento Mountains of south-central New Mexico. New Mexico alumroot, *H. novomexicana,* with greenish to yellow flowers, is found on damp slopes from north-central to southwestern New Mexico.

93. **Saxifrage**   *Saxifraga rhomboidea*   Saxifrage family

Perennial herb 4–12 in. (10–30 cm) tall. *Leaves* basal, ovate, shallowly toothed, mostly glabrous, the margins and petioles ciliate, the petioles usually longer than the blades. *Flowers* borne in tight clusters at the summit of an often branched, leafless flowering stem bearing glandular hairs, the 5 calyx lobes oval or ovate, the 5 petals oblong-ovate, white and about $^1/_8$ in. (3–4 mm) long, narrowed at the base, and 10 stamens. *Fruit* of small pods $^1/_8$–$^3/_{16}$ in. (3–5 mm) long, each usually spreading at the tip.
Range and Habitat: Montana to Colorado and New Mexico. Usually found in moist areas in northern and central New Mexico; 7,000–13,000 ft.
Key Characters: This saxifrage may be recognized by the ovate basal leaves, the dense clusters of flowers, and the absence of reddish purple hairs on the leaves.
Related Species: Another saxifrage, *S. eriophora,* differs in bearing conspicuous reddish purple hairs on the petioles and lower leaf surfaces. It ranges from southern New Mexico to southern Arizona and is found on rocky slopes at altitudes of 7,000–8,500 ft.

94. **Spotted saxifrage**   *Saxifraga bronchialis*   Saxifrage family

Perennial somewhat matted herb, the flowering stems to 6 in. (15 cm) tall. *Leaves* mostly crowded at the base, narrowly oblong to lanceolate, spine-tipped, with a fringe of stiff hairs on the margins, the stem leaves scattered and much reduced. *Flowers* borne in open, loose clusters, with 5 blunt calyx lobes, and 5 oblong to oblong-lanceolate petals about $^1/_4$ in. (4–6 mm) long, these white, often dotted with yellow or reddish purple. *Fruit* of small pods $^3/_{16}$–$^3/_8$ in. (5–9 mm) long. Spotted saxifrage is a delicately beautiful little plant.
Range and Habitat: Alberta and British Columbia to Washington, Utah, Colorado, and New Mexico. Commonly found on moist rocky ledges, especially along streams and canyons, from northern to south-central New Mexico; 7,000–12,000 ft.
Key Characters: Spotted saxifrage is distinguished by the matted bases, the flowering stems with a few small leaves, the oblong to oblong-ovate basal leaves, and the often yellow- or purple-dotted white petals.

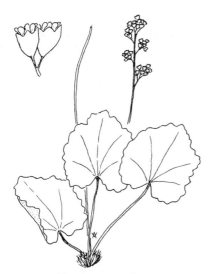

Heuchera parvifolia

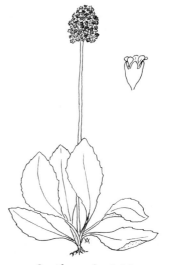

Saxifraga rhomboidea

Saxifraga bronchialis

| 95. Fendlerella | *Fendlerella utahensis* | Saxifrage family |

Shrub, the young branches with short hairs, the stems to 40 in. (1 m) tall. *Leaves* opposite, lanceolate to oblanceolate, bearing short hairs, sessile, entire on the margins, ³/8–1 in. (10–25 mm) long. *Flowers* borne in branching, open, many-flowered clusters, with 5 small sepals, and 5 white petals ¹/8–¹/4 in. (3–5 mm) long. *Fruit* a capsule larger than the calyx. The small but numerous white flowers make this an attractive shrub.

Range and Habitat: New Mexico to southern Arizona and northern Mexico. Usually found on dry slopes and in open pine forests of southern New Mexico; 5,000–8,000 ft.

Key Characters: Fendlerella may be identified by the opposite leaves, the partly inferior ovary, the 10 stamens, and the clusters of many white flowers.

| 96. Fendlerbush | *Fendlera rupicola* | Saxifrage family |

Much-branched shrub with shreddy grayish bark, to 6 ft. (2 m) tall. *Leaves* opposite, linear-lanceolate to elliptic, sometimes scythe-shaped, often rolled on the margins, from glabrous or nearly so to bearing whitish matted-hairs (tomentose). *Flowers* borne in small clusters of 2 or 3, or solitary, with 4 sepals united at the base, and 4 irregularly margined, white or pink-tinged petals ⁵/8–³/4 in. (15–20 mm) long, these constricted to form a stalklike base. *Fruit* a capsule ³/8–⁵/8 in. (10–15 mm) long. Fendlerbush is a very conspicuous shrub.

Range and Habitat: Texas to Colorado, New Mexico, Arizona, and Mexico. Commonly found on rocky slopes and canyon walls throughout New Mexico; 5,000–8,000 ft.

Key Characters: Fendlerbush may be recognized by the opposite leaves, the flowers solitary or 2 or 3 in a cluster, with 4 large petals and 8 stamens.

Related Species: The three varieties of *F. rupicola* differ mainly in the shape and hairiness of the leaves, and somewhat in their distribution.

| 97. Mock-orange | *Philadelphus occidentalis* | Saxifrage family |

Shrub, the stems much-branched, to 40 in. (1 m) tall, sometimes taller. *Leaves* opposite, ovate or oblong-ovate, entire on the margins, sparsely hairy on both surfaces, ³/8–³/4 in. (10–20 mm) long and ³/16–³/8 in. (5–11 mm) wide. *Flowers* borne in clusters of 3 or solitary, the calyx 4-lobed, the 4 (rarely 5) petals white, obovate, ³/16–³/8 in. (5–10 mm) long, with 15 or more stamens. *Fruit* a broadly ellipsoid pod about ³/16 in. (5 mm) long and wide. This is another strikingly handsome shrub of rocky hills and canyon walls.

Range and Habitat: Wyoming to California, New Mexico, Arizona, and Mexico. Found occasionally on rocky hillsides and in canyons of central and southern New Mexico; 5,000–8,000 ft.

Key Characters: Mock-orange may be distinguished by the opposite leaves, the small flowers with 4 white petals, and the 15 or usually more stamens.

Fendlerella utahensis

Fendlera rupicola

Philadelphus occidentalis

107

98. Gooseberry currant — *Ribes montigenum* — Saxifrage family

Erect or spreading shrub, the stems to 32 in. (80 cm) long, bearing 1–3 spines at each node, sometimes bristly between the nodes. *Leaves* alternate, petioled, rounded and notched at the base, with glandular hairs, usually 5-lobed, the segments toothed or cleft. *Flowers* with the ovary completely inferior, the floral cup very short, saucer-shaped, bearing glandular hairs, the 5 calyx lobes reddish purple, the 5 petals reddish, shorter than the calyx lobes. *Fruit* a red berry $^1/_4$–$^3/_8$ in. (6–10 mm) in diameter bearing glandular bristles. The berries of this plant have been used for food but are not very palatable.

Range and Habitat: Montana to British Columbia, southward to New Mexico, Arizona, and California. Often found on open slopes throughout New Mexico; 7,500–11,000 ft.

Key Characters: Gooseberry currant may be distinguished by the spiny stems, the leaf petioles with glandular hairs, the floral cup and fruit bearing glandular bristles, and the flower stalks jointed below the ovary.

Related Species: Orange gooseberry, *R. pinetorum,* occurs in open woods from west-central to south-central and southwestern New Mexico, and differs in having the leaf petioles hairy but not glandular, the fruit bristly but not glandular, and the flower stalks not jointed below the ovary.

99. Agrimony — *Agrimonia striata* — Rose family

Perennial herb, the stems glandular and with spreading hairs, 20–40 in. (5–10 cm) tall. *Leaves* alternate, pinnately compound, copiously hairy, often glandular beneath, the 7–13 leaflets coarsely toothed, alternately larger and smaller in size. *Flowers* borne in long, narrow clusters (racemes), small, with 5 sepals and 5 yellow petals, the floral tube about $^1/_6$–$^1/_5$ in. (4–5 mm) long, bearing a ring of hooked bristles at the summit, these spreading upward. *Fruit* of 1 or 2 achenes.

Range and Habitat: Widespread in North America except the extreme West. Frequently found in moist woods throughout New Mexico; 7,000–9,000 ft.

Key Characters: Agrimony may be recognized by the slender racemes of small yellow flowers, the hypanthium bearing hooked bristles at the summit, and the 5 to numerous stamens.

Related Species: Tall agrimony, *A. grypsosepala,* occurring mostly in northern New Mexico, differs in having glabrous or sparsely hairy leaves and downward-pointing bristles on the floral cup.

100. Wild strawberry — *Fragaria americana* — Rose family

Low perennial herb from short rootstocks, producing slender runners which root and produce new plants. *Leaves* basal, divided into 3 leaflets, these obovate to rhombic-ovate, usually sparsely hairy on both surfaces, the margins toothed from the apex to below the middle, the long petioles bearing spreading or downward-pointing hairs. *Flowers* in loose clusters at the top of a slender, hairy flowering stalk, with 5 sepals alternating with 5 bractlets, 5 white petals about twice as long as the sepals, and 20 stamens. Wild strawberry is a favorite food of many animals.

Range and Habitat: Widespread in North America except for the far-western part. Common in meadows from north-central to south-central New Mexico; 6,500–10,000 ft.

Key Characters: Wild strawberry is distinguished by the low growth habit, the presence of runners producing new plants, the basal leaves, the numerous stamens, and the red fleshy berry.

Related Species: Another strawberry, *F. ovalis,* differs in having the hairs of the flowering stem appressed and the leaflets toothed mostly above the middle. It occurs mostly in northern New Mexico.

Ribes montigenum

Agrimonia striata

Fragaria americana

109

101. Western thimbleberry　　　　*Rubus parviflorus*　　　　Rose family

Perennial herb with stems erect or ascending, to 39 in. (1 m) tall, woody at the base, prickles or sharp bristles absent, the older bark shredding. *Leaves* simple, 2³/₈–6¹/₂ in. (6–18 cm) wide, rounded and notched at the base, unevenly toothed on the margins, palmately 3- to 5-lobed, the petioles glandular and hairy. *Flowers* white, 1–2 in. (25–50 mm) in diameter, with 5 ovate, spreading or reflexed sepals, slenderly pointed at the apex, and 5 petals. *Fruit* red, ⁵/₈–³/₄ in. (15–18 mm) wide. The fruit of the thimbleberry may be eaten by animals but is not very palatable.

Range and Habitat: Ontario to Alaska, southward to Michigan, New Mexico, California, and Mexico. Common in woods throughout New Mexico; 7,000–9,500 ft.

Key Characters: Western thimbleberry is easily recognized by the large, white, usually solitary flowers, the unarmed stems, and the large, lobed leaves.

102. Red raspberry　　　　*Rubus strigosus arizonicus*　　　　Rose family

Erect perennial, the stems woody, to 6¹/₂ ft. (2 m) tall, bearing stiff, slender, sharp bristles and often with stalked glands. *Leaves* pinnately compound, with 5–9 leaflets, these long-pointed at the apex, toothed on the margins, sparsely hairy beneath, the terminal leaflet 2⁷/₈– 4 in. (7–10 cm) long. *Flowers* in clusters of 4–7, or sometimes solitary in the axils of the leaves, the 5 sepals long-pointed at the tip and with glandular hairs, the 5 petals white. *Fruit* red, about ³/₈ in. (10 mm) in diameter. The wild raspberry fruit is edible and is a favorite food of many wild animals, especially bears.

Range and Habitat: Colorado to New Mexico and Arizona. Common in open woods throughout New Mexico; 6,500–12,000 ft.

Key Characters: Red raspberry is easily recognized by the numerous sharp bristles on the stem, the pinnately compound leaves with large terminal leaflets, and the red fruit.

103. Shrubby cinquefoil　　　　*Potentilla fruticosa*　　　　Rose family

Shrub, to 40 in. (1 m) tall, the stems much-branched, the older ones with brown shreddy bark. *Leaves* alternate, with silky hair above, densely covered with white hairs beneath, pinnately 3- to 7-foliolate, the leaflets linear to oblong or oblanceolate, ¹/₄–³/₄ in. (5–20 mm) long. *Flowers* borne in loose clusters or solitary, with 5 calyx lobes alternating with 5 longer bractlets, 5 bright yellow, nearly round petals ¹/₄–⁵/₈ in. (5–15 mm) long and longer than the sepals, and 20–25 stamens. *Fruits* of densely hairy achenes with the styles attached to one side. The flowers of this shrub are quite showy and have been used in summer ceremonies by some Native Americans.

Range and Habitat: Labrador to Alaska, southward to New Jersey, New Mexico, and California; also Eurasia. Commonly found in damp meadows and on moist slopes and streambanks in mountains throughout New Mexico; 7,000–11,500 ft.

Key Characters: Shrubby cinquefoil is distinguished by the many stamens, the 5 bractlets alternating with the calyx lobes, the shrubby habit, the 5 bright yellow petals, and the densely hairy achenes.

Rubus parviflorus

Rubus strigosus arizonicus

Potentilla fruticosa

104. **Cinquefoil**   *Potentilla hippiana*   Rose family

Perennial herb, the stems with silky hairs, 4–20 in. (10–50 cm) tall. *Leaves* alternate,
pinnately compound with 7–13 leaflets, these oblanceolate, coarsely toothed on the margins,
variously hairy. *Flowers* borne in loose, open clusters, the 5 sepals alternating with 5 shorter
bractlets, the 5 petals yellow and longer than the sepals, with 20 stamens. *Fruits* of achenes
with the styles attached at the tip. Cinquefoils are showy plants.
Range and Habitat: Saskatchewan and Alberta to New Mexico and Arizona. Common in
meadows throughout New Mexico; 7,000–10,500 ft.
Key Characters: This cinquefoil is distinguished by the pinnately compound leaves with 7–
13 leaflets bearing whitish hairs, the 5 yellow petals, and the fruits with styles terminally
placed.
Related Species: Norway cinquefoil, *P. norvejica,* occurring from northern to south-central
and western New Mexico, has digitately 3-foliolate leaves and bractlets about as long as the
petals. Brook cinquefoil, *P. rivalis,* occurs in wet ground throughout most of New Mexico,
and has leaves with 3–5 leaflets, flowers with 10 stamens, and glabrous achenes.

105. **Red cinquefoil**   *Potentilla thurberi*   Rose family

Perennial herb, the stems erect, hairy, 12–24 in. (30–60 cm) tall. *Leaves* digitately compound
with 5–7 obovate to oblong leaflets, these 1¹/₈–2 in. (3–5 cm) long and often with some
silky hairs on the lower surface. *Flowers* in loose, open clusters, the 5 sepals long-pointed, the
5 petals wine red, nearly round, longer than the sepals. *Fruits* of glabrous achenes with the
styles attached at the tip. This is one of the most attractive of New Mexico's wildflowers.
Range and Habitat: New Mexico to Arizona and northern Mexico. Found along streams and
in moist meadows in most of New Mexico except the eastern part; 7,000–9,000 ft.
Key Characters: Red cinquefoil is characterized by the dark red flowers, the nearly naked
flowering cymes, and the terminal styles.

106. **Cinquefoil**   *Potentilla pulcherrima*   Rose family

Perennial herb, the stems 10–24 in. (25–60 cm) tall. *Leaves* digitately or pinnately compound
with 5–11, usually 7, leaflets, these oblanceolate to obovate, toothed on the margins, green
and glabrous to sparsely hairy on the upper surface, whitish with densely matted hairs
beneath. *Flowers* in somewhat crowded clusters, the 5 sparsely hairy sepals alternating with 5
shorter bractlets, the 5 petals yellow and longer than the sepals, and 20 stamens. *Fruits* of
achenes with the styles attached at the tip. This cinquefoil is an attractive meadow flower.
Range and Habitat: Manitoba to British Columbia, southward to South Dakota, New
Mexico, Arizona, and Nevada. Frequently found in mountain meadows throughout New
Mexico; 7,500–11,500 ft.
Key Characters: This cinquefoil is characterized by having the leaflets pinnately or digitately
arranged, green and nearly glabrous above and woolly with whitish hairs beneath, and yellow
petals.

Potentilla hippiana

Potentilla thurberi

Potentilla pulcherrima

107. Yellow avens   *Geum strictum*   Rose family

Perennial herb, the stems hairy, to 40 in. (1 m) or more tall. *Leaves* of 2 types, the basal ones pinnate, with an enlarged terminal segment and 4–8 lateral leaflets alternating with much smaller ones, all leaflets toothed or cleft and hairy on both surfaces, the upper stem leaves 3-foliolate. *Flowers* in loose clusters or solitary, the 5 calyx lobes about ¹/₄ in. (5–6 mm) long, alternating with 5 much smaller bractlets, the 5 yellow petals obovate and usually longer than the sepals. *Fruits* of achenes covered with appressed hairs, each with a jointed, 2-parted style, the lower portion hooked and persistent. Avens superficially resembles cinquefoil.
Range and Habitat: Newfoundland to British Columbia, southward to Pennsylvania, Missouri, New Mexico, California, and Mexico. Often found in damp woods, especially along streams, throughout New Mexico; 7,000–9,500 ft.
Key Characters: Yellow avens is characterized by the 5 yellow petals, the 5 sepals alternating with 5 bractlets, and by the jointed styles with the lower portion persistent and hooked.
Related Species: Avens, *G. turbinatum,* occurring in montane habitats above 9,000 ft. from northern to south-central New Mexico, differs in having 11 or more leaflets per leaf, and smooth unjointed styles.

108. Wild rose   *Rosa woodsii*   Rose family

Shrub to 40 in. (1 m) tall, the stems brown or gray, usually bearing scattered, straight, slender prickles between the nodes, also with 1 or 2 prickles just below the nodes. *Leaves* pinnately compound with 5–7 leaflets, stipulate, the leaflets oval to obovate, toothed, ³/₈–1¹/₈ in. (1–3 cm) long. *Flowers* solitary or in a loose cluster, the flowering branches often without prickles, the 5 calyx lobes gradually tapering to a point, arising from a glabrous calyx tube, the 5 petals pink or rose purple, about ⁵/₈–³/₄ in. (15–20 mm) long. The *R. woodsii* complex in New Mexico is composed of 7 varieties, including Fendler rose, paleleaf rose, Macoun rose, New Mexico rose, Arizona rose, and two varieties without common names. The description given is based on the Fendler rose, *R. woodsii* var. *fendleri.*
Range and Habitat: Minnesota to British Columbia, southward to Mexico. Found on plains and mountain slopes throughout New Mexico; 6,000–9,000 ft.
Key Characters: The wild rose is easily recognized by the large rose purple to pink flowers, the stems with prickles between the nodes and with 1 or 2 prickles next to the nodes, and the gradually tapering calyx lobes arising from the globose calyx tube.
Related Species: The different varieties of *R. woodsii* are diverse in range, elevation, and distribution in New Mexico, but all are similar in general description.

109. Apache plume   *Fallugia paradoxa*   Rose family

Much-branched shrub with slender, whitish branches. *Leaves* small, in clusters, pinnately 3- to 7-lobed, each lobe linear-oblong, obtuse, the edges somewhat rolled under. *Flowers* numerous, showy, white, roselike, the calyx tube hairy inside, extending into 5 gradually tapering lobes and alternating with 5 narrower bractlets, the 5 petals rounded or obovate and easily knocked off, the stamens numerous. *Fruits* of numerous achenes, each bearing a persistent, long, twisted, hairy style to 2 in. (5 cm) long. Apache plume is so named because of the conspicuous reddish bundle of fruits. The plant has been used in several ways by Native Americans.
Range and Habitat: Colorado and Utah to Texas, New Mexico, Arizona, and Mexico. Common, often abundant, on dry slopes and along arroyos throughout New Mexico; 5,000–7,500 ft.
Key Characters: Apache plume is easily recognized by the small, linear-lobed leaves borne in clusters, the shrubby nature, the large white flowers, and the fruits of numerous achenes with conspicuous, persistent, reddish or pinkish styles.

Geum strictum

Rosa woodsii

Fallugia paradoxa

115

110. **Cliffrose**   *Cowania stansburiana*   Rose family

Resinous shrub, the stems to 6 1/2 ft. (2 m) tall, with spreading branches. *Leaves* alternate, simple, 3/8–5/8 in. (10–15 mm) long, pinnately lobed into 5 or fewer linear or oblong lobes, glandular above and with matted hairs beneath. *Flowers* solitary, terminal on the branches, with 5 calyx lobes and 5 pale yellow, broadly obovate petals 1/4–3/8 in. (6–10 mm) long. *Fruits* of about 5 densely hairy achenes, bearing persistent, feathery styles 5/8–2 in. (15–50 mm) long.
Range and Habitat: Colorado to Utah, New Mexico, Arizona, and California. Usually found on dry slopes and mesas from northern to western and southwestern New Mexico; 5,000–7,500 ft.
Key Characters: Cliffrose is characterized by the glandular, narrowly lobed leaves, the small yellow flowers, and the usually 5 achenes with long, featherlike, persistent taillike styles.

111. **Mesquitilla; Fairy duster**   *Calliandra humilis*   Legume family

Perennial herb, sometimes woody at the base, the stems to about 8 in. (20 cm) tall. *Leaves* usually densely hairy, bipinnate, the primary rib with 4–9 pairs of pinnae, each pinna bearing 10–18 pairs of linear or narrowly oblong leaflets, these usually about 1/12–1/6 in. (2–4 mm) long, 1/16–1/12 in. (1–2 mm) wide. *Flowers* whitish, borne in dense, globose, axillary or terminal clusters on stalks 3/8–1 1/8 in. (1–3 cm) long, the calyx 5-toothed, about 1/12 in. (2 mm) long, the corolla 5-lobed, about 1/4 in. (6 mm) long, the stamens numerous. *Fruit* a pod 1 5/8–2 3/4 in. (4–7 cm) long, hairy when young but glabrous in age. Mesquitilla without flowers or fruits closely resembles a young mesquite without thorns.
Range and Habitat: New Mexico to Arizona and Mexico. Frequently found on dry slopes, or in open wooded areas among oaks or pines, from central to southern and western New Mexico; 4,500–9,000 ft.
Key Characters: This mesquitilla is characterized by the bipinnate leaves, the whitish globose heads of flowers, the herbaceous nature, and by the short, numerous, hairy leaflets.
Related Species: Another mesquitilla, *C. reticulata,* is very similar but differs in having glabrous to sparsely hairy leaflets 1/4–1/2 in. (6–12 mm) long. It is found mostly in southwestern New Mexico.

112. **Catclaw acacia; Devil's claw**   *Acacia greggii*   Legume family

Shrub or small tree, the stems usually armed with short, curved, pricklelike spines. *Leaves* bipinnate, 1 1/8–2 in. (3–5 cm) long, with 2–6 pinnae, each with 4–14 oblong to obovate, prominently nerved leaflets, these oblique at the base and rounded or truncate at the apex. *Flowers* yellowish or white, borne in dense, cylindrical spikelike clusters 3/4–1 1/2 in. (2–4 cm) long. *Fruit* a flat, linear pod, 3 1/4–4 1/4 in. (8–12 cm) long, irregularly constricted between the seeds. The spines of catclaw acacia can be devastating to clothing or skin.
Range and Habitat: Texas to Nevada, Arizona, and California, southward to New Mexico. Found along streams and washes in southern New Mexico; 3,500–5,000 ft.
Key Characters: Catclaw acacia may be recognized by the curved spines, the flowers borne in cylindrical spikes, and the numerous small leaflets.
Related Species: Whitethorn acacia or mescat acacia, *A. constricta,* also occurs in southern New Mexico and differs in having straight spines, yellow flowers in dense globose heads, and leaves with 2–7 pairs of pinnae.

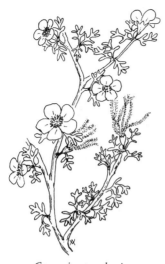

Cowania stansburiana

Calliandra humilis

Acacia greggii

113. **Whiteball acacia**   *Acacia angustissima*   Legume family

Perennial, woody only toward the base or on the lower stems, the upper stems and branches herbaceous and unarmed. *Leaves* bipinnate with 3–6 pairs of pinnae, each pinna with 18–30 thick, linear-oblong, obtuse, glabrous to hairy leaflets $^1/_8$–$^1/_4$ in. (2.5–5 mm) long. *Flowers* whitish, borne in round, tight, headlike clusters about $^5/_8$ in. (15 mm) in diameter, on hairy stalks. *Fruit* a broadly linear pod $1^3/_{16}$–$2^3/_8$ in. (3–6 cm) long, $^1/_4$–$^1/_3$ in. (6–8 mm) wide, abruptly narrowed at the tip.

Range and Habitat: Missouri to Texas and Arizona, southward into Guatemala; also southern Florida. Occurring on rocky or grassy slopes or woodlands of east-central and southern New Mexico; 4,000–6,000 ft.

Key Characters: Whiteball acacia is characterized by the absence of spines, the round heads of whitish flowers, and by the herbaceous stems and branches.

114. **Honey mesquite and Torrey mesquite**   *Prosopis glandulosa*   Legume family

Shrub to 10 ft. (3 m) tall, the stems rigid, tough, with many zigzag branches, armed with stout, sharp spines to 2 in. (5 cm) long. *Leaves* bipinnate with 4–8 pinnae, each with 12–60 linear or oblong leaflets, these $1^1/_8$–2 in. (3–5 cm) long in honey mesquite, $^5/_8$–1 in. (15–25 mm) long in Torrey mesquite. *Flowers* yellow, in a dense, cylindrical, spikelike cluster $1^1/_2$–$3^1/_8$ in. (4–8 cm) long. *Fruit* a narrow, straight or slightly curved pod 4–8 in. (10–20 cm) long, somewhat constricted between the seeds. Wood from this shrub has been used for fence posts.

Range and Habitat: Kansas to Texas, westward to Arizona and Mexico. Common on plains and prairies and in valleys of eastern to central, south-central, and southwestern New Mexico; 3,000–6,000 ft.

Key Characters: Honey and Torrey mesquites may be recognized by the glabrous leaflets and twigs, and by the 16–24 leaflets on each pinna. Leaflet length is the distinguishing character separating these two mesquites.

Related Species: Velvet mesquite, *P. velutina,* differs in having has finely hairy twigs and leaflets. It ranges from western Texas to Arizona and occurs from eastern to southwestern New Mexico at altitudes of 4,500–6,000 ft.

115. **Western sensitive briar**   *Schrankia occidentalis*   Legume family

Perennial herb, sometimes woody, the stems mostly prostrate, 16–48 in. (4–12 dm) long, armed with recurved prickles. *Leaves* bipinnate, sensitive (folding up when touched), with 4–14 pinnae, each with 20–32 oblong or linear-oblong leaflets $^1/_8$–$^1/_4$ in. (4–6 mm) long. *Flowers* pink, borne in dense, globose heads on stalks $1^1/_8$–$2^3/_4$ in. (3–7 cm) long. *Fruit* a prickly, angled, beaked pod, $2^3/_8$–$3^1/_2$ in. (6–9 cm) long and about $^1/_8$ in. (2–3 mm) wide. The sensitive briar is unusual in its ability to fold up its leaflets when touched.

Range and Habitat: Texas to southeastern Colorado and New Mexico. Usually found in deep sands of plains in eastern New Mexico; 3,500–4,500 ft.

Key Characters: Western sensitive briar may be easily recognized by the sensitive leaflets, the dense heads of pink flowers, and the prostrate, prickly stems.

Acacia angustissima

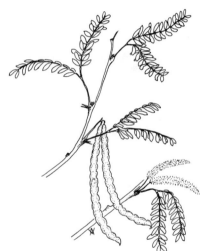

Prosopis glandulosa

Schrankia occidentalis

116. **Prairie bundleflower**   *Desmanthus illinoensis*   Legume family

Unarmed perennial, the stems often woody at the base, spreading to ascending, 12–40 in. (30–100 cm) tall. *Leaves* bipinnate, with 16–30 pinnae, each with numerous linear to oblong leaflets, these about $^1/_8$ in. (2–3 mm) long, the primary rib bearing a circular gland between the pinnae of one or more pairs. *Flowers* greenish white, borne in dense, headlike axillary clusters, the calyx about $^1/_{25}$ in. (1 mm) long, the petals about twice as long, with 5 stamens. *Fruit* borne in compact heads, the pods strongly curved and slightly twisted, $^1/_2$–1 in. (12–25 mm) long, $^1/_6$–$^1/_4$ in. (4–7 mm) wide.

Range and Habitat: Ohio to South Dakota, southward to Florida, Texas, and New Mexico. Common in valleys, along streambanks and roadsides, and on prairies throughout New Mexico; 3,000–6,500 ft.

Key Characters: Prairie bundleflower can be recognized by the bipinnate leaves, the absence of spines or prickles, the greenish white heads of flowers, and the compact clusters of strongly curved fruits.

Related Species: Another bundleflower, *D. obtusus,* is occasionally found in New Mexico and differs in having straight fruits, a lower, more spreading nature, only 1–6 pairs of pinnae, and leaflets with raised netted veins, at least beneath.

117. **Wait-a-bit**   *Mimosa biuncifera*   Legume family

Shrub to 60 in. (1.5 m) tall, the branches armed with curved spines. *Leaves* bipinnate, wih 8–20 pinnae, each with 10–24 linear to oblong, densely hairy leaflets $^1/_{16}$–$^1/_6$ in. (1–4 mm) long. *Flowers* white or pale pink, fragrant, borne in globose headlike clusters, the calyx and corolla with 4 or 5 lobes, hairy. *Fruit* a linear pod, constricted between the seeds, $^3/_4$–1$^1/_2$ in. (2–4 cm) long, about $^1/_8$ in. (3–4 mm) wide. The curved spines of wait-a-bit are extremely rude to clothing and skin.

Range and Habitat: Central Texas to New Mexico, Arizona, and Mexico. Usually found on rocky slopes and mesas in central and southern New Mexico; 3,500–6,000 ft.

Key Characters: Wait-a-bit may be recognized by the globose heads of flowers, the 4–10 pairs of pinnae per leaf, the fruits glabrous and constricted between the seeds.

Related Species: Fragrant mimosa, *M. borealis,* occurs in canyons and on rocky slopes of eastern and southern New Mexico, and differs in having 1–3 pairs of pinnae, the leaflets glabrous or nearly so and $^1/_{12}$–$^1/_4$ in. (2–6 mm) long, and fruits $^1/_4$–$^1/_3$ in. (6–8 mm) wide.

118. **Prostrate ratany**   *Krameria lanceolata*   Legume family

Perennial herbs, sometimes woody at the base, the stems prostrate or nearly so. *Leaves* alternate, simple, oblanceolate to narrowly oblong or linear, $^3/_8$–1$^1/_8$ in. (1–3 cm) long, not petioled. *Flowers* crimson, solitary on slender axillary stalks $^3/_4$–1$^1/_8$ in. (2–3 cm) long, the sepals 4 or 5, petallike, ovate-lanceolate, acute at the tip, about $^3/_8$ in. (8–10 mm) long, with 5 petals shorter than the sepals, and 4 stamens. *Fruit* a spiny, globose, single-seeded pod $^1/_4$–$^5/_{16}$ in (7–9 mm) in diameter. Fruit of the prostrate ratany has been known as "sandbur" and can puncture the skin when stepped on with bare feet.

Range and Habitat: Arkansas and Kansas to Texas and Arizona, southward into Mexico. Commonly found in sandy soil of open plains from eastern to central and southern New Mexico; 4,000–6,500 ft.

Key Characters: Prostrate ratany is characterized by the prostrate, herbaceous nature, the simple leaves, and the spiny, globose fruit.

Related Species: White ratany, *K. grayi,* a low, much-branched shrub to 2 ft. (60 cm) tall, has similar flowers, but differs in having fruits with barbed spines. It occurs on plains, dry rocky ridges, and slopes of southern New Mexico at 3,500–4,000 ft.

Desmanthus illinoensis

Mimosa biuncifera

Krameria lanceolata

119. Senna *Cassia bauhinioides* Legume family

Perennial herb to 17 in. (40 cm) tall, the stems branching, densely covered with spreading hairs. *Leaves* pinnate, with 2 oblong-ovate, obtuse leaflets, these oblique at the base, hairy on both surfaces, ³/₈–1¹/₂ in. (1–4 cm) long, and ⁵/₁₆–⁵/₈ in. (8–16 mm) wide. *Flowers* in axillary pairs borne near the ends of the branches, the calyx 5-toothed, the corolla nearly regular, with 5 dark yellow petals ⁵/₈–³/₄ in. (15–18 mm) long, much longer than the sepals. *Fruit* a straight or slightly curved, somewhat flattened pod, ³/₄–1¹/₂ in. (2–4 cm) long. The dark yellow flowers of senna are very attractive.

Range and Habitat: Texas to Arizona and Mexico. Commonly found on rocky slopes and mesas from west-central to central and southern New Mexico; 4,000–5,500 ft.

Key Characters: This senna is easily recognized by the nearly regular, dark yellow flowers, and the leaves with 2 leaflets.

Related Species: A similar senna, *C. roemeriana,* differs in having bright green lanceolate leaflets 1¹/₄–2¹/₂ in. (3–6 cm) long, 2–4 flowers per cluster, and petals about ¹/₂ in. (12–14 mm) long. It occurs on dry plains, mesas, and foothills in eastern and southern New Mexico at 3,500–5,500 ft.

120. Poinciana *Caesalpinia gilliesii* Legume family

Ill-smelling, sparingly branched shrub, the stems green, with glandular hair, to 10 ft. (3 m) tall. *Leaves* large, bipinnate, with 6–12 pairs of pinnae, each with 5–9 pairs of oblong leaflets ¹/₈–¹/₄ in. (3–6 mm) long. *Flowers* yellow, borne in terminal, open, glandular clusters, the 5 calyx lobes petallike with the lower lobe larger and overlapping the others, the 5 petals unequal, the 10 stamens with conspicuous red, curved filaments. *Fruit* a flat, oblong pod.

Range and Habitat: Introduced from Argentina into cultivation in the southern United States and frequently escaped. Found around dwelling sites and waste places, mostly in southern New Mexico; 3,500–6,000 ft.

Key Characters: Poinciana may be readily identified by the coarse stems with glandular, hairy, ill-smelling herbage, and the yellow flowers with conspicuous red filaments.

121. Rushpea *Hoffmanseggia jamesii* Legume family

Perennial herb, the stems branching at the base, erect or ascending, finely hairy with blackish glands, 4–14 in. (10–35 cm) long. *Leaves* bipinnate with 5–7 pinnae, each with 10–20 oblong to ovate leaflets about ¹/₈ in. (3–5 mm) long, these with blackish glands. *Flowers* somewhat irregular, with blackish glands, in narrow clusters, the calyx 5-lobed, the 5 petals dark yellow, glandular, less than twice as long as the calyx. *Fruit* a somewhat moon-shaped pod bearing blackish glands, ³/₄–1 in. (20–25 mm) long and about ⁵/₁₆ in. (8–9 mm) wide.

Range and Habitat: Kansas to Colorado, southward to Texas, New Mexico, and Arizona. Common on sandy hills and plains throughout New Mexico; 4,000–6,000 ft.

Key Characters: Rushpea is characterized by the bipinnate leaves with 10–20 leaflets per pinna, the moon-shaped fruit, and the blackish glands on leaflets, flowers, and fruits.

Cassia bauhinioides

Caesalpinia gilliesii

Hoffmanseggia jamesii

122. Hog potato — *Hoffmanseggia densiflora* — Legume family

Perennial herb, the stems usually branched at the base, the branches erect or ascending, to 12 in. (30 cm) tall. *Leaves* bipinnate, with 5–11 pinnae, each with 10–22 oblong, obtuse leaflets, these not glandular-dotted, ¹/₆–¹/₃ in. (4–8 mm) long. *Flowers* yellow, borne in terminal, glandular, narrow clusters, the calyx with glandular hairs and 5 linear to linear-oblong lobes about ¹/₃ in. (7–8 mm) long, the 5 petals yellow, somewhat unequal, the 10 stamens with red filaments. *Fruit* of linear, usually somewhat curved pods ³/₄–1¹/₂ in. (2–4 cm) long. This is a common roadside plant.

Range and Habitat: Kansas to Arizona and southern California, southward to central Mexico. Common in alkaline soils of plains and valleys in central and southern New Mexico; 3,500–6,000 ft.

Key Characters: Hog potato is characterized by the flower clusters with glandular hairs, the leaflets lacking black glands, and the dark yellow flowers with slightly unequal petals.

Related Species: The rushpea, *H. drepanocarpa,* is similar but differs in having the flower clusters not glandular and the fruit strongly curved, often forming a semicircle. It is usually found in central and southern New Mexico.

123. Big golden-pea — *Thermopsis pinetorum* — Legume family

Perennial herb, the stems erect, branching, 12–24 in. (30–60 cm) tall, with ovate or lanceolate stipules at the base of the petioles. *Leaves* palmately compound, with 3 ovate-oblong to elliptic leaflets 1¹/₈–2³/₈ in. (3–6 cm) long. *Flowers* in narrow, often dense, terminal clusters, the calyx 5-lobed, the 5 petals yellow and pealike. *Fruit* a usually slightly curved pod angled upward to spreading, hairy when young, 1¹/₂–3¹/₈ in. (4–8 cm) long.

Range and Habitat: Wyoming to Colorado, Utah, New Mexico, and Arizona. Common in open woods and clearings in the mountains of New Mexico; 7,000–9,500 ft.

Key Characters: Big golden-pea may be recognized by the palmately 3-foliolate leaves, the bright yellow, pealike flowers in dense, narrow, terminal clusters, and the fruits angled upward or spreading.

Related Species: Mountain golden-pea, *T. montanum,* differs in having lanceolate stipules and pods that are mostly erect. It is found mostly in northern New Mexico at 7,000–10,000 ft. Prairie thermopsis, *T. rhombifolia,* usually does not exceed 12 in. (30 cm) in height, has smaller leaflets, and has curved, widely spreading to drooping pods. It occurs on dry, sandy hills and plains of northern New Mexico at 5,000–9,000 ft.

124. King lupine — *Lupinus kingii* — Legume family

Annual or biennial herb, the stems erect or widely spreading, 2¹/₂–8 in. (6–20 cm) tall, branched near the base, with spreading, silky, tannish hairs. *Leaves* alternate, palmately compound, with 5–15 leaflets, these oblanceolate to oblong-lanceolate, bearing silky hairs on both surfaces, ³/₈–1¹/₈ in. (1–3 cm) long. *Flowers* pealike, borne in dense, terminal clusters, almost headlike, usually not more than ³/₄ in. (2 cm) long, usually not projecting beyond the leaves, the calyx 2-lipped, and with a hump on one side, the petals usually blue or purple, about ¹/₄–³/₈ in. (7–10 mm) long, irregular, the upper petal broad and with bent-back edges, the 2 lower (keel) petals united. *Fruit* an ovoid or rhombic pod about ³/₈ in. (10 mm) long, densely hairy, 2-seeded.

Range and Habitat: Colorado to Utah, New Mexico, and Arizona. Common in open woods from northern to southwestern New Mexico; 6,000–8,000 ft.

Key Characters: King lupine is distinguished by the dense flower clusters, the short pods, and the short stems bearing scattered leaves.

Related Species: Another lupine, *L. hillii,* found on wooded slopes of west-central New Mexico, has flowers in loose clusters, and longer pods. Palmer lupine, *L. palmeri,* with stems to 2 ft. (60 cm) tall, may be found in wooded canyons and on slopes in western and north-central New Mexico.

Hoffmanseggia densiflora

Thermopsis pinetorum

Lupinus kingii

125. **Silvery lupine**   *Lupinus argenteus*   Legume family

Perennial herb, the stems erect or ascending, branching, slender, 12–20 in. (30–50 cm) tall, the herbage with short, silvery appressed hairs. *Leaves* palmately compound, with 5–8 narrowly lanceolate leaflets, these 1 1/8–2 in. (3–5 cm) long, acute, glabrous or nearly so on the upper surface. *Flowers* pealike, borne in loose, elongate clusters (racemes) 2–6 in. (5–15 cm) long, the calyx 2-lipped and with a hump on one side, the upper lip broad and 2-toothed, the lower one nearly entire, the petals blue, cream-colored, or purplish, the upper petal broad and bent back on the edges. *Fruit* a pod 3/4–1 3/8 in. (20–35 mm) long, 3- to 6-seeded. Silvery lupine is a striking and attractive plant.

Range and Habitat: North Dakota to Montana, southward to Nebraska, New Mexico, and Arizona. Found in meadows and open woods from northern to south-central New Mexico; 7,000–10,000 ft.

Key Characters: Silvery lupine may be recognized by the loose, elongate clusters of flowers, the flowers about 1/3–1/2 in. (8–12 mm) long, and the minute, silvery hairs on stems and leaves.

Related Species: Another lupine, *L. alpestris,* occurs in moist mountain meadows of northern and western New Mexico at 7,000–10,000 ft. The leaflets are obtuse and with a short point (cusp) at the tip, and the corolla is blue with a purple spot.

126. **Narrowleaf bean**   *Phaseolus angustissimus*   Legume family

Perennial herb, the stems twining, usually at least 12 in. (30 cm) long. *Leaves* pinnate with 3 linear, narrowly oblong, or sometimes linear-lanceolate leaflets 1 3/16–2 in. (3–5 cm) long. *Flowers* several, in axillary, long-stalked, narrow clusters, the calyx 5-toothed, subtended by a pair of small bractlets, the petals purplish pink with a yellow keel, pealike, about 1/4–3/8 in. (8–10 mm) long. *Fruit* a flat pod 1/4–5/16 in. (6–8 mm) wide, tipped with a beak about 1/12 in. (2 mm) long.

Range and Habitat: New Mexico and Arizona. Commonly found on dry hills and plains from south-central to west-central and southwestern New Mexico; 4,000–7,000 ft.

Key Characters: Narrowleaf bean may be recognized by the perennial nature, the twining stems, the small bractlets subtending the calyx, and the narrow leaflets.

Related Species: Texas bean, *P. acutifolius,* is very similar but is an annual plant. Another wild bean, *P. grayanus,* differs in having the leaflets mostly strongly 3-lobed and hairy pods. In New Mexico, both of these beans are found in generally the same range and habitat as the narrowleaf bean.

Lupinus argenteus

Phaseolus angustissimus

127

127. **Scurfpea**   *Psoralea tenuiflora*   Legume family

Perennial herb, the stems much-branched, erect or angled upward, hairy, glandular-dotted, to
2 ft. (60 cm) tall. *Leaves* pinnate or palmate, with 3–5 leaflets, these almost hairless above,
hairy beneath, glandular-dotted, linear to oblong-oblanceolate, $^3/_8$–$1^5/_8$ in. (1–4 cm) long.
Flowers pealike, borne in slender clusters $^3/_8$–$1^5/_8$ in. (1–4 cm) long, on stalks $^1/_{12}$–$^1/_6$ in. (2–
4 mm) long, the calyx about $^1/_8$ in. (2–3 mm) long, 2-lipped, glandular, the petals blue or
purple, $^1/_6$–$^5/_{16}$ in. (4–7 mm) long. *Fruit* an ovoid, glabrous, glandular-dotted pod about $^1/_3$
in. (7–8 mm) long, tipped by a short beak. Scurfpea is an abundant plant, especially on
roadsides, but the flowers are individually rather inconspicuous.
Range and Habitat: North Dakota to Montana, southward to Kansas, Texas, Arizona, and
northern Mexico. Frequently found on dry plains and low hills throughout New Mexico;
4,500–7,500 ft.
Key Characters: This scurfpea may be distinguished by the small, blue flowers, the absence
of silvery or whitish hairs, and the linear-oblanceolate leaves.
Related Species: Lemon scurfpea or lemonweed, *P. lanceolata,* differs in having stems usually
not exceeding 16 in. (4 dm) tall, leaves with 3 usually linear leaflets, and white flowers. It
occurs in sandy soil of mesas and wooded slopes from northern to central and western New
Mexico at 5,000–7,000 ft.

128. **Feather indigobush**   *Dalea formosa*   Legume family

Much-branched shrub, the stems to 24 in. (60 cm) long, the branches glabrous. *Leaves*
pinnate, with 7–11 oblong or spatulate leaflets about $^1/_8$ in. (2–3 mm) long, these glabrous
and glandular-dotted beneath. *Flowers* 2–10 in narrow, somewhat dense clusters, each flower
subtended by an ovate, glandular bract, the glandular calyx tube about $^1/_8$–$^3/_{16}$ in. (3–4 mm)
long, with long hairs, and 5 narrow, featherlike lobes longer than the tube, the petals
pealike, mostly rose-colored, sometimes yellowish. *Fruit* a hairy, glandular-dotted pod.
Range and Habitat: Colorado to New Mexico, Arizona, and Mexico. Frequently found on
dry plains and low hills, often among rocks, throughout New Mexico; 4,000–7,000 ft.
Key Characters: Feather indigobush is characterized by the usually rose-colored flowers, often
with yellowish markings, the shrubby, low, much-branched habit, the hairy calyx tube, and
the 11 or fewer leaflets per leaf.
Related Species: Black indigobush, *D. frutescens,* is similar but differs in having mostly
unbranched stems and glabrous calyx tubes. It ranges from Texas to New Mexico and Mexico,
occurring on dry open slopes in southeastern and south-central New Mexico at 6,500–8,000
ft. Another indigobush, *D. greggii,* found on limestone hills of southern New Mexico at
2,500–6,000 ft., has hairy leaves and stems, and sessile flowers.

129. **Hairy indigobush**   *Dalea lanata*   Legume family

Perennial herb, the stems reclining, branched at the base, densely hairy with grayish hairs, to
2 ft. (60 cm) long, glandular-dotted. *Leaves* pinnate with 7–13 obovate, densely hairy leaflets,
these $^1/_5$–$^1/_2$ in. (5–12 mm) long glandular-dotted. *Flowers* pealike, borne in slender, many-
flowered, spikelike clusters $^3/_4$–4 in. (2–10 cm) long, each flower subtended by an ovate,
long-pointed bract, the calyx 5-lobed, about $^1/_8$ in. (3–4 mm) long, each lobe lanceolate or
nearly triangular, the petals usually purplish red, $^1/_6$–$^1/_4$ in. (4–6 mm) long. *Fruit* a hairy
pod.
Range and Habitat: Kansas to Colorado, southward to Texas and New Mexico. Common on
plains and prairies, often in sandy soil, from eastern to central and south-central New Mexico;
4,500–5,500 ft.
Key Characters: This indigo bush is characterized by the low, spreading habit, the stems
and leaves with dense grayish hairs, the small flowers, and the densely hairy calyx.
Related Species: Spreading indigobush, *D. terminalis,* is very similar but the calyx tube is
glabrous. It is common on dry fields and plains throughout New Mexico at 4,000–5,500 ft.

Psoralea tenuiflora

Dalea formosa

Dalea lanata

130. **Silktop indigobush**   *Dalea aurea*   Legume family

Perennial herb, sometimes woody at the base, the stems erect or nearly so, with silky hairs, to 2 ft. (60 cm) tall. *Leaves* pinnate with 5, rarely 7, leaflets, these oblong, oblanceolate, or obovate, bearing silky hairs, minutely glandular-dotted beneath, $^3/_8-^3/_4$ in. (1–2 cm) long. *Flowers* pealike, borne in dense, cylindrical, spikelike clusters $^3/_4-2^3/_8$ in. (2–6 cm) long, each flower subtended by a bract with silky hairs, the calyx $^5/_{16}-^3/_8$ in. (8–10 mm) long, 5-lobed, the dense hairs silky, the petals yellow. *Fruit* a pod with silky hairs..
Range and Habitat: South Dakota to Wyoming, Texas, New Mexico, Arizona, and Mexico. Found occasionally on plains and open hills in eastern and central New Mexico; 4,500–6,000 ft.
Key Charcters: Silktop indigobush may be recognized by its tall, slender habit, the large dense spike of yellow flowers, and the silky-hairy herbage.
Related Species: James indigobush, *D. jamesii,* usually does not exceed 8 in. (20 cm) in height and has palmately compound leaves with 3 nonglandular leaflets.It occurs on dry, often sandy plains throughout New Mexico at 5,000–6,500 ft.

131. **Red clover**   *Trifolium pratense*   Legume family

Biennial or perennial herb, the stems leafy, erect to spreading, the herbage pubescent. *Leaves* palmately compound with 3 ovate to obovate or oval leaflets, these $^3/_4-2$ in. (2–5 cm) long, usually minutely toothed, sparsely hairy. *Flowers* pealike, borne in dense, headlike clusters $^3/_4-1^1/_8$ in. (2–3 cm) in diameter, the clusters sessile or nearly so and subtended by 1 or 2 leaves, the calyx hairy, 5-toothed, greenish white, the petals reddish purple, $^1/_2-^3/_4$ in. (12–20 mm) long. *Fruit* a 1- or 2-seeded pod. Red clover is a low but very attractive plant of roadsides.
Range and Habitat: Introduced from Europe; now widespread in the United States and Canada. Found occasionally in fields and waste ground throughout most of New Mexico; 4,000–9,000 ft.
Key Characters: Red clover may be recognized by the sessile heads of reddish purple flowers, the leafy stems, and the hairy calyx.

132. **Woods clover**   *Trifolium pinetorum*   Legume family

Perennial herb, the stems ascending to spreading, leafy, glabrous or sparsely hairy, to 20 in. (50 cm) long. *Leaves* palmately compound with 3 obovate or oblanceolate leaflets, these usually blunt at the tip, $^1/_3-^3/_4$ in. (8–20 mm) long. *Flowers* pealike, borne in dense, headlike clusters subtended by an involucre cleft nearly to the base into narrowly lanceolate or linear divisions, the clusters $^3/_8-^3/_4$ in. (1–2 cm) wide, more than 10-flowered, on often hairy stalks, the calyx 5-toothed, glabrous or nearly so, the teeth longer than the tube, the petals purple, $^1/_3-^3/_8$ in. (8–10 mm) long.
Range and Habitat: New Mexico and Arizona. Found occasionally in moist woods from central to southern New Mexico; 6,500–10,000 ft.
Key Characters: Woods clover may be distinguished by the glabrous calyx, the leafy stems, the hairy flowering stalks, and the deeply cleft involucres subtending the flower heads.
Related Species: White clover, *T. repens,* occurs throughout New Mexico in fields and waste ground at 4,500–8,500 ft. The flowers are white or pink-tinged, not subtended by an involucre, and the calyx is glabrous. Alsike clover, *T. hybridum,* is similar to white clover but differs in having leaflets rounded at the tip instead of notched. It is found mostly in damp meadows from north-central to western New Mexico.

Dalea aurea

Trifolium pratense

Trifolium pinetorum

131

133. **Brandegee alpine-clover**   *Trifolium brandegei*   Legume family

Perennial herb without stems, the flowering stalks angled upward or spreading, to 6 in. (15 cm) long, the herbage glabrous or nearly so. *Leaves* basal, palmately compound with 3 oval to oblong-elliptic leaflets, ¹/₄–1¹/₈ in. (7–30 mm) long, these glabrous or nearly so, entire or with minute teeth on the margins. *Flowers* pealike, borne in loose, headlike clusters above the leaves on stout stalks, the subtending involucre minute or absent, all flowers becoming reflexed, the calyx glabrous or nearly so, often tinged with purple, ¹/₄–³/₈ in. (6–10 mm) long, with 5 lanceolate teeth about as long as the tube, the petals purple, ¹/₂–³/₄ in. (1–2 cm) long. *Fruit* a 2- to 7-seeded pod

Range and Habitat: Colorado and New Mexico. Found occasionally in montane and alpine meadows of north-central New Mexico; 11,000–13,000 ft.

Key Characters: Brandegee alpine-clover is characterized by the 6–15 drooping purple flowers in somewhat loose heads, the glabrous calyx, and the basal leaves.

Related Species: Dwarf alpine-clover, *T. nanum,* differs in having 1–3 rose purple flowers per head. It occurs in much the same area. Alpine clover, *T. dasyphyllum,* occurs in much the same range and habit, but has 10–30 flowers per head, a hairy calyx, and entire leaflets.

134. **Alfalfa**   *Medicago sativa*   Legume family

Perennial herb the stems mostly erect, branched, glabrous or sparsely hairy, to 40 in. (1 m) tall. *Leaves* pinnate with 3 oblong to obovate leaflets ³/₈–1¹/₈ in. (1–3 cm) long, these obtuse at the apex and minutely toothed toward the apex. *Flowers* borne in dense, narrow, axillary clusters ³/₈–2 in. (1–5 cm) long, the calyx tube bell-shaped with 5 equal lobes, the corolla pealike, violet, about ⁵/₁₆ in. (7–9 mm) long. *Fruit* a hairy, coiled, several-seeded pod. Alfalfa is commonly cultivated and often escapes.

Range and Habitat: Introduced from Europe to temperate areas of North America. Frequently found along roadsides and waste ground throughout New Mexico; 4,000–8,000 ft.

Key Characters: Alfalfa may be easily identified by the small clusters of violet flowers, the 3 leaflets minutely toothed above the middle, and the coiled fruit.

135. **Yellow sweet clover**   *Melilotus officinalis*   Legume family

Biennial herb, the stems mostly erect, branched, usually glabrous, to about 6¹/₂ ft. (2 m) tall. *Leaves* pinnate with 3 oblong to oval, sharply toothed, glabrous leaflets ³/₈–1¹/₈ in. (1–3 cm) long. *Flowers* in slender axillary clusters ³/₄–4³/₄ in. (2–12 cm) long, the corolla pealike, yellow, about ¹/₄ in. (5–6 mm) long. *Fruit* a straight, sparsely hairy pod about ¹/₈ in. (3–4 mm) long. Yellow sweet clover is very fragrant when cut or crushed.

Range and Habitat: Introduced from Europe throughout the United States. Frequently found along roadsides and in waste or cultivated ground throughout New Mexico; 4,000–8,000 ft.

Key Characters: Yellow sweet clover may be identified by the slender clusters of small yellow pealike flowers, the leaves with 3 sharply toothed leaflets, and the small, straight, wrinkled fruit.

Related Species: White sweet clover, *M. albus,* differs in having white flowers and only slightly wrinkled pods. It is also widespread in New Mexico.

Trifolium brandegei

Medicago sativa

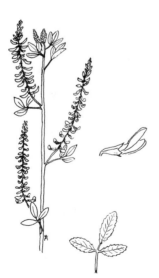

Melilotus officinalis

133

136. Wright deervetch   *Lotus wrightii*   Legume family

Perennial herb, the stems numerous, erect or angled upward, with grayish hairs, to 16 in. (40 cm) tall. *Leaves* sessile, appearing palmate, with 3–5 hairy, linear to narrowly oblong leaflets ¼–¾ in. (6–20 mm) long. *Flowers* pealike, borne in groups of 1–3 in the leaf axils, sessile or nearly so, the calyx ¼–⅓ in. (6–8 mm) long, with slender teeth about as long as the tube, the petals yellow or orange, becoming reddish orange in age, ½–⅝ in. (12–15 mm) long. *Fruit* a linear, hairy pod ¾–1 in. (20–25 mm) long.
Range and Habitat: Colorado to Utah, New Mexico, and Arizona. Found frequently in open, usually dry woods from northern to south-central and western New Mexico; 6,000–9,000 ft.
Key Characters: Wright deervetch is characterized by the absence of large stipules, and apparently palmately compound leaves with 3–5 leaflets.
Related Species: Another deervetch, *L. oroboides,* occurs occasionally on wooded slopes. It has leaves that are pinnate with 4–13 leaflets.

137. Ground milkvetch   *Astragalus humistratus*   Legume family

Perennial herb, the stems prostrate, to about 2 ft. (60 cm) long, the herbage sparsely hairy with appressed hairs. *Leaves* pinnate with 11–17 elliptic to oblanceolate leaflets, these glabrous on the upper surface. *Flowers* pealike, borne in axillary clusters, the calyx 5-toothed, sparsely hairy, ¼–⅓ in. (6–8 mm) long, the corolla greenish white or pale yellowish white, sometimes tinged with purple, the upper petal (banner) 5/16–½ in. (9–12 mm) long. *Fruit* an oblong or ellipsoid, somewhat curved pod 9/16–¾ in. (14–18 mm) long, with dark brown seeds.
Range and Habitat: Colorado to New Mexico, Arizona, and northern Mexico. Found on dry mesas, hills, and gravelly areas throughout New Mexico; 4,500–8,500 ft.
Key Characters: Ground milkvetch is characterized by the long, prostrate stems, the 11–17 leaflets per leaf, and the pods at least 3 times longer than wide.
Related Species: Another milkvetch, *A. brandegei,* differs in having 5–15 narrow leaflets and whitish flowers, with the upper petal (banner) 1/6–¼ in. (4–7 mm) long. It occurs on dry rocky areas, usually among pinyons and junipers from central to western New Mexico at 5,500–8,500 ft.

138. Giant milkvetch   *Astragalus giganteus*   Legume family

Perennial herb, the stems stout, erect, 8–24 in. (20–60 cm) tall, the herbage densely covered with often somewhat matted hairs. *Leaves* pinnate, with 17–35 flat, oblong-elliptic to ovate leaflets, these acute at the apex and densely hairy on the midnerve beneath. *Flowers* pealike, borne in elongate, narrow clusters exceeding the leaves, the flowers becoming reflexed in age, the calyx 5-toothed, hairy, ⅜–⅝ in. (10–15 mm) long, the corolla pale yellow, the upper petal (banner) ⅝–¾ in. (15–20 mm) long, shallowly notched. *Fruit* an erect, laterally compressed, glabrous, ovoid or ellipsoid pod ⅝–1 in. (15–25 mm) long. Giant milkvetch is a conspicuous showy flower of gravelly meadows.
Range and Habitat: Texas to New Mexico and Mexico. Frequent in gravelly areas of south-central New Mexico; 6,000–9,000 ft.
Key Characters: Giant milkvetch is easily recognized by the erect habit and tall stems, the grayish appearance, and the long narrow clusters of conspicuous yellow flowers exceeding the leaves.
Related Species: Another milkvetch, *A. flexuosus,* occurs on dry grassy slopes and sandy hills throughout New Mexico, and differs in having decumbent stems, greenish herbage, and the white to cream-colored or purple corolla, with the banner petal ⅓–½ in. (7–11 mm) long.

Lotus wrightii

Astragalus humistratus

Astragalus giganteus

139. Wooton milkvetch — *Astragalus wootonii* — Legume family

Annual or biennial herb, the stems decumbent to ascending, to 12 in. (30 cm) tall, or sometimes taller, the herbage with appressed to spreading hairs. *Leaves* 1⁵/₈–4 in. (4–10 cm) long, pinnate, with 11–23 leaflets, these linear-oblong to oblanceolate, blunt at the apex, usually folded, glabrous on the upper surface. *Flowers* pealike, the stalks spreading in fruit, the calyx 5-toothed, about ¼ in. (5–7 mm) long, with white or black hairs, the corolla whitish or tinged with pink or blue, the upper petal (banner) ¹/₅–¼ in. (5–8 mm) long. *Fruit* an inflated, ovoid to subglobose pod ⁵/₈–1⁵/₈ in. (15–40 mm) long.

Range and Habitat: New Mexico to Arizona, southern California, and Mexico. Found occasionally on plains, slopes, and in valleys from north-central to south-central and western New Mexico; 4,000–8,500 ft.

Key Characters: Wooton milkvetch may be identified by the leaves with 11–23 leaflets, the inflated pods, the small banner petal, and the usually white flowers.

Related Species: Lotus milkvetch, *A. lotiflorus,* occurs in gravelly soils from central to northeastern New Mexico, and differs in having the stems reclining, usually less than 4 in. (10 cm) long, the corolla greenish white, the banner petal ³/₈–⁵/₈ in. (9–14 mm) long, and the pods not inflated.

140. Ground plum — *Astragalus crassicarpus* — Legume family

Perennial herb, the stems curving upward from reclining bases, to 20 in. (50 cm) long, usually hairy. *Leaves* alternate, pinnate, with 15–29 leaflets, these broadest above the middle or elliptic. *Flowers* in dense axillary clusters, pealike, purple or lilac or occasionally white with purple spots, the upper petal (banner) ⁵/₈–1 in. (16–25 mm) long. *Fruit* a smooth, plumlike, fleshy pod ⁵/₈–1 in. (15–25 mm) long.

Range and Habitat: Manitoba and Alberta to Missouri, Texas, and New Mexico. Usually found on open plains and waste ground, often along roadsides, in eastern and southern New Mexico; 4,500–7,500 ft.

Key Characters: Ground plum may be identified by the upward curving stems, the compound leaves with 15 or more leaflets, the usually purple or lilac pealike flowers, and the fleshy, spongy fruits.

141. Woolly locoweed — *Astragalus mollissimus* — Legume family

Short-stemmed or stemless perennial herb, the stems usually less than 4 in. (10 cm) long, both stems and leaves woolly with silky hairs. *Leaves* alternate, pinnate, the 15–29 leaflets oval or broader above the middle, blunt at the tip, ³/₈–³/₄ in. (1–2 cm) long. *Flowers* pealike, yellowish purple to pinkish purple, the upper petal (banner) mostly ¹/₂–⁷/₈ in. (13–22 mm) long. *Fruit* an ellipsoid, abruptly curved pod as long as the flowers. Although relatively unpalatable, this plant is poisonous to livestock. This description includes the six varieties of woolly locoweed found in New Mexico.

Range and Habitat: Nebraska and Wyoming to Texas and Arizona. Mostly on dry, open plains or slopes, sometimes in rocky areas throughout New Mexico; 4,000–8,500 ft.

Key Characters: Woolly locoweed is characterized by the very short stems or the lack of stems, the elongate flower stalks, the yellowish purple to pinkish purple flowers, and the strongly curved pods.

Astragalus wootonii

Astragalus crassicarpus

Astragalus mollissimus

137

142. **Hassayampa milkvetch**   *Astragalus allochrous*   Legume family

Biennial herb, the stems angled upward, to 20 in. (50 cm) long, the leaves and stems mostly sparsely hairy with appressed hairs. *Leaves* pinnate, with 11–21 leaflets, these oblong-obovate to oblanceolate or elliptic, sometimes glabrous on the upper surface. *Flowers* pealike, on ascending to spreading stalks, the calyx 5-toothed, 1/6–1/4 in. (4–6 mm) long, often with black hairs, the corolla pinkish purple, becoming violet when dry, the upper petal (banner) 1/3–3/8 in. (7–10 mm) long. *Fruit* an ellipsoid, inflated, somewhat hairy pod 1–15/8 in. (25–40 mm) long.

Range and Habitat: Trans-Pecos Texas to Arizona and northern Mexico. Usually found on plains, in valleys, and on open slopes from west-central to south-central and southwestern New Mexico; 4,000–7,000 ft.

Key Characters: Hassayampa milkvetch may be identified by the inflated pods, the banner 1/3–3/8 in. (7–10 mm) long, and by the flower clusters with 10–25 flowers.

143. **Bush peavine**   *Lathyrus eucosmus*   Legume family

Perennial herb, the stems erect to climbing or twining, often angled or winged, 6–20 in. (15–50 cm) long. *Leaves* subtended by conspicuous stipules, pinnate, with 6–8 thick, narrowly oblong to oblong-elliptic leaflets, the leaf rachis ending in a twining tendril. *Flowers* pealike, borne in loose axillary clusters of 2–5, the calyx 3/8–5/8 in. (10–15 mm) long, 5-toothed, the teeth slightly shorter than the tube, the corolla showy, rose pink or purple, 3/4–11/8 in. (2–3 cm) long, with 10 stamens. *Fruit* of glabrous pods about 1/6 in. (4–5 mm) long. Bush peavine is a low-growing but very attractive roadside plant.

Range and Habitat: Colorado and Utah to New Mexico and Arizona. Commonly found in open woods and on waste ground from northern to south-central and southwestern New Mexico; 5,000–7,000 ft.

Key Characters: Bush peavine is characterized by the large, pinkish to purple flowers borne 2–5 in axillary clusters, the leaf rachis terminating in a twining tendril, the 6–8 oblong to ovate leaflets, and the calyx teeth shorter than the tube.

144. **Peavine**   *Lathyrus leucanthus*   Legume family

Perennial herb, the stems erect to climbing or trailing, angled, nearly glabrous, 6–16 in. (15–40 cm) long. *Leaves* pinnately compound, subtended by narrow stipules, with 4 to 6 or, rarely, 10 leaflets, ending in a bristlelike or twining tendril, the leaflets linear-elliptic to ovate, prominently veined, 1–2 in. (25–50 mm) long. *Flowers* pealike, borne 2–5 in loose clusters, the calyx 3/16–3/8 in. (7–9 mm) long, 5-toothed, the teeth shorter than the tube, the corolla white, becoming yellow or yellowish brown in age, 1/2–7/8 in. (14–22 mm) long, the stamens 10.

Range and Habitat: Wyoming to Colorado, Utah, New Mexico, and Arizona. Common in meadows, woods, and on open slopes from northern to south-central New Mexico; 7,000–10,500 ft.

Key Characters: This peavine may be recognized by the white to yellowish-brown flowers that are 1/2–7/8 in. (14–22 mm) long.

Related Species: Arizona peavine, *L. arizonicus,* occurs frequently in open woods of New Mexico at 7,000–10,000 ft. It has bristlelike tendrils, 2–6 leaflets per leaf, and flowers usually 3/8–5/8 in. (11–14 mm) long.

Astragalus allochrous

Lathyrus eucosmus

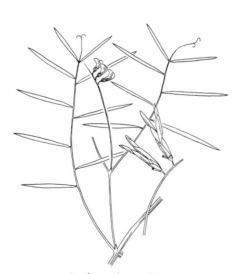

Lathyrus leucanthus

139

145. **American vetch**   *Vicia americana*   Legume family

Perennial herb, the stems smooth, climbing or trailing, to 3 ft. (1 m) long. *Leaves* pinnately compound, with 8–18 variable leaflets ⁵/₈–1³/₈ in. (15–35 mm) long and ¼–½ in. (6–14 mm) wide, the leaf rachis ending in a tendril. *Flowers* in small clusters, pealike, the corolla bluish purple, ⁵/₈–³/₄ in. (15–20 mm) long. *Fruit* a slender, flattened pod about 1¼ in. (3 cm) long.

Range and Habitat: Canada and Alaska to Virginia, New Mexico, and Arizona. Usually found on open or wooded slopes in the mountains of New Mexico; 5,000–10,000 ft.

Key Characters: American vetch may be recognized by the smooth, elongate stems, the pinnately compound tendrilled leaves with 8–18 leaflets, and the large bluish flowers about ³/₄ in. (20 mm) long.

146. **Sweet vetch**   *Hedysarum boreale*   Legume family

Perennial herb, the stems grooved, finely hairy, 16–24 in. (40–60 cm) tall. *Leaves* pinnately compound, subtended by stipules, with 9–15 linear-oblong to elliptic or obovate leaflets, these glabrous to sparsely hairy above, hairy beneath, ³/₈–³/₄ in. (1–2 cm) long. *Flowers* pealike, borne in loose, narrow clusters (racemes), the lower ones sometimes reflexed, the calyx hairy, 5-toothed, the teeth ⅛–¼ in. (3–5 mm) long, as long or longer than the tube, the corolla reddish to rose purple, ½–³/₄ in. (12–20 mm) long, and 10 stamens. *Fruit* a pod constricted between the seeds to form 2–5 rounded, conspicuously nerved, hairy segments ¼–⅓ in. (6–8 mm) long. Sweet vetch superficially resembles milkvetch and is a strikingly beautiful plant when in flower.

Range and Habitat: Montana to Colorado, Utah, and New Mexico. Usually found in canyons and valleys and on slopes in northern New Mexico; 4,500–7,000 ft.

Key Characters: Sweet vetch may be easily identified by the pinnate leaves, the narrow racemes of rose purple flowers, and the segmented pods.

147. **Wild licorice**   *Glycyrrhiza lepidota*   Legume family

Perennial herb from thick, sweet roots, the stems erect, to 40 in. (1 m) tall, both stems and leaves with sticky glands. *Leaves* pinnately compound, with 13–19 oblong to lanceolate leaflets ³/₈–1⁵/₈ in. (1–4 cm) long, the apex bearing a small, sharp point. *Flowers* pealike, borne in short, axillary clusters 1⅛–3⅛ in. (3–8 cm) long, the calyx 5-toothed with the 2 upper teeth shorter than the lower ones, the corolla blue or white, ¼–½ in. (7–12 mm) long, with 10 stamens. *Fruit* an ellipsoid pod ⅓–³/₄ in. (8–18 mm) long, covered with numerous hooked prickles.

Range and Habitat: Ontario to Washington, southward into Mexico. Frequent in meadows, prairies, and low places, often along sandy roadsides or in wet ground, throughout New Mexico; 3,500–6,500 ft.

Key Characters: Wild licorice may be easily identified by the sticky, glandular herbage, the dark green appearance, the spikes or racemes of white or bluish flowers, and the pods covered with hooked prickles.

Vicia americana

Hedysarum boreale

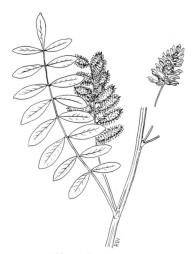

Glycyrrhiza lepidota

141

148. **Prairie clover**   *Petalostemum compactum*   Legume family

Perennial herb, the stems erect or ascending, glabrous, marked with longitudinal lines, 24–32 in. (60–80 cm) tall, the stems and leaves glandular-dotted. *Leaves* pinnately compound, with 5–7 oblong to oblong-lanceolate, glabrous leaflets, these glandular-dotted beneath, $^1/_8$–1 in. (3–25 mm) long. *Flowers* pealike, borne in dense, cylindrical, often long-stalked clusters (spikes), each flower subtended by a lanceolate, bract bearing silky hairs, the calyx with silky hairs, $^1/_8$–$^1/_6$ in. (3–4 mm) long, with 5 lanceolate lobes about as long as the tube, the corolla whitish, drying pinkish or purplish, the petals constricted to form a stalklike base, the upper petal (banner) about $^1/_{12}$ in. (2 mm) long. *Fruit* a sparsely hairy pod about $^1/_8$ in. (3 mm) long.

Range and Habitat: Nebraska and Wyoming to Colorado and New Mexico. Occasionally found on sandy plains in New Mexico; 4,000–6,000 ft.

Key Characters: This prairie clover is characterized by the leaves with 5–7 leaflets, the dense spikes of white flowers, and the hairy calyx.

Related Species: Another prairie clover, *P. candidum,* is very similar but differs in having 7–9 leaflets and the glabrous calyx. It is frequently found on open slopes and prairies throughout New Mexico at 4,500–8,000 ft.

149. **Prostrate prairie clover**   *Petalostemum scariosum*   Legume family

Perennial fragrant herb, the stems prostrate, to 32 in. (80 cm) long, the stems and leaves glandular-dotted. *Leaves* pinnately compound with 7–9 cuneate-oblanceolate leaflets $^1/_5$–$^3/_8$ in. (5–10 mm) long. *Flowers* pealike, borne in dense cylindrical clusters (spikes) mostly about $^3/_8$ in. (8–10 mm) wide, the calyx 5-toothed, 10-ribbed, and usually glabrous, the corolla small, rose purple. *Fruit* an obovoid to nearly round, glabrous pod. This species inhabits a very limited range in central New Mexico and is often overlooked due to its low, prostrate nature, but it has a very pleasant odor.

Range and Habitat: Apparently restricted to the Rio Grande Valley and adjacent sandy plains of central New Mexico; 4,000–5,000 ft.

Key Characters: Prostrate prairie clover is easily distinguished by the prostrate habit, the short, wide spikes of rose purple flowers, and the oblanceolate leaflets.

150. **Narrow-leaved false indigo**   *Amorpha fruticosa*   Legume family

Much-branched shrub to about 10 ft. (3 m) tall. *Leaves* pinnate, to 8 in. (20 cm) long, with 9–25 gland-dotted leaflets $^3/_4$–1$^5/_8$ in. (2–4 cm) long, these acutely pointed or slightly notched at the tip. *Flowers* in groups of 1–4 dense spikes, each spike to 8 in. (20 cm) long, the corolla pealike, purplish, the upper petal (banner) about $^1/_4$ in. (5 mm) long, the other petals missing. *Fruit* a curved, resin-dotted pod about $^5/_{16}$ in. (8 mm) long.

Range and Habitat: Wisconsin to Saskatchewan, southward to Mexico. Mostly found in canyons and along streams throughout much of New Mexico; 4,500–7,500 ft.

Key Characters: Narrow-leaved false indigo is distinguished by the pinnately compound leaves with gland-dotted leaflets and the dense spikes of purplish flowers having only one petal.

Related Species: Stinking willow or California false indigo, *A. californica,* occurring in moist canyons from central to southern and western New Mexico at 5,000–7,000 ft., differs in having stems and petioles bearing pricklelike glands.

142

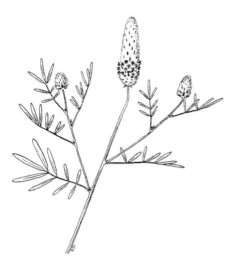

Petalostemum compactum

Petalostemum scariosum

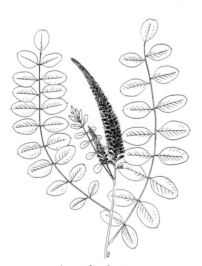

Amorpha fruticosa

143

151. **Leadplant amorpha**   *Amorpha canescens*   Legume family

Perennial, mostly herbaceous but woody at the base, the stems to 40 in. (1 m) tall, the stems and leaves densely whitish-hairy throughout. *Leaves* curved, 2–4³/₄ in. (5–12 cm) long, short-stalked, pinnate, with 15–47 crowded, ovate to lanceolate leaflets, these rounded at the base, ³/₈–³/₄ in. (9–18 mm) long. *Flowers* borne in clusters of dense, narrow spikes 2–6 in. (5–18 cm) long, each flower short-stalked, the calyx about ¹/₄ in. (5 mm) long, 5 narrowly lanceolate lobes about ¹/₈ in. (2–3 mm) long, the upper petal (banner) light blue, about ¹/₄ in. (5 mm) long, the other petals absent. *Fruit* a 1-seeded pod about ¹/₆ in. (4 mm) long, densely covered with matted whitish hairs.
Range and Habitat: Indiana to Manitoba, southward to Louisiana, Texas, and New Mexico. Found occasionally on dry plains and hills from northern to south-central New Mexico; 4,500–6,000 ft.
Key Characters: Leadplant amorpha is characterized by the single, light blue petal, the herbage densely hairy with whitish hairs, the 1-seeded pods, and the 5 similar calyx teeth.
Related Species: Fragrant false indigo, *A. nana,* occurring on plains and hills from eastern to south-central New Mexico at 5,000–6,500 ft., differs in having woody stems, glabrous herbage, and usually solitary flower clusters not exceeding 3¹/₄ in. (8 cm) in length.

152. **Dune broom**   *Parryella filifolia*   Legume family

Low, much-branched, somewhat rushlike shrub, the numerous stems about 30 in. (75 cm) tall, the stems and leaves glandular-dotted, glabrous or sparsely hairy. *Leaves* mostly 2³/₈–4³/₄ in. (6–12 cm) long, pinnate, with 11–45 mostly linear-filiform leaflets ¹/₅–⁵/₈ in. (5–15 mm) long and less than ¹/₁₂ in. (2 mm) wide. *Flowers* pealike, yellow, borne in terminal, dense, often branched clusters ³/₄–1¹/₈ in. (2–3 cm) long, the calyx ¹/₈–¹/₆ in. (3–4 mm) long, 5-toothed, 10-ribbed, the tube glabrous, the teeth hairy on the margins, the petals absent. *Fruit* a small, glandular-dotted pod about ¹/₄ in. (5–6 mm) long.
Range and Habitat: New Mexico and Arizona. Occasionally found on sandy hills and plains from northern to central and southwestern New Mexico; 4,500–6,500 ft.
Key Characters: Dune broom may be recognized by the absence of petals, the narrow leaflets, the rushlike, much-branched stems, and the glabrous, glandular-dotted stems and leaves.

153. **New Mexico locust**   *Robinia neomexicana*   Legume family

Tree or large shrub to about 25 ft. (8 m) tall, the twigs with straight or slightly curved short spines. *Leaves* alternate, pinnately compound, with 9–19 oblong or elliptic leaflets, these hairy, rounded at both ends, and with a tiny point at the tip. *Flowers* pealike, in glandular, hairy clusters about 2–4 in. (5–10 cm) long, the corolla rose pink, about ³/₄–1 in. (20–25 mm) long, the upper petal recurved. *Fruit* a pod bearing gland-tipped hairs. This plant is extremely attractive in flower and has much potential as a protective cover for wildlife.
Range and Habitat: Colorado to Nevada, southward to northern Mexico. Locally common in canyons or on slopes in open or partially shaded areas in the mountains of New Mexico; 6,000–9,500 ft.
Key Characters: New Mexico locust can be identified by the treelike or shrubby habit, the twigs with short spines, the compound leaves with leaflets rounded at both ends, and the rose pink flowers.

Amorpha canescens

Parryella filifolia

Robinia neomexicana

154. Silvery locoweed — *Oxytropis sericea* — Legume family

Perennial herb without true stems or the stems very short, but with flowering stalks to 16 in. (40 cm) tall. *Leaves* basal, pinnately compound with 11–21 oblong or lance-shaped, silvery hairy leaflets. *Flowers* many, in narrow clusters at the summit of the flower stalks, the corolla showy, pealike, white but lower petals purple-tipped. *Fruit* an oblong pod, beaked at the tip. Like many other species of the locoweed genus, this plant is considered to be toxic to foraging livestock.

Range and Habitat: Saskatchewan to British Columbia, southward to Colorado, Utah, and New Mexico. Usually found on open slopes throughout New Mexico; 6,500–9,000 ft.

Key Characters: Silvery locoweed is distinguished by the grayish silvery stems and leaves in a basal cluster, the leaves with 11–21 leaflets, and the showy, irregular white flowers at the summit of the flower stalks.

Related Species: Lambert locoweed, *O. lambertii,* is widespread on plains and montane slopes in New Mexico at 5,000–9,000 ft. It is very similar to silvery locoweed but has purple flowers. Like silvery locoweed, it is also considered to be toxic to livestock.

155. Red bladderpod — *Sphaerophysa salsula* — Legume family

Perennial herb, the stems erect, with grayish hairs. *Leaves* alternate, pinnately compound, 1¹/₄–4 in. (3–10 cm) long, the 15–25 oblong leaflets mostly ¹/₈–³/₄ in. (3–18 mm) long. *Flowers* in loose, narrow clusters, the corolla showy, pealike, dull red, the upper petal (banner) about ¹/₂ in. (12 mm) long. *Fruit* an inflated, nearly spherical, papery-walled pod.

Range and Habitat: Native of Asia, now occasionally found in the western United States. Occasionally found on moist streambanks or along ditches throughout New Mexico; 4,500-6,000 ft.

Key Characters: Red bladderpod can be identified by the compound leaves with 15 or more leaflets and the conspicuous, dull red, pealike flowers.

156. Richardson's geranium — *Geranium richardsonii* — Geranium family

Perennial herb, the stems ascending or spreading, 16–32 in. (40–80 cm) long, usually with spreading gland-tipped hairs. *Leaves* alternate, long-stalked, palmately lobed, the primary lobes variously lobed or toothed. *Flowers* loosely arranged or solitary on the flower stalks, regular, the 5 petals white, separate, ³/₈–³/₄ in. (10–20 mm) long, the sepals hairy, the flower stalks with purple-tipped hairs, the styles forming an elongated, column bearing glandular hairs and tipped by 5 style branches, with 10 stamens. *Fruit* a long-beaked capsule with a persistent central column, the 5 carpels curling away from the base toward the tip.

Range and Habitat: Saskatchewan to British Columbia, southward to New Mexico, Arizona, and California. Usually associated with damp wooded areas in the mountains of all but eastern New Mexico; 7,000–11,000 ft.

Key Characters: Richardson's geranium is distinguished by the palmately lobed leaves, the purple-tipped hairs on the flower stalks, and the large, white or purple-tinged petals, these often ⁵/₈–³/₄ in. (15–20 mm) long.

Related Species: Mogollon geranium, *G. lentum,* a species of the mountains of southern New Mexico, differs in having smaller flowers with petals about ³/₈ in. (8 mm) long and the hairs of the flower stalks without purple tips.

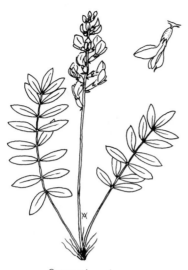

Oxytropis sericea

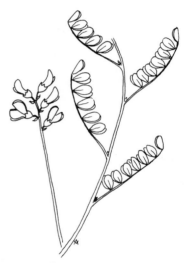

Sphaerophysa salsula

Geranium richardsonii

147

157. **Purple geranium** *Geranium caespitosum* Geranium family

Perennial herb, the stems clustered, spreading or ascending, much branched, to about 30 in. (75 cm) long, covered with backward-pointing hairs. *Leaves* alternate, stalked, the blades palmately divided into about 5 lobes, the primary lobes coarsely toothed or lobed. *Flowers* loosely arranged or sometimes solitary on the flower stalks, the petals purple, mostly ½–¾ in. (12–18 mm) long, the hairs of the flower stalks not purple-tipped, the sepals about ⅜ in. (10 mm) long, the margins fringed with stiff hairs, the style elongating into a column about ¾ in. (20 mm) long, tipped with 5 style branches, the 5 carpels separating from the base at maturity, curling upward and leaving behind a persistent central column.
Range and Habitat: Colorado and Utah to Mexico. Found on moist slopes, sometimes in waste ground throughout New Mexico; 6,000–9,500 ft.
Related Species: The very similar Fremont's geranium, *G. fremontii,* differs in having pinkish purple petals and the stylar column usually more than ¾ in. (20 mm) long.

158. **Yellow woodsorrel** *Oxalis stricta* Woodsorrel family

Perennial herb, the stems often spreading, to 20 in. (50 cm) long, usually densely hairy. *Leaves* compound, with 3 leaflets, the leaflets obcordate (heart-shaped with the leaf stalk attached at the small end), ⅝–¾ in. (15–20 mm) wide. *Flowers* perfect, in few-flowered clusters or solitary, yellow, the petals separate, ³⁄₁₆–⅜ in. (5–10 mm) long, the sepals about ³⁄₁₆ in. (4 mm) long, the 10 stamens, united at the base into a tube and of 2 lengths, 5 long and 5 short, the filaments glabrous. *Fruit* a capsule.
Range and Habitat: Nova Scotia to Florida, westward to Wyoming, Arizona, and Mexico. Open fields or slopes, often in waste ground throughout New Mexico; 5,000–9,000 ft.
Key Characters: Yellow woodsorrel is distinguished by the stems usually solitary, the stems, leaf stalks, and flower stalks bearing septate (divided transversely into cells) hairs, and the yellow flowers.
Related Species: The widespread, sometimes common, violet woodsorrel, *O. violaceae,* differs in having violet petals and hairy staminal filaments. In canyons and damp woods in southern areas there is *O. grayi,* differing in having leaves with 4–7 leaflets and violet flowers. *O. metcalfei,* of shaded montane slopes of southern New Mexico, differs in having the leaflets very broadly and somewhat shallowly notched and the longer staminal filaments hairy, the shorter ones glabrous.

159. **Western blue flax** *Linum lewisii* Flax family

Glabrous perennial herb, the stems erect, mostly 8–26 in. (20–65 cm) tall, often clustered. *Leaves* alternate, crowded along the stem, linear, ⅜–1¼ in. (10–30 mm) long, sometimes inrolled lengthwise. *Flowers* in loose, often 1-sided clusters, on slender stalks, the petals blue or white, separate, ⅜–⅝ in. (10–15 mm) long, 5 separate styles, and 5 stamens alternating with 5 short sterile filaments (staminodes). *Fruit* a rounded capsule.
Range and Habitat: Alaska to Wisconsin, Texas, California, and northern Mexico. Often abundant in open meadows throughout New Mexico; 5,000–11,500 ft.
Key Characters: Western blue flax can be identified by the erect, slender stems, the alternate linear leaves, and the conspicuous blue flowers with 5 separate styles. These are poor bouquet flowers because the petals tend to fall with even a moderate amount of disturbance.
Related Species: The similar meadow flax, *L. pratense,* differs in having an annual habit, the leaves crowded at the base of the stem, and petals less than ⅜ in. (10 mm) long.

Geranium caespitosum

Oxalis stricta

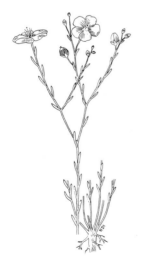

Linum lewisii

160.   **Plains yellow flax**   *Linum aristatum*   Flax family

Erect, glabrous annual, the stems slender, angled, branching, to 12 in. (30 cm) tall. *Leaves* linear, inrolled lengthwise, scattered along the stem, to ³/₈ in. (10 mm) long, with 1 vein. *Flowers* in loose clusters, yellow, the 5 petals mostly ⁵/₈–⁷/₈ in. (15–22 mm) long, the 5 sepals often glandular, the tips projecting as elongated bristles, and 5 styles united nearly to the apex. *Fruit* an ovoid or ellipsoid capsule.
Range and Habitat: Western Texas to Arizona and Mexico. Usually found on sandy plains and mesas in southern New Mexico; 4,000–7,500 ft.
Key Characters: Plains yellow flax is easily recognized by the slender stems with linear leaves, the yellow flowers, and the sepals with bristlelike tips.
Related Species: Two other species of yellow flaxes include the widely distributed *L. puberulum,* differing in having the stems covered with short hairs and petals only ⁵/₁₆–⁵/₈ in. (8–15 mm) long, and *L. neomexicanum* of mountain slopes in the southwestern part of the state, differing in having the styles separate and petals only ³/₁₆–³/₈ in. (5–8 mm) long.

161.   **Goathead**   *Tribulus terrestris*   Caltrop family

Prostrate annual, the stems often 20 in. (50 cm) or more long, forming extensive radiating mats. *Leaves* opposite, pinnate, with mostly 4–6 pairs of oblong leaflets about ³/₁₆ in. (5 mm) long, the members of a pair usually unequal. *Flowers* solitary, axillary, yellow, with mostly 5 oblong petals about ¹/₈–³/₁₆ in. (2–5 mm) long, and 10 stamens. *Fruit* mostly 5-angled, ultimately separating into as many triangular nutlets bearing a pair of sharp spines. These plants have attractive little flowers, but goathead is one of our more troublesome weeds.
Range and Habitat: Native of Europe and widely established in the United States. Common in disturbed ground throughout New Mexico; 3,000–7,000 ft.
Key Characters: Goathead is easily recognized by the prostrate, often radiating stems with pinnately compound leaves, the relatively small yellow flowers, and the spiny, bony fruits.

162.   **Arizona poppy**   *Kallstroemia grandiflora*   Caltrop family

Prostrate annual, the stems hairy, often 12 in. (30 cm) long or longer. *Leaves* pinnately compound, with 5–9 pairs of leaflets, each ⁵/₈–1 in. (15–25 mm) long, the members of a pair usually unequal in size. *Flowers* solitary, axillary, orange, with petals ³/₄–1¹/₄ in. (20–30 mm) long, and with 10–12 stamens. *Fruit* forming a slender beak at the summit. This plant closely resembles the much smaller goathead, *Tribulus terrestris.*
Range and Habitat: Texas to Arizona and Mexico. Typically found on dry flats, slopes, and hills in southern New Mexico; 4,000– 5,500 ft.
Key Characters: Arizona poppy is easily recognized by the prostrate hairy stems, the pinnately compound leaves, and the large, solitary orange flowers.
Related Species: Two similar species of widespread distribution include hairy caltrop, *K. hirsutissima,* differing in having the leaflets in 3 or 4 pairs and the petals ³/₁₆–¹/₄ in. (4–6 mm) long, and *K. parviflora,* differing in having the leaves glabrous, the petals ¹/₅-¹/₂ in. (5–12 mm) long, and the beak of the fruit about ¹/₄ in. (5–6 mm) long.

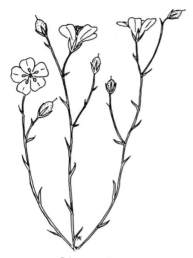

Linum aristatum

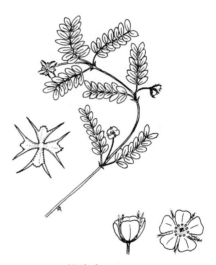

Tribulus terrestris

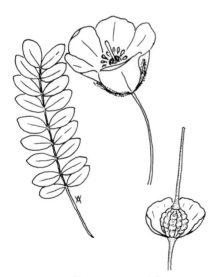

Kallstroemia grandiflora

163. **Peganum**   *Peganum harmala*   Caltrop family

Branching perennial herb, the stems to 18 in. (45 cm) tall, glabrous. *Leaves* alternate, glabrous, pinnately divided into linear segments. *Flowers* regular, mostly solitary, the 4 or 5 petals white, the sepals linear, the stamens 8–10 with the filaments expanded at the base. *Fruit* a many-seeded capsule. Although a relatively new introduction into New Mexico, this plant because of its competitive, perennial nature will probably spread rapidly along the roadsides of the southern part of the state.
Range and Habitat: Introduced from Africa and Asia; occasionally escaped from cultivation, and found growing wild in the Western Hemisphere. Occasionally found on dry plains or along roadsides in southern New Mexico; 4,000–5,000 ft.
Key Characters: Peganum is distinguished by the leaves pinnately lobed into narrow segments and the large white flowers with 4 or 5 petals.

164. **White milkwort**   *Polygala alba*   Milkwort family

Perennial herb, the stems clustered, to about 14 in. (35 cm) tall, grooved and angled. *Leaves* alternate, linear to narrowly lance-shaped, sometimes in whorls at the base. *Flowers* numerous, in dense, spikelike clusters, the petals white with green centers, not spreading, forming an irregular corolla, one of the petals appearing as a fringed, often purplish, keellike structure.
Range and Habitat: Kansas to Washington, southward to Mexico. Usually on dry plains and slopes throughout New Mexico; 5,000–7,500 ft.
Key Characters: White milkwort is distinguished by the clustered stems with slender leaves and the numerous whitish flowers in dense, spikelike, often somewhat lax clusters.
Related Species: Two milkworts having a more restricted southerly distribution include *P. tweedyi,* differing in having very short, incurved hairs on the stem, purple flowers, and the keel petal without a fringed crest, and *P. longa,* differing in having the lower leaves ¼–½ in. (6–12 mm) wide, the stems with minute hairs, the flowers purple or greenish purple, and the keel without a fringed crest.

165. **Poison ivy**   *Rhus radicans*   Sumac family

Plant shrubby or sometimes vining, ours usually not more than 3 ft. (1 m) tall when in shrub form. *Leaves* alternate, pinnately compound with 3 ovate, usually coarsely toothed, stalked, bright green leaflets. *Flowers* in small dense axillary clusters, with 5 greenish yellow petals about ⅛ in. (3 mm) long, the ovary surrounded by a flattened, lobed, ringlike disk, the 5 stamens attached on or under the disk. *Fruit* a smooth, shiny, whitish or yellowish white berry about 3/16 in. (5 mm) in diameter.
Range and Habitat: Common or at least locally abundant throughout North America. Usually in wooded areas or along the margins of clearings throughout New Mexico; 5,500–8,500 ft.
Key Characters: Poison ivy is easily recognized by the compound leaves with 3 stalked, lobed or toothed leaflets, the small yellowish white flowers about ¼ in. (6–7 mm) in diameter, and the whitish or yellowish white smooth fruits. All forms of this species are capable of causing dermatitis among many people who come in contact with it.

Peganum harmala

Polygala alba

Rhus radicans

153

Low shrub, mostly less than 3 ft. (1 m) tall, much branched, the branches often spine-tipped and with grayish appressed hairs. *Leaves* alternate, narrowly elliptic or oblong, 3/8–1 1/2 in. (10–35 mm) long, with 3 longitudinal veins from the base of the leaf, without teeth or lobes, bearing dense appressed hairs beneath. *Flowers* in clusters at the tip of the branches, white, the petals about 1/8 in. (3 mm) long, about twice as long as the sepals. *Fruit* a small capsule.

Range and Habitat: Wyoming to western Texas, Arizona, and northern Mexico. Typically found on open or brushy slopes in all but eastern New Mexico; 5,500–9,000 ft.

Key Characters: Buckbrush can be identified by the much-branched, shrubby aspect, the branches often strongly spine-tipped and the alternate leaves with 3 longitudinal veins from the base.

Related Species: Deer brush, *C. integerrimus,* a species of the southwestern part of the state, differs in having flexible, nonspiny branches, leaves mostly 1 1/4–2 5/8 in. (30–70 mm) long, and flowers with white, blue, or pink petals.

Erect perennial herb, the stems unbranched, to about 32 in. (80 cm) tall, glabrous below the flower clusters. *Leaves* alternate, stalked, rounded in outline, 1 5/8–6 in. (4–15 cm) wide, glabrous on the upper surface, hairy beneath, the basal leaves with 7 rounded, coarsely toothed lobes, the upper leaves deeply parted into several narrow segments. *Flowers* conspicuous, in terminal clusters, the 5 petals white or cream-colored, 5/8–1 in. (15–25 mm) long, the calyx covered with numerous stellate (star-shaped) hairs, the stamens numerous, united into a tube around the style. *Fruit* eventually splitting into 5–9, 1-seeded segments.

Range and Habitat: Wyoming to Colorado, Nevada, and New Mexico. Mostly found in damp meadows or clearings in the mountains of northern, central, and south-central New Mexico; 6,500–11,000 ft.

Key Characters: White prairie mallow is easily distinguished by the tall, unbranched, usually glabrous stems, the rounded but palmately lobed, stalked leaves, and the large, white or cream-colored flowers with numerous stamens united into a tube.

Related Species: New Mexico prairie mallow, *S. neomexicana,* one of our most spectacular wildflowers, differs in having leaves hairy on both surfaces and purple flowers.

Low annual or biennial herb, the stems creeping but pointing upward at the tip, to about 16 in. (45 cm) long. *Leaves* alternate, long stalked, the blades rounded in outline, 3/4–2 3/8 in. (20–60 mm) wide, with rounded teeth on the margins and sometimes shallow lobes. *Flowers* in clusters in the axils of the leaves, stalked, the petals white to pale blue, about 3/8 in. (10 mm) long, the calyx about half as long as the corolla, subtended by a series of narrow bractlets nearly as long as the sepals, the stamens numerous, united into a tube around the style. *Fruit* of about 15 segments, these splitting apart at maturity.

Range and Habitat: Introduced from Europe and well established throughout North America. Usually associated with waste ground throughout New Mexico; 3,500–7,500 ft.

Key Characters: Common mallow is easily recognized by the more or less creeping stems with rounded or somewhat kidney-shaped leaves, these hairy on both sides, the whitish or bluish flowers with the calyx subtended by a series of narrow bractlets, and the fruit with about 15 segments.

Related Species: Two other weedy mallows that may occur nearly anywhere in the state include curled mallow, *M. crispa,* differing in having the stems erect, the margins of the leaves irregularly curled, and the segments of the fruit conspicuously net-veined, and *M. parviflora,* differing in having erect stems, nearly glabrous leaves, and smaller flowers, the petals about as long as the calyx.

Ceanothus fendleri

Sidalcea candida

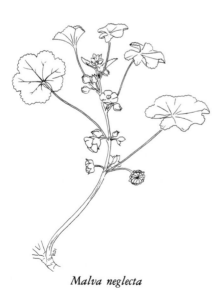

Malva neglecta

155

169. **Poppy mallow**   *Callirhoe involucrata*   Mallow family

Creeping perennial herb, the stems to about 24 in. (60 cm) long, both stems and leaves hairy. *Leaves* alternate, stalked, rounded in outline, parted into 5–7 narrow, toothed segments. *Flowers* showy, in the axils of the upper leaves, long-stalked, the petals red to purple, squared-off and irregularly toothed at the apex, ³/₄–1¹/₄ in. (20–30 mm) long, the calyx subtended by 3 slender bractlets, the stamens numerous, in a single series, forming a tube around the style. *Fruit* of 10–20 prominently net-veined segments.
Range and Habitat: North Dakota to Missouri, Oklahoma, Texas, and New Mexico. Occasionally found on open plains and prairies in northeastern New Mexico; 5,000–6,000 ft.
Key Characters: Poppy mallow is distinguished by the creeping stems, the leaves rounded in outline but palmately divided into several narrow, toothed segments, and the showy, red to purple flowers with irregularly toothed petals and numerous stamens.
Related Species: The widely distributed prairie poppy mallow, *C. alcaeoides,* differs in having erect stems, somewhat heart-shaped lower leaves and white to pink petals.

170. **Wild hollyhock**   *Iliamna grandiflora*   Mallow family

Tall perennial herb, from rhizomes, the stems to 3 ft. (1 m) or more tall, both stems and leaves hairy. *Leaves* alternate, large, stalked, about as long as broad, 4–6 in. (10–15 cm) wide, 3– to 7-lobed, toothed on the margins. *Flowers* showy, in slender clusters terminating the branches, 1¹/₄–2 in. (3–5 cm) in diameter, the 5 petals white to purple, constricted and densely hairy at the base, the calyx of united sepals, subtended by 3 narrow bractlets, the stamens numerous, in a column surrounding the style. *Fruit* of several segments surrounding a central axis.
Range and Habitat: Colorado and New Mexico. Typically found in damp meadows in the mountains of northern New Mexico; 7,000–10,000 ft.
Key Characters: Wild hollyhock is distinguished by the tall stems, the hairy 3– to 7-lobed leaves, these often 6 in. (15 cm) wide, the conspicuous white to purple flowers with the petals constricted and hairy at the base, and the fruit segments hairy on the back but glabrous on the sides.

171. **Lanceleaf globe-mallow**   *Sphaeralcea subhastata*   Mallow family

Erect to sprawling perennial herb, the stems mostly 12–20 in. (30–50 cm) long, both stems and leaves variously hairy. *Leaves* alternate, lance-shaped to ovate in outline, with 3 major veins diverging from the base, the margins sometimes irregularly toothed and usually with an angled lobe or large tooth at the base, the blades to about 2 in. (50 mm) long. *Flowers* in a racemelike cluster, usually 1 flower at each node, the petals orange red, ³/₈–³/₄ in. (10–18 mm) long, the calyx with slender tips and subtended by 2 or 3 very narrow bractlets, the stamens numerous, forming a ring around a central axis.
Range and Habitat: Western Texas to Arizona and northern Mexico. Scattered on open plains, mesas, low hills, or rocky slopes from central to southern and western New Mexico; 5,000–7,000 ft.
Key Characters: Lanceleaf globe-mallow is distinguished by the usually lance-shaped or ovate leaves with few or no teeth and with a pair of small lobes at the base of the blade, and by the conspicuous orange red flowers.
Related Species: Another species with orange red flowers, *S. parvifolia,* mostly from the northwestern part of the state, differs in having leaves broadly triangular to nearly round in outline with 5 major veins diverging from the base of the blade.

Callirhoe involucrata

Iliamna grandiflora

Sphaeralcea subhastata

157

172. **Red globe-mallow**   *Sphaeralcea coccinea*   Mallow family

Perennial herb, the stems often prostrate at the base, to 20 in. (50 cm) long, both stems and leaves covered with star-shaped hairs. *Leaves* alternate, divided into several lobes, the lobes often toothed or parted as well. *Flowers* in a narrow cluster, orange red, the petals ³/₈–³/₄ in. (10–20 mm) long, the calyx subtended by 2 or 3 slender bractlets, the stamens numerous, united into a column surrounding the style.
Range and Habitat: Southern Canada to Texas, New Mexico, and Arizona. Mostly found on open hills, plains, waste ground, or roadsides throughout New Mexico; 4,500–8,000 ft.
Key Characters: Red globe-mallow can be distinguished by the pinnately parted or divided leaves, the primary lobes often toothed or parted, both stems and leaves densely covered by numerous stellate (star-shaped) hairs, the orange red flowers, and the numerous stamens in a column. Like the preceding species, the red globe-mallow is represented in our area by several varieties, often difficult to distinguish. The globe-mallow genus is a most difficult one taxonomically.

173. **Fendler globe-mallow**   *Sphaeralcea fendleri*   Mallow family

Perennial herb, the stems to 3 ft. (1 m) or more tall, clothed with stellate (star-shaped) hairs. *Leaves* alternate, stalked, broadly ovate in outline, the blades ³/₄–2¹/₂ in. (2–6 cm) long, 3-lobed below the middle, the midlobe toothed or cleft into small lobes, the upper surface green, paler green or whitish beneath, often densely hairy. *Flowers* in narrow, interrupted clusters, stalked, the petals orange red to violet, ³/₈–¹/₂ in. (9–12 mm) long, the calyx subtended by 2 or 3 slender, greenish bractlets, the stamens numerous, united into a somewhat hairy column. *Fruit* of 11–15 segments surrounding a central axis.
Range and Habitat: Colorado to Texas, Arizona, and Mexico. Usually found in dry ground on open slopes or sparsely wooded areas throughout New Mexico; 5,000–8,000 ft.
Key Characters: Fendler globe-mallow is distinguished by the leaves ovate in outline and 3-lobed below the middle, the flowers in a narrow, interrupted cluster, and the orange red to violet petals. There are three very similar varieties of this species in New Mexico.
Related Species: Narrowleaf globe-mallow, *S. angustifolia,* found in eastern, central, and southern parts of the state, differs in having leaves lance-shaped in outline and mostly unlobed. A species of central, southern, and western parts of the state, *S. incana,* differs in having densely hairy leaves with yellowish hairs, triangular ovate blades with 5 diverging veins, and red or pink flowers.

174. **Scurfy mallow**   *Sida leprosa*   Mallow family

Perennial herb, the stems often prostrate, to 16 in. (40 cm) long, both stems and leaves densely covered with star-shaped hairs. *Leaves* alternate, somewhat triangular, ³/₄–1⁵/₈ in. (20–40 mm) long, toothed on the margins. *Flowers* solitary or in small clusters, white or pale yellow, the petals ³/₈–¹/₂ in. (10–12 mm) long.
Range and Habitat: Western Texas to Arizona. Usually found in dry fields and on open plains in southern New Mexico; 3,500–4,000 ft.
Key Characters: Scurfy mallow is distinguished by the prostrate stems covered with scalelike hairs, the somewhat triangular leaves, and by the white to pale yellow flowers.
Related Species: The widespread but not common *S. hederacea,* usually in damp soils near streams below 5,000 ft., differs in having leaves broader than long and the calyx subtended by 2 or 3 bractlets. From southern and western parts of the state comes *S. neomexicana,* differing in having linear to oblong leaves and yellow to orange flowers.

Sphaeralcea coccinea

Sphaeralcea fendleri

Sida leprosa

175. **Western St. John's-wort** *Hypericum formosum* St. John's-wort family

Erect perennial herb, the stems mostly 12–26 in. (30–65 cm) tall. *Leaves* opposite, without teeth, oblong, ¹/₂–1⁵/₈ in. (12–40 mm) long, usually glandular-dotted throughout but black-dotted along the margins. *Flowers* in loose leafy clusters, bright yellow, with a few black glands on the petals, the stamens numerous, in 3–5 clusters. *Fruit* a 3-celled capsule with numerous pitted seeds.

Range and Habitat: Wyoming to California, southward to Mexico. Occasionally found in moist ground in meadows or open coniferous forests throughout New Mexico; 7,000–9,000 ft.

Key Characters: Western St. John's-wort is easily identified by the opposite, oblong leaves and the conspicuous flowers with bright yellow petals marked by a few black dots and numerous stamens in 3–5 clusters.

176. **Tamarisk** *Tamarix pentandra* Tamarisk family

Large shrub or small tree, to 20 ft. (6 m) or more tall, the branches slender, flexible, and green. *Leaves* very small and scalelike, triangular, clothing the branchlets. *Flowers* pinkish, numerous, in slender-branched or unbranched clusters, the petals about ¹/₁₆ in. (2 mm) long. This plant is also known as "salt cedar" because of its superficial resemblance to the juniper.

Range and Habitat: Introduced from the Old World and established along watercourses, often in saline conditions over much of New Mexico; 3,000–6,500 ft.

Key Characters: Tamarisk is distinguished by the slender, flexible green branchlets with tiny, scalelike leaves and the clusters of small pinkish flowers.

177. **Northern bog violet** *Viola nephrophylla* Violet family

Stemless perennial herb, the flower stalks mostly 2–8 in. (5–20 cm) tall. *Leaves* broadly heart-shaped to kidney-shaped, toothed on the margins. *Flowers* solitary, the petals ³/₈–⁵/₈ in. (10–15 mm) long, violet, but lighter and purplish veined at the base, the lower petal bearded and bearing a spur about a fourth as long as the petal.

Range and Habitat: Newfoundland to British Columbia, southward to Connecticut, New Mexico, and California. Typically located in wooded areas of the mountains from northern to south-central and western New Mexico; 6,500–9,000 ft.

Key Characters: Northern bog violet is readily identified by the basal leaves with heart-shaped or kidney-shaped blades and the violet, spurred, irregular flowers with the lower petal bearded.

178. **Canada violet** *Viola canadensis* Violet family

Erect perennial herb, the stems mostly 6–12 in. (15–30 cm) tall. *Leaves* alternate, stalked, heart-shaped, 1¹/₄–2 in. (3–5 cm) wide, with lance-shaped stipules. *Flowers* solitary on slender axillary stalks, irregular, the petals white but often tinged with violet or purple-veined, the lateral ones bearded, the lower petal with a short spur and yellowish at the base.

Range and Habitat: New Brunswick to British Columbia, southward to South Carolina, New Mexico, and Arizona. Locally common in shady places in damp woods in the mountains throughout New Mexico; 6,500–11,500 ft.

Key Characters: Canada violet is easily distinguished by the stems with heart-shaped leaves, the flowers solitary on slender axillary stalks, and the petals whitish and often purple-veined.

Hypericum formosum

Tamarix pentandra

Viola nephrophylla

Viola canadensis

179. **Wavyleaf cevallia**   *Cevallia sinuata*   Loasa family

Perennial herb, the stems to 24 in. (60 cm) tall, both stems and leaves with typical hairs as well as some stinging hairs. *Leaves* alternate, sessile, pinnately wavy-lobed. *Flowers* small, in dense, conspicuous terminal heads, the petals and sepals similar, feathery, somewhat yellowish, $^1/_5$-$^5/_{16}$ in. (5–8 mm) long, and 5 stamens.
Range and Habitat: Western Texas to Arizona and Mexico. Usually found in dry soil on mesas and plains, or along roadsides in central and southern New Mexico; 3,500–6,500 ft.
Key Characters: Wavyleaf cevallia can be identified by the wavy-lobed leaves and the flowers in dense, feathery, terminal heads.

180. **Plains stickleaf**   *Mentzelia stricta*   Loasa family

Erect perennial herb, the stems to about 28 in. (70 cm) tall, whitish, bearing short, stiff, barbed hairs. *Leaves* alternate, linear to oblong, sinuately toothed, to 4 in. (10 cm) long, with short, stiff, barbed hairs on both surfaces, short-stalked or sessile. *Flowers* solitary or clustered, white, with seemingly 10 petals $^3/_4$–$1^1/_2$ in. (20–35 mm) long, the calyx subtended by bracts cut into narrow segments, the stamens numerous, the outer 5 filaments becoming petallike and longer than the inner filaments. *Fruit* a cylindrical, flat-topped capsule about 1 in. (25 mm) long with numerous seeds.
Range and Habitat: South Dakota and Montana to Texas and New Mexico. Usually found on dry open plains and hills throughout New Mexico; 5,000–6,500 ft.
Key Characters: Plains stickleaf is distinguished by the whitish stems, typically rough to the touch, the whitish flowers with 5 typical petals and an inner series of 5 petallike expanded staminal filaments, and the calyx tube subtended by toothed bracts.
Related Species: Two similar species are *M. nuda,* differing in having the calyx tube without bracts or sometimes subtended by bracts with untoothed margins, and *M. decapetala,* differing in having petals mostly 2–3 in. (50–80 mm) long and calyx lobes about 1 in. (25 mm) long.

181. **Common stickleaf**   *Mentzelia pumila*   Loasa family

Biennial herb, the stems stout, often more than 24 in. (60 cm) tall, grayish or yellowish. *Leaves* alternate, lance-shaped, $1^3/_8$–4 in. (3–10 cm) long, with minute, barbed hairs, wavy-lobed or wavy-toothed on the margins. *Flowers* in small clusters, bright yellow, the petals pointed, $3/5$–$^5/_8$ in. (10–15 mm) long, with a few hairs at the tip, the stamens numerous, the outer series of filaments flattened and petallike, the flowers appearing to have more than 5 petals. *Fruit* a flat-topped capsule with numerous winged seeds.
Range and Habitat: Wyoming to Texas, westward to California. Usually associated with sandy or gravelly soils thoroughout New Mexico; 4,500–8,000 ft.
Key Characters: Common stickleaf can be identified by the stout grayish or yellowish stems, the wavy-toothed leaves, and the bright yellow flowers with the outer staminal filaments appearing petallike.
Related Species: Another widespread species of montane slopes, *M. rusbyi,* differs in having the calyx tube subtended by a pair of pinnately lobed bracts and the outer staminal filaments not expanded and petallike.

Cevallia sinuata

Mentzelia stricta

Mentzelia pumila

163

182.   **Club cholla**   *Opuntia clavata*   Cactus family

Low perennial, the stems matted, to about 4 in. (10 cm) high, the joints club-shaped, about 2 in. (5 cm) long and half as wide, with conspicuous tubercles about ¹/₂ in. (15 mm) long. *Spines* 10–20 per cluster, grayish, strongly recurved, to 1 in. (25 mm) long with 1 spine in each cluster flattened. *Flowers* funnel-shaped, yellow, about 1¹/₄–2 in. (3–5 cm) wide. *Fruit* a yellowish berry.

Range and Habitat: New Mexico and Arizona. Associated with dry plains and valleys from northern to south-central New Mexico; 6,000–8,000 ft.

Key Characters: Club cholla is distinguished by the club-shaped joints with conspicuous tubercles, the grayish recurved spines, and the yellow flowers.

Related Species: Another species with matted habit and occurring in the northern part of the state, little prickly pear (*O. fragilis*) differs in having the stem joints only slightly longer than wide and 5–7 red or reddish brown spines in each cluster.

183.   **Plains prickly pear**   *Opuntia macrorhiza*   Cactus family

Clump-forming perennial, the stems to about 6 in. (15 cm) high, the joints flattened in cross section, tapering from near the summit to the base or sometimes nearly round. *Spines* 1–6 in each cluster, whitish or grayish, to about 2 in. (5 cm) long, usually strongly turned downward, mostly on only the upper spine-bearing areas. *Flowers* about 2¹/₂ in. (5–6 cm) wide, the petaloid parts yellow or tinged with red. *Fruit* a fleshy, purplish berry.

Range and Habitat: Michigan to Louisiana, westward to California. Usually associated with rocky or sandy plains or hills throughout New Mexico; 3,000–5,000 ft.

Key Characters: Plains prickly pear is distinguished by the clumped, low-growing stems, the flattish joints, the whitish to grayish spines, and the conspicuous yellow flowers, the parts often tinged with red, especially at the base.

Related Species: A species with several very similar varieties, *O. polyacantha* differs in having usually 6–10 spines in each cluster, often brownish, and the fruit dry, brownish, and usually spiny at maturity.

184.   **Green pitaya**   *Echinocereus viridiflorus*   Cactus family

Fleshy perennial, the stems mostly ovoid, to about 8 in. (20 cm) tall and about 3 in. (75 mm) thick, with 10–14 parallel ribs. *Spines* about 12–18 per cluster, reddish or brownish or white. *Flowers* funnel-shaped, green or sometimes purplish, about ³/₄–2 in. (20–25 mm) wide. *Fruit* a green berry.

Range and Habitat: South Dakota to Texas and New Mexico. Usually found on rocky or sandy slopes or mesas or in draws in all but western New Mexico; 4,000–8,000 ft.

Key Characters: Green pitaya is distinguished by the ovoid stems with 10–14 parallel ribs and the usually green flowers or fruit.

Opuntia clavata

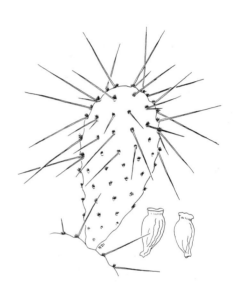

Opuntia macrorhiza

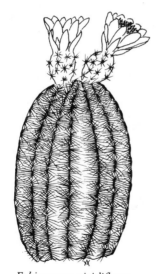

Echinocereus viridiflorus

165

185. **Hedgehog cactus**   *Echinocereus triglochidiatus*   Cactus family

Fleshy perennial, the stems in small clusters, cylindrical, to about 12 in. (30 cm) tall and 2³/₄ in. (7 cm) thick, with 5–12 parallel ribs. *Spines* mostly 3–15 per cluster, usually pink, gray, or tan. *Flowers* red or scarlet, funnel-shaped, about 1⁵/₈–2 in. (4–5 cm) wide. *Fruit* a red, fleshy berry, usually spiny when young. This species is represented by several similar varieties in New Mexico and often called claret cup or strawberry hedgehog cactus.
Range and Habitat: Colorado to Nevada, southward to Mexico. Usually found on rocky, gravelly, or sandy slopes or canyon walls or in grassy areas, often among pinyon and juniper trees, throughout New Mexico; 4,500–7,000 ft.
Key Characters: Strawberry hedgehog cactus is distinguished by the cylindrical stems with 5–12 parallel ribs and 3–15 spines per cluster, and the red or scarlet funnel-shaped flowers.
Related Species: Two related species include *E. enneacanthus,* which differs in the stems often forming large mounded clusters and in the flowers being purplish, and *E. fasciculatus* which has larger purplish flowers.

186. **Fendler's hedgehog cactus**   *Echinocereus fendleri*   Cactus family

Fleshy perennial, the stems cylindrical or ovoid, to about 10 in. (25 cm) tall and 2³/₈ in. (6 cm) wide, with 8–10 parallel ribs. *Spines* mostly 8–12 per cluster, white to gray or yellow. *Flowers* reddish purple, funnel-shaped, about 2–3 in. (5–7 cm) wide. *Fruit* a greenish or reddish berry.
Range and Habitat: Texas to Arizona and northern Mexico. Usually found on open sandy or gravelly plains or slopes throughout New Mexico; 6,000–8,000 ft.
Key Characters: Fendler's hedgehog cactus is distinguished by the mostly cylindrical stems with 8–10 parallel ribs and spines 8–12 in a cluster, and the reddish purple flowers.
Related Species: A species of the eastern, often brushy, plains or prairies, *E. reichenbachii,* differs in having 12–18 ribs per stem, 12–20 spines per cluster, and pink or pale purple flowers.

187. **Turk's head**   *Echinocactus horizonthalonius*   Cactus family

Stems solitary, rounded or ovoid, to about 12 in. (30 cm) tall, mostly with 8–10 ribs. *Spines* 6–9 per cluster, stout, recurved, transversely ridged. *Flowers* funnel-shaped, pink, about 2–2³/₈ in. (5–6 cm) wide. *Fruit* a red, fleshy, woolly berry.
Range and Habitat: Texas to New Mexico and Mexico. Typically found on open, rocky slopes, often on limestone, in southern New Mexico; 3,000–5,000 ft.
Key Characters: Turk's head can be identified by the rounded to ovoid stems with usually 8–10 ribs, the stout transversely ridged and recurved spines, and the pink flowers.
Related Species: The hemispherical-stemmed, lower-growing horse crippler, *E. texensis,* differs mainly in having 13–21 ribs per stem and stems to only 6 in. (15 cm) high.

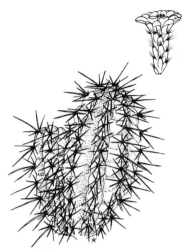

Echinocereus triglochidiatus

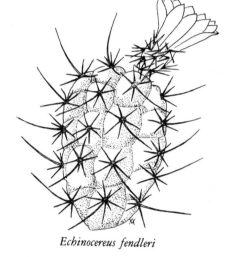

Echinocereus fendleri

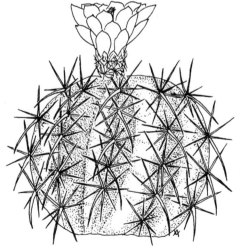

Echinocactus horizonthalonius

167

188. **Barrel cactus**   *Ferocactus wislizenii*   Cactus family

Stems usually solitary, cylindrical to ovoid, to 6 ft. (2 m) tall, often 12 in. (30 cm) or more in diameter, with numerous ribs. *Spines* stout, the centrally located ones about 4 per cluster, reddish, strongly transversely ridged, to 2 in. (5 cm) long, the lower spines hooked, the radial or outer spines in each cluster grayish and not transversely ridged. *Flowers* yellow, about 2¼ in. (55 mm) wide. *Fruit* yellowish, covered by rounded scales.
Range and Habitat: Western Texas to Arizona and Mexico. Usually found on rocky or gravelly slopes or canyons in southern New Mexico; 4,000–5,000 ft.
Key Characters: Barrel cactus is easily identified by the thick stems with numerous ribs, the stout, usually transversely ridged spines, at least 1 of which is hooked, and the yellow flowers.
Related Species: An uncommon species of the southern part of the state, *F. hamatacanthus*, differs in having shorter stems, usually not more than 14 in. (35 cm) tall and spines not or only slightly transversely ribbed.

189. **Plains pincushion cactus**   *Coryphantha vivipara*   Cactus family

Short, fleshy, very spiny perennial, the stems rounded to ovoid, usually clustered, mostly less than 4 in. (10 cm) tall and 2¼ in. (6 cm) wide, clothed with spirally arranged tubercles, each bearing at the tip 16–45 straight reddish or pinkish spines ³/₈–⁵/₈ in. (10–15 mm) long. *Flowers* borne at the summit of the stem, pink to purple, funnel-shaped, about 1¼–2 in. (30–50 mm) wide. *Fruit* a greenish, smooth, fleshy berry.
Range and Habitat: Southern Canada to Texas and New Mexico. Usually associated with open plains, grasslands, or sandy or rocky slopes throughout New Mexico; 4,500–9,000 ft.
Key Characters: Plains pincushion cactus may be recognized by the short, broad, fleshy stems with numerous reddish or pinkish spines and the pink to purple funnel-shaped flowers, usually less than 2 in. (50 mm) wide.

190. **Simpson's pediocactus**   *Pediocactus simpsonii*   Cactus family

Dwarf perennial, the stems mostly ³/₄–4½ in. (2–12 cm) high and often nearly as wide, ribbed. *Spines* mostly 20–40 per cluster, those in the center of the cluster reddish or brownish, the outer ones whitish or cream-colored and ¼–³/₈ in. (6–10 mm) long. *Flowers* pink to white or somewhat yellowish, ½–1 in. (12–25 mm) wide. *Fruit* greenish, tinged with red, dry at maturity.
Range and Habitat: Idaho and Oregon to New Mexico and Arizona. Associated with dry hills, valleys, and open rocky slopes in northern New Mexico; 6,000–9,000 ft.
Key Characters: Simpson's pediocactus is distinguished by the short, globose or ovoid stems, the spines mostly 20–40 per cluster with the outer spines in a cluster white or cream-colored and at least ¼ in. (6 mm) long, and the small, mostly pink or white flowers.

191. **California loosestrife**   *Lythrum californicum*   Loosestrife family

Perennial herb, the stems slender, angled, to 3 ft. (1 m) tall, the outer layers peeling away. *Leaves* usually alternate, simple, sessile, smooth on the margins, linear to oblong, to about 1¼ in. (30 mm) long. *Flowers* usually solitary and axillary, short-stalked, the 4–7 petals rose purple, ³/₁₆–¼ in. (4–6 mm) long, the calyx longitudinally lined, with 4–7 teeth and a small appendage in the sinuses between the teeth, and 8–12 stamens. *Fruit* a cylindrical, several-seeded capsule.
Range and Habitat: Texas to California and Mexico. Usually found in wet ground, often in the vicinity of springs, streams, or marshes in central and southern New Mexico; 3,500–6,000 ft.
Key Characters: California loosestrife can be identified by the slender, angled stems with narrow alternate leaves and pink or purple flowers with 4–7 petals and 8–12 stamens.

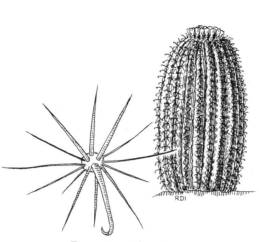

Ferocactus wislizenii

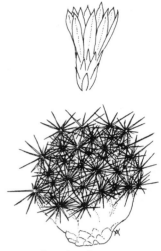

Coryphantha vivipara

Pediocactus simpsonii

Lythrum californicum

192. **Small-flowered gaura**   *Gaura parviflora*   Evening primrose family

Annual or biennial herb, the stems with both long, soft hairs and gland-tipped hairs. *Leaves* alternate, hairy, 1¼–6 in. (3–15 cm) long, the basal ones broadest above the middle and tapering to the base, wavy-toothed, the upper leaves lance-shaped. *Flowers* in slender, spikelike, often nodding clusters, the petals pink, broadest toward the tip, about ¹/₁₆ in. (2 mm) long, the sepals ¹/₁₆ in. (2–3 mm) long, recurved in flower.
Range and Habitat: Indiana to Washington, southward to Texas, California, Mexico, and Argentina. Usually found in waste ground or on open plains throughout New Mexico; 4,000–7,500 ft.
Key Characters: Small-flowered gaura is identified by the coarse stems with soft hairs and the flowers in slender spikes which nod at the tip.
Related Species: A species of eastern areas, *G. villosa,* differs in lacking glandular hairs on the stem and in having flowers with petals white, turning red, and about ³/₈ in. (8 mm) long.

193. **Scarlet gaura**   *Gaura coccinea*   Evening primrose family

Perennial herb, the stems spreading or ascending, to 16 in. (40 cm) long. *Leaves* alternate, linear to lance-shaped or oblong, to 2³/₈ in. (6 cm) long, wavy-toothed or the margins smooth. *Flowers* in slender, spikelike clusters, the petals white to pink or red, elliptic, about ¹/₄ in. (3–6 mm) long, the sepals ¹/₄–³/₈ in. (5–10 mm) long, recurved in flower. This is a weedy plant with flowers often appearing irregular.
Range and Habitat: Southern Canada to Texas, California, and Mexico. Mostly associated with open plains and hills, often in waste ground, throughout New Mexico; 3,500–7,500 ft.
Key Characters: Scarlet gaura is distinguished by the narrow, often wavy-toothed leaves and the white to red flowers in slender, spikelike clusters.
Related Species: The also widespread New Mexico gaura, *G. neomexicana,* is superficially similar but differs in having the stem leaves at least 2 in. (5 cm) long and the sepals red and mostly ³/₈–⁵/₈ in. (10–15 mm) long.

194. **Fireweed**   *Epilobium angustifolium*   Evening primrose family

Perennial herb, the stems erect, to 6 ft. (2 m) tall. *Leaves* alternate, lance-shaped, 2–6 in. (5–15 cm) long, the margins smooth or nearly so, the lateral veins curled into loops below the margins of the blades. *Flowers* numerous, in racemes, stalked, the 4 petals constricted at the base, purple to pink or white, ³/₈–³/₄ in. (8–18 mm) long, with 8 stamens, the style hairy at the base, projecting into 4 slender lobes at the tip. *Fruit* a capsule with numerous hairy seeds.
Range and Habitat: Quebec to Alaska, southward to New Mexico and California, also Eurasia. Found in clearings, recently burned areas, and damp ground in the mountains throughout New Mexico; 7,000–12,000 ft.
Key Characters: Fireweed may be recognized by the 4 purple to pink or white, smooth-margined petals, the 8 stamens, and the floral tube extending only slightly, if at all, beyond the ovary.

Gaura parviflora

Gaura coccinea

Epilobium angustifolium

171

195. Dwarf yellow evening primrose   *Oenothera flava*   Evening primrose family

Perennial herb, the stems absent or nearly so. *Leaves* oblong to lance-shaped in outline, to about 8 in. (20 cm) long and 3/8–3/4 in (10–20 mm) wide, stalked, deeply and irregularly pinnately lobed. *Flowers* opening in early evening, the petals pale yellow, rounded, 3/8–3/4 in. (10–20 mm) long, the calyx tube slender, 3/4–4 1/2 in. (2–12 cm) long. *Fruit* an ovoid, winged capsule with numerous seeds.

Range and Habitat: Wyoming to California, southward to New Mexico and Arizona. Scattered on open plains and meadows throughout New Mexico; 5,000–11,000 ft.

Key Characters: This evening primrose is distinguished by the stemless habit, the relatively large irregularly lobed leaves, and the yellow flowers.

196. Hairythroat evening primrose   *Oenothera coronopifolia*   Evening primrose family

Perennial herb, the stems to 10 in. (25 cm) tall, mostly finely hairy. *Leaves* alternate, simple, the lower leaves 5/8–1 in. (15–25 mm) long, with wavy-toothed margins, the upper ones deeply and regularly divided into usually narrow lobes. *Flowers* borne in the upper leaf axils, nodding in bud, the 4 white petals becoming pink in age, 1/3–5/8 in. (8–15 mm) long, the calyx tube 3/8–1 1/4 in. (10–30 mm) long, with long conspicuous hairs in the throat. *Fruit* a cylindrical, many-seeded capsule.

Range and Habitat: South Dakota to Kansas, New Mexico, and Arizona. Found in open ground in a variety of habitats throughout New Mexico; 5,000–8,000 ft.

Key Characters: Hairythroat evening primrose is distinguished by the short stems, the wavy-toothed to pinnately lobed leaves, the white flowers, becoming pinkish in age, and the conspicuous hairs in the throat of the calyx tube.

197. Palestem evening primrose   *Oenothera albicaulis*   Evening primrose family

Slender annual, the stems about 12–18 in. (30–45 cm) tall, hairy. *Leaves* alternate, the basal leaves broadest toward the tip and tapering to the base, to 2 3/8 in. (6 cm) long, the margins smooth or lobed, the upper leaves pinnately divided into narrow lobes. *Flowers* solitary in the leaf axils, nodding in bud, the petals white, sometimes pinkish in age, 5/8–1 5/8 in. (15–40 mm) long, the calyx tube hairy, 5/8–1 1/2 in. (15–35 mm) long. *Fruit* a cylindrical, many-seeded capsule.

Range and Habitat: South Dakota and Montana to Texas, Arizona, and Mexico. Usually found on open, often sandy plains or in disturbed ground throughout New Mexico; 4,000–7,500 ft.

Key Characters: Whitestem evening primrose is distinguished by the whitish, hairy stem, the upper leaves pinnately divided into narrow lobes, and the conspicuous white petals, these often 1 in. (25 mm) or more long and about as wide.

Related Species: Two other relatively common white-flowered species include the pale evening primrose, *O. pallida,* and its several similar varieties, differing in having the stems glabrous and the whitish outer layer splitting away, and the smaller petals, these 5/8–3/4 in. (15–20 mm) long, and *O. neomexicana,* differing in having a western and southern distribution, the stems with conspicuous long hairs above, and the calyx tube 1 1/4–2 in. (3–5 cm) long.

Oenothera flava

Oenothera coronopifolia

Oenothera albicaulis

198. **Great plains evening primrose**   *Calylophus serrulatus*   Evening primrose family

Perennial herb, sometimes woody at the base, the stems erect to spreading, 6–20 in. (15–50 cm) long, the dense hairs appressed. *Leaves* alternate, mostly linear to lance-shaped, ⁵/₈–2³/₈ in. (15–60 mm) long. *Flowers* borne in the axils of the upper leaves, opening in the evening, the petals yellow, ¹/₈–¹/₂ in. (3–12 mm) long, the calyx tube ³/₁₆–⁵/₈ in. (5–15 mm) long, shorter than the ovary, the style 4-lobed at the tip. *Fruit* a cylindrical capsule with numerous dark brown seeds.

Range and Habitat: Manitoba to Alberta, southward to Texas and Arizona. Usually found on dry, open plains in eastern and central New Mexico: 4,500–6,000 ft.

Key Characters: This evening primrose is distinguished by the often broadly spreading stems with appressed hairs, the yellow flowers, and the style with 4 short lobes at the tip.

Related Species: The widely distributed, also spring-flowering *C. hartwegii* and its several varieties differ in having the petals ⁵/₈–1 in. (15–30 mm) long and the tip of the style disklike and unlobed.

199. **Osha**   *Ligusticum porteri*   Carrot family

Coarse perennial, the stems 24–36 in. (60–90 cm) tall, much branched, glabrous except with minute hairs in the flowering cluster. *Leaves* alternate, to about 12 in. (30 cm) long, repeatedly divided into numerous, often toothed or lobed segments, with the base of the stalk sheathing the stem. *Flowers* in loose umbels consisting of 11–24 primary branches, each bearing at the tip an umbellet of small flowers with 5 white or pink petals, with neither primary branches (rays) or umbellets subtended by bracts. *Fruit* ovoid, about ¹/₄ in. (6 mm) long, ribbed, and winged laterally and dorsally.

Range and Habitat: Wyoming to Colorado, Nevada, and Mexico. Associated with damp ground, usually in wooded areas, throughout New Mexico; 7,000–11,000 ft.

Key Characters: Osha is distinguished by the somewhat fernlike, repeatedly divided leaves with petioles sheathing the stem, the stems longitudinally ridged and hollow, the small flowers in compound umbels, and the absence of bracts at the base of both the primary rays of the flower cluster and the individual clusters (umbellets). A distinctive pungent odor is given off by this plant. Its roots are highly prized in folk medicine. Because many species of the carrot family tend to be very similar, osha can be confused with poisonous members of this family. Most species are best left alone unless one is absolutely certain of the identification.

200. **Cow-parsnip**   *Heracleum lanatum*   Carrot family

Coarse perennial, the stems longitudinally ridged, hollow, to about 6 ft. (2 m) tall, both stems and leaves hairy. *Leaves* alternate, compound, each leaf with 3 large, lobed, toothed leaflets attached to a strongly dilated leaf stalk. *Flowers* in huge compound umbels with 15–20 primary stalks (rays), each ray bearing a large umbellet of small, white, 5-petalled flowers at the summit. *Fruit* about ³/₈ in. (10 mm) long, strongly flattened, hairy, and longitudinally ribbed.

Range and Habitat: Newfoundland to Alaska, southward to Georgia, Arkansas, New Mexico, and California; also in Asia. Typically found in wet, often marshy areas near streams in the mountains of northern New Mexico; 7,500–9,000 ft.

Key Characters: Cow-parsnip is easily recognized by the tall, very stout stems, the leaves divided into 3 large, lobed and irregularly toothed, leaflike segments, and the conspicuous umbel of small white flowers.

Calylophus serrulatus

Ligusticum porteri

Heracleum lanatum

175

201. **Mountain parsley**   *Pseudocymopterus montanus*   Carrot family

Perennial herb, the stems longitudinally ridged, usually 8–32 in. (20–80 cm) tall or sometimes nearly absent. *Leaves* successively divided into 3-part segments, the final divisions linear to oval, on petioles often having papery or purplish margins. *Flowers* in loose compound umbels, the primary branches or rays without subtending bracts, each bearing at the summit a small umbellet of yellow or purplish flowers, the umbellet subtended by a series of small slender bractlets.
Range and Habitat: Wyoming to Texas, Arizona, and Mexico. Usually found in open meadows or coniferous woods in the mountains of New Mexico; 6,000–12,000 ft.
Key Characters: Mountain parsley is distinguished by the leaves divided into numerous divisions and the small yellowish or purple flowers in compound umbels.

202. **Poison hemlock**   *Conium maculatum*   Carrot family

Tall biennial herb, the stems branched, purple-spotted, to 10 ft. (3 m) tall. *Leaves* alternate, repeatedly pinnately divided into coarsely toothed segments. *Flowers* in compound umbels, with numerous primary stalks or rays subtended by small membranaceous bracts, each ray with a small umbellet of small, white, 5-petalled flowers, the umbellet subtended by a series of small membranaceous bractlets. *Fruit* ovoid, slightly flattened, and prominently ribbed, 1/8 in. (3 mm) long.
Range and Habitat: Introduced from Europe and widely established in the United States. Found in damp ground near streams, occasionally found on slopes, in the mountains of New Mexico; 5,000–7,500 ft.
Key Characters: Poison hemlock is distinguished by the tall, coarse, longitudinally ridged stems marked with purple spots, the compound leaves with the ultimate segments coarsely toothed or incised, and the umbels subtended by small membranaceous bracts. Beware of this plant; it is extremely poisonous.

203. **Fendler cowbane**   *Oxypolis fendleri*   Carrot family

Erect perennial herb, the stems unbranched, mostly 12–24 in. (30–60 cm) tall, both stems and leaves glabrous. *Leaves* alternate, pinnately compound with coarsely toothed segments, the leaf stalks expanded at the base and sheathing the stem. *Flowers* in loose compound umbels, the several primary stalks or rays with an umbellet of small, white or purple, 5-petalled flowers, neither primary rays nor umbellets subtended by bractlets. *Fruit* ovoid, about 3/16 in. (4 mm) long, compressed, ribbed, with broad, thin, lateral wings.
Range and Habitat: Wyoming to New Mexico and Arizona. Found mostly in marshy ground near streams from northern to south-central and western New Mexico; 7,000–10,000 ft.
Key Characters: Fendler cowbane is distinguished by the glabrous stems and leaves, the once-pinnate leaves with coarsely toothed segments, and the fruit with broad, thin, lateral wings.

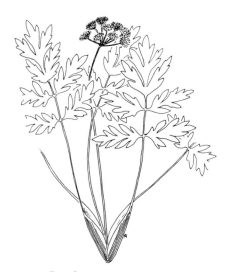

Pseudocymopterus montanus

Conium maculatum

Oxypolis fendleri

177

204. **Water-parsnip**   *Berula erecta*   Carrot family

Aquatic perennial herb, the stems erect, branching, 8–20 in. (20–50 cm) tall, both stems and leaves glabrous. *Leaves* pinnately compound, with 5–9 pairs of usually coarsely toothed leaflets. *Flowers* in compound umbels, the primary branches or rays subtended by a series of conspicuous bracts, each ray with an umbellet of small, white, 5-petalled flowers, the umbellet subtended by conspicuous bractlets. *Fruit* nearly round, notched at the base, compressed, ribbed, less than 1/8 in. (3 mm) long.
Range and Habitat: Ontario to British Columbia, southward to Florida, California, and Mexico; also Europe. Typically found in marshes and streams throughout New Mexico; 4,500–9,000 ft.
Key Characters: Water parsnip is distinguished by the smooth stems and leaves, the stems not more than 20 in. (50 cm) tall, the leaves once-pinnate and with coarsely toothed leaflets, and the rays of the umbel with linear or lance-shaped bracts.

205. **Water-hemlock**   *Cicuta douglasii*   Carrot family

Stout, smooth perennial, the stems longitudinally ridged, to 6 ft. (2 m) tall. *Leaves* once-, twice-, or thrice-pinnately compound, the leaflets lance-shaped, 1 1/4–4 in. (3–10 cm) long, toothed, the lateral veins ending at the base of the notches between the teeth. *Flowers* in compound umbels, the primary rays subtended by few bracts or none, each ray with an umbellet of small, white to greenish white, 5-petalled flowers, each umbellet subtended by several narrow bractlets. *Fruit* ovoid to nearly round, ribbed, about 1/8 in. (3 mm) long.
Range and Habitat: Alaska to South Dakota, New Mexico, California, and Mexico. Found in wet ground near streams or in marshy situations throughout New Mexico; 4,500–8,500 ft.
Key Characters: Water-hemlock is distinguished by the once- to thrice-pinnately compound leaves with coarsely toothed leaflets and the lateral veins ending at the base of the notch between the teeth, and the compound umbels of small whitish flowers.

206. **Dwarf cornel**   *Cornus canadensis*   Dogwood family

Low herb from a woody base, the stems to 10 in. (25 cm) tall. *Leaves* 4–6 in a whorl near the apex of the stem, oval or sometimes broadest above the middle, pointed at the tip, tapered at the base, 1 1/4–2 3/8 in. (3–6 cm) long, stiffly hairy on the upper surface, smooth beneath. *Flowers* in a headlike cluster subtended by 4 petallike bracts 3/8–5/8 in. (10–15 mm) long, the petals tiny, yellow to purple. *Fruit* red, berrylike.
Range and Habitat: Greenland to Alaska, southward to West Virginia, New Mexico, and California. Associated with wooded slopes in northern New Mexico; 7,500–11,000 ft.
Key Characters: Dwarf cornel is easily identified by the whorled leaves near the stem tip and by the headlike cluster of small flowers subtended by petallike bracts.
Related Species: The red-osier dogwood, *C. stolonifera*, widespread in the mountains of New Mexico, differs in having woody stems to 6 ft. (2 m) tall, numerous opposite leaves, and the flower clusters not subtended by petallike bracts.

Berula erecta

Cicuta douglasii

Cornus canadensis

207. **Myrtle whortleberry**   *Vaccinium myrtillus*   Heath family

Low shrub, to about 16 in. (40 cm) high, with conspicuously angled branchlets and spreading branches. *Leaves* alternate, ovate, mostly ⁵/₈–1¼ in. (15–30 mm) long, minutely toothed and nearly sessile. *Flowers* solitary in the axils of the leaves, the corolla globular, pink or white, 5-lobed. *Fruit* a purplish black berry about ¼ in. (6 mm) in diameter.

Range and Habitat: Alberta and British Columbia to New Mexico and Arizona. Usually found in open woods and meadows in the mountains of northern and west-central New Mexico; 8,000–11,500 ft.

Key Characters: Myrtle whortleberry is easily recognized by the woody, low-growing, spreading stems and angled branchlets, the alternate leaves with minute teeth, and the globular, pink or white flowers.

Related Species: The similar but usually shade-loving littleleaf whortleberry, *V. scoparium*, differs in having leaves usually less than ⁵/₈ in. (15 mm) long and red fruit less than ³/₁₆ in. (5 mm) in diameter. In the northern mountains at elevations above 10,000 ft., usually in wooded areas, grows the creeping wintergreen, *Gaultheria humifusa*, differing in having creeping stems, the corolla bell-shaped and attached below the ovary, and the ovary subtended by a fleshy disk.

208. **Pinedrops**   *Pterospora andromedea*   Heath family

Parasitic or saprophytic nongreen perennial, the stems purplish to reddish brown, clothed with glandular hairs, 12–20 in. (30–50 cm) tall. *Leaves* alternate, scalelike. *Flowers* small, pendulous, in a terminal raceme, the petals united to forn an urn-shaped white corolla with 5 short lobes, the calyx deeply parted, with 10 stamens, each anther with a pair of awns. *Fruit* a many-seeded capsule.

Range and Habitat: Canada, southward to Pennsylvania, New Mexico, California, and northern Mexico. Usually found in partial shade in coniferous forests in the mountains throughout New Mexico; 7,000–9,000 ft.

Key Characters: Pinedrops is distinguished by the brownish or purplish stems and leaves, the scalelike leaves, and the white, urn-shaped corolla.

209. **Pinesap**   *Monotropa latisquama*   Heath family

Parasitic or saprophytic nongreen perennial, the stems red to brown, 6–12 in. (15–30 cm) tall, usually clustered, somewhat fleshy. *Leaves* alternate, reduced to reddish scales. *Flowers* several, nodding at first, in terminal racemes, the 3–5 petals oblong, about ³/₈ in. (10 mm) long, hairy and with a fringe of hairs on the margins. *Fruit* an erect capsule with numerous minute seeds.

Range and Habitat: Montana to British Columbia, southward to New Mexico, California, and Mexico. Scattered in damp woods in the mountains throughout New Mexico; 7,000–9,500 ft.

Key Characters: Pinesap is easily recognized by the reddish or brownish stems and nongreen, scalelike leaves, the herbage often becoming black in drying and the racemes of flowers with 3–5 oblong, separate petals.

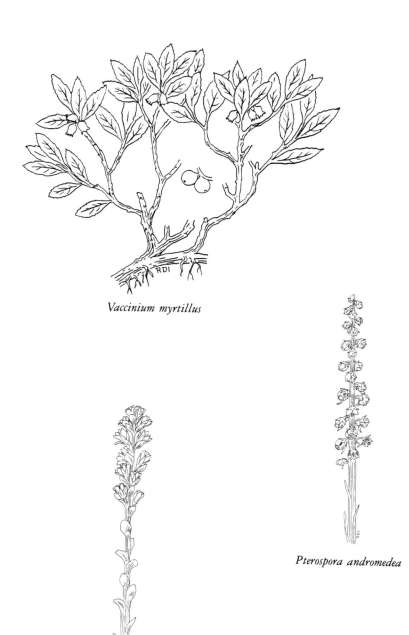

Vaccinium myrtillus

Monotropa latisquama

Pterospora andromedea

210. **Pipsissewa**   *Chimaphila umbellata*   Heath family

Low perennial from creeping rootstocks, the stems mostly 4–8 in. (10–20 cm) tall. *Leaves* crowded on the stem, often whorled, broadest above the middle and tapering to the base, ³/₄– 1⁵/₈ in. (20–40 mm) long, toothed, evergreen. *Flowers* mostly in umbellike clusters, fragrant, nodding, the 5 petals purplish, pinkish, or whitish, about ¹/₄ in. (6 mm) long, and 10 stamens, each anther with 2 small horns. *Fruit* a nearly globose capsule with numerous seeds. **Range and Habitat:** Colorado to New Mexico and Arizona. Usually found in shaded areas in coniferous forests in the mountains throughout New Mexico; 8,000–11,500 ft. **Key Characters:** Pipsissewa is characterized by the low-growing stems, the crowded, often whorled, shiny, toothed leaves, and the nodding, usually pinkish or purplish flowers in umbellike clusters.

211. **Sidebells**   *Ramischia secunda*   Heath family

Low perennial without true stems, the flowering stalks 6–8 in. (15–20 cm) tall. *Leaves* in basal clusters, ovate to oval, about ³/₈–1⁵/₈ in. (1–4 cm) long, stalked, minutely toothed. *Flowers* in 1-sided racemes, nodding, the petals greenish white, about ³/₁₆ in. (5 mm) long, each with a pair of small projections on the inner surface, with 10 stamens, the ovary surrounded at the base by a toothed, fleshy disk. *Fruit* a 5-lobed capsule. **Range and Habitat:** Labrador to Alaska, southward through Canada to New Jersey, Illinois, New Mexico, and California; also in Europe and Asia. Usually in shaded areas in deep woods from northern to western New Mexico; 7,000–9,500 ft. **Key Characters:** Sidebells is distinguished by the basal leaves, the leafless flower stalks, the small, greenish white flowers, and the ovary surrounded by a 10-toothed fleshy disk. **Related Species:** The beautiful woodnymph, *Moneses uniflora,* also known as one-flowered wintergreen, is found in similar habitats; it differs in having a solitary, much larger flower at the summit of a single flower stalk.

212. **Roundleaf wintergreen**   *Pyrola chlorantha*   Heath family

Small, evergreen perennial herb without true stems, the flower stalks mostly 4–8 in. (10–20 cm) tall. *Leaves* basal, usually broad elliptic to round, ³/₈–1¹/₄ in. (1–3 cm) long, stalked. *Flowers* nodding, in short terminal racemes, not 1-sided, the petals 5, greenish white, about ¹/₄ in. (6 mm) long, separate, the 10 stamens curved upward, the style curved upward, with a thickened collar below the stigma. *Fruit* a nearly globose capsule having many seeds. **Range and Habitat:** Labrador to British Columbia, southward to Massachusetts, South Dakota, New Mexico, and California; also in Europe. Found in deep woods in northern, central, and western New Mexico; 7,000–10,000 ft. **Key Characters:** Roundleaf wintergreen is distinguished by the often rounded, stalked leaves in basal clusters, the greenish white flowers in short racemes on leafless flower stalks, and the stamens and style curving upward. **Related Species:** Similar species of wintergreen include *P. picta,* differing in having leaves mottled with white along the veins, and *P. elliptica,* differing in having leaves mostly oval and with petioles not exceeding the blade in length.

Chimaphila umbellata

Ramischia secunda

Pyrola chlorantha

183

213. **Southern shooting star**   *Dodecatheon pulchellum*   Primrose family

Smooth perennial with basal leaves, the flower stalks 6–16 in. (15–40 cm) tall. *Leaves* in basal clusters, dull green, broadest above the middle and tapering to the petioles, usually without marginal teeth. *Flowers* often in terminal clusters, pink to purple, yellowish in the tube, both petals and sepals strongly reflexed, the stamens projecting to a point and giving the flower a dartlike appearance.
Range and Habitat: South Dakota to New Mexico, Arizona, and Mexico. Often locally common in wet meadows or near streams in the mountains of New Mexico; 7,000–11,000 ft.
Key Characters: Southern shooting star is easily recognized by the basal leaf cluster, the leafless flowering stem, and the pinkish or purplish flowers with petals and sepals strongly bent backward, the flower similar in appearance to a shooting star.
Related Species: A less common species of coniferous forests of central and southwestern parts of the state, *D. ellisiae,* differs in having frequently toothed leaves and white petals.

214. **Rusby primrose**   *Primula rusbyi*   Primrose family

Perennial herb with basal leaves and leafless flowering stalks 6–10 in. (15–25 cm) tall. *Leaves* mostly broadest above the middle and tapering to the base, with short hairs beneath, toothed, to about 4 in. (10 cm) long. *Flowers* few to many in terminal clusters, purplish, $3/8$–$3/4$ in. (10–20 mm) wide, funnel-shaped, the lobes notched, the calyx and individual flower stalks with a mealy covering.
Range and Habitat: New Mexico and Arizona. Often found on damp rocky ledges from north-central to southwestern New Mexico; 7,500–10,000 ft.
Key Characters: Rusby primrose may be identified by the basal leaf cluster, the leafless flowering stalks, and by the calyx and flowering stalks with a mealy covering.
Related Species: The similar and perhaps not distinct *P. ellisiae differs in having leaves to about 10 in. (25 cm) long and the calyx about $1/4$ in. (6–7 mm) long.*

215. **Bog Primrose**   *Primula parryi*   Primrose family

Perennial herb with basal leaves and leafless flowering stalks about 6–20 in. (15–50 cm) tall. *Leaves* crowded, glabrous, smooth on the margins, broadest above the middle and tapering to the base, to about 12 in. (30 cm) long. *Flowers* clustered at the top of the flower stalks, funnel-shaped, about $3/4$–1 in. (20–25 mm) wide, the lobes often shallowly notched, the calyx and individual flower stalks densely glandular.
Range and Habitat: Montana and Idaho to New Mexico and Arizona. Typically found in bogs and damp rocky places in the mountains of northern New Mexico; 10,000–12,000 ft.
Key Characters: Bog primrose is distinguished by the crowded basal leaves with smooth margins, the purple or pink flowers in clusters at the summit of the flower stalks, and the densely glandular calyx.

216. **Sea lavender**   *Limonium limbatum*   Plumbago family

Perennial herb with basal leaves and flower stalks to about 12 in. (30 cm) tall. *Leaves* simple, leathery, broadest above the middle and tapering to the base, smooth on the margins. *Flowers* small, blue, in dense clusters, the corolla with an elongate slender tube and the lobes spreading at right angles, the calyx with a 10-ribbed, glandular tube, and 5 stamens.
Range and Habitat: Texas and New Mexico. Usually associated with alkaline soil in central and southern New Mexico; 3,000–6,000 ft.
Key Characters: Sea lavender is distinguished by the basal leathery leaves that are smooth on the margins, the dense clusters of small blue flowers, the corolla with an elongate slender tube, and the 10-ribbed calyx.

Dodecatheon pulchellum

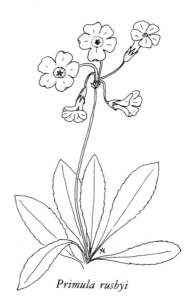

Primula rusbyi

Primula parryi

Limonium limbatum

217. **Rough menodora**   *Menodora scabra*   Olive family

Perennial herb, usually woody at the base, the stems mostly 6–12 in. (15–30 cm) tall, both stems and leaves usually rough to the touch. *Leaves* usually alternate, broadest above the middle, ³/₈–1 in. (10–25 mm) long. *Flowers* scattered, showy, bright yellow, the corolla 5- or 6-lobed and about ⁵/₈ in. (15 mm) wide, the calyx having 7–15 slender lobes, and 2 or 3 stamens.

Range and Habitat: Western Texas to Arizona and Mexico. Usually found on dry hills and mesas, often in rocky soils, throughout New Mexico; 4,000–7,000 ft.

Key Characters: Rough menodora is characterized by the rough stems and leaves, the showy yellow flowers, and the many-lobed calyx.

218. **Prairie gentian**   *Eustoma russellianum*   Gentian family

Smooth perennial, the stems to 24 in. (60 cm) tall. *Leaves* opposite, without teeth, sessile, clasping the stem, elliptic to lance-shaped, to about 3¹/₄ in. (8 cm) long and 1¹/₄ in. (3 cm) wide. *Flowers* showy, blue, white, or yellowish, stalked, the corolla somewhat funnel-shaped, with 5 or 6 lobes 1¹/₄–1⁵/₈ in. (30–40 mm) long, the calyx lobes slender, about half as long as the corolla, the stamens 5 or 6, recurved. *Fruit* a capsule with numerous seeds.

Range and Habitat: Nebraska and Colorado to Louisiana, New Mexico, and Mexico. Mostly associated with moist ground in open fields, meadows, and prairies in all but western New Mexico; 4,000–6,500 ft.

Key Characters: Prairie gentian is distinguished by the opposite clasping leaves and the showy blue, white, or yellowish flowers with both corolla and calyx of 5 or 6 parts.

Related Species: A smaller-flowered species, *E. exaltatum,* differs in having the corolla lobes not more than 1 in. (25 mm) long.

219. **Deer's ears**   *Swertia radiata*   Gentian family

Erect, stout perennial herb, the stems to about 6 ft. (2 m) tall. *Leaves* in whorls of 3–7, the lower ones oblong or ovate, to about 12 in. (30 cm) long, the upper ones often linear. *Flowers* in a narrow cluster, each flower subtended by a leaflike bract, the corolla deeply 4-lobed, the lobes ¹/₂–1¹/₄ in. (12–30 mm) long, greenish white and dotted with purple, each with 2 conspicuously fringed glands on the inner surface near the base, the calyx lobes linear, often slightly longer than the corolla.

Range and Habitat: South Dakota to Washington, southward to New Mexico, California, and Mexico. Typically found in wet meadows in the mountains throughout New Mexico; 7,000–10,000 ft.

Key Characters: Deer's ears is distinguished by the tall stout stems with leaves in whorls of 3–7 and the conspicuous greenish white flowers, these dotted with purple.

Menodora scabra

Eustoma russellianum

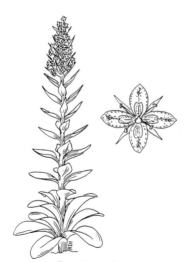

Swertia radiata

220.   **Pleated gentian**   *Gentiana affinis*   Gentian family

Erect perennial herb, the stems to about 12 in. (30 cm) long, usually clustered. *Leaves* opposite, not stalked, lance-shaped to ovate, not more than 5 times longer than wide. *Flowers* in short, often dense clusters, funnel-shaped, blue or purple, 1–1¼ in. (25–30 mm) long, 5-lobed, sinuses between the lobes with toothed appendages, the calyx lobes linear to lance-shaped, unequal.

Range and Habitat: Saskatchewan to British Columbia, southward to New Mexico, Arizona, and California. Occasionally found in open meadows in the mountains of New Mexico; 7,000–9,000 ft.

Key Characters: Pleated gentian is easily distinguished by the numerous, opposite leaves, the blue or purple, 5-lobed corolla with toothed appendages in the sinuses between the lobes, and the calyx with lobes unequal in length.

Related Species: A somewhat similar but annual and widespread species, *G. heterosepala,* differs in having the flowers solitary or in 2s or 3s in the axils of the upper leaves, the corolla with a fringed crown inside at the base of the lobes, and the calyx strongly unequal, with 2 of the lobes greatly enlarged and leaflike.

221.   **Western fringed gentian**   *Gentiana thermalis*   Gentian family

Erect, smooth annual, the stems mostly 4–16 in. (10–40 cm) tall. *Leaves* opposite, the basal ones tapering from above the middle to the base, to about 1¼ in. (30 mm) long, the upper leaves linear or narrowly lance-shaped, sessile. *Flowers* solitary at the summit of the stem, blue to purple, the corolla funnel-shaped, 1–2 in. (25–50 mm) long, the 5 lobes toothed and fringed, the calyx often 4-lobed, angled, and sometimes spotted with purple.

Range and Habitat: Western Canada to New Mexico and Arizona. Often abundant in moist meadows, bogs, or slopes in the mountains of northern and central New Mexico; 8,000–9,500 ft.

Key Characters: Western fringed gentian is distinguished by the solitary, terminal, blue or purple flowers with the lobes toothed and fringed toward the apex.

Related Species: The very dwarf, also annual, alpine fringed gentian, *G. tenella,* differs in having stems not more than 4 in. (10 cm) tall and the corolla ⅜–⅝ in. (10–15 mm) long.

222.   **Spreading dogbane**   *Apocynum androsaemifolium*   Dogbane family

Perennial herb, the stems to 3 ft. (1 m) or more tall, branching. *Leaves* opposite, ovate to oblong, to 4 in. (10 cm) long, short-stalked, somewhat drooping, smooth-margined, hairy and much paler on the lower surface. *Flowers* in loose clusters, the corolla somewhat bell-shaped, ¼–½ in. (6–12 mm) long, the 5 lobes spreading or recurved at the tip, usually pinkish. *Fruits* a pair of slender pods 2⅜–6 in. (6–15 cm) long, the seeds with a tuft of hair at one end.

Range and Habitat: Canada to Georgia, Louisiana, Texas, and Arizona. Usually in open areas in waste or disturbed ground, often along roadsides, throughout New Mexico; 7,000–9,000 ft.

Key Characters: Spreading dogbane is easily distinguished by the opposite, spreading or drooping leaves, the blades whitish and hairy beneath, the pinkish bell-shaped flowers, and the slender pods borne in pairs.

Related Species: Several other species of dogbane, including *A. medium, A. suksdorfii, A. sibericum,* and *A. cannabinum,* are very similar, differing mostly in amount of leaf pubescence, shape of leaf base and apex, and flower color. This is a very difficult group. The use of the tough fibrous bark by American Indians for various purposes has promoted the use of the name Indian hemp for members of the genus, especially the white-flowered *A. cannabinum.*

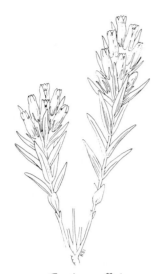

Gentiana affinis

Gentiana thermalis

Apocynum androsaemifolium

223. **Long-flowered amsonia**   *Amsonia longiflora*   Dogbane family

Erect perennial herb, the stems much branched, to about 24 in. (60 cm) tall, both stems and leaves glabrous. *Leaves* alternate but often nearly whorled, narrowly linear to narrowly lance-shaped, to about 1 in. (25 mm) long and $^1/_{16}$ in. (1–2 mm) wide. *Flowers* pale blue, in small terminal clusters, the corolla tubular but the lobes usually spreading at wide angles, the tube usually about 1$^1/_2$ in. (35 mm) long, constricted at the top, the lobes about $^1/_2$ in. (12 mm) long, the calyx with 5 bristle-tipped lobes. *Fruits* a pair of slender pods about 3 in. (8 cm) long.
Range and Habitat: Western Texas to New Mexico and Mexico. In dry rocky ground in southern New Mexico; 4,000–5,000 ft.
Key Characters: Long-flowered amsonia is distinguished by the long, tubular, pale blue flowers with conspicuous spreading lobes and the very narrow, usually crowded leaves.
Related Species: The sand-loving *A. arenaria,* of about the same elevational range, differs in having woolly stems and leaves, wider leaves, and the flower cluster with numerous flowers.

224. **Plains milkweed**   *Asclepias asperula*   Milkweed family

Perennial herb, the stems spreading, to about 24 in. (60 cm) long. *Leaves* alternate but often nearly opposite, mostly 2–6 in. (5–15 cm) long, linear to lance-shaped, tapered or rounded at the base. *Flowers* in terminal, umbellike clusters, the 5 petals reflexed and white to greenish white, about $^3/_8$ in. (8 mm) long, the 5 hoodlike appendages within mostly purplish brown to pink or rose and shorter than the corolla lobes. *Fruit* of smooth or slightly spiny pods, these in pairs or solitary and containing seeds with tufts of soft hairs.
Range and Habitat: Kansas to California, southward to Mexico. Usually found on dry open plains and slopes throughout New Mexico; 4,000–8,000 ft.
Key Characters: Plains milkweed is characterized by the alternate leaves, the reflexed greenish white petals, and the pinkish or purplish brown hoodlike appendages inside the flowers.
Related Species: Two other species, mostly of southern and western parts of the state, are *A. macrotis,* differing in having the leaves opposite, very narrowly linear, and with the margins rolled under, and *A. quinquedentata,* having narrowly linear, opposite leaves, pale green corolla lobes, and with erect hoodlike appendages containing a hornlike projection within.

225. **Butterflyweed**   *Asclepias tuberosa*   Milkweed family

Perennial herb, the stems mostly 12–32 in. (30–80 cm) tall, usually hairy. *Leaves* alternate, numerous, lance-shaped, mostly 1$^1/_4$–3$^5/_8$ in. (30–90 mm) long. *Flowers* in groups of umbellike clusters, the corolla yellow to reddish orange, about $^1/_4$–$^3/_8$ in. (5–9 mm) long, the petals and sepals turned backward, the inner flower with 5 bright orange or yellow hoodlike structures. Few plants in our flora can match the butterflyweed for beauty and showiness.
Range and Habitat: Ohio to Utah, southward to Texas and Arizona. Found in scattered populations, usually in gravelly canyons throughout New Mexico; 4,000–8,000 ft.
Key Characters: Butterflyweed is easily identified by the erect, relatively tall, usually hairy stems, the alternate leaves, and the conspicuous yellow to reddish orange flowers.

Amsonia longiflora

Asclepias asperula

Asclepias tuberosa

191

226. **Poison milkweed**   *Asclepias subverticillata*   Milkweed family

Erect or somewhat spreading perennial herb, the stems mostly 12–36 in. (30–100 cm) tall,
usually with short branches in the axils of the leaves. *Leaves* usually in whorls, smooth,
narrow, mostly 1¹/₂–4¹/₂ in. (3–11 cm) long, short-stalked. *Flowers* in umbels mostly at the
upper nodes, the corolla whitish to greenish purple and both petals and sepals reflexed, the
inner flower with 5 nearly erect, hoodlike structures, these toothed at the base and bearing a
hornlike appendage within. *Fruit* of slender pods 2–4 in. (5–10 cm) long.
Range and Habitat: Idaho to Kansas, Texas, New Mexico, Arizona, and Mexico. Usually
found in disturbed areas in plains and valleys throughout New Mexico; 4,000–7,500 ft.
Key Characters: Poison milkweed is distinguished by the stems with short branches in the
axils of the leaves, the whorled leaves, and the whitish or sometimes greenish purple flowers.
Related Species: A closely related species from the northeastern plains, *A. verticillata,* differs
in having no short axillary branches. The dwarf milkweed from northern and eastern parts of
the state, *A. pumila,* differs in having stems not more than 10 in. (25 cm) tall, and alternate,
extremely narrow leaves.

227. **Showy milkweed**   *Asclepias speciosa*   Milkweed family

Unbranched perennial herb, the stems mostly 16–45 in. (4–12 dm) or more tall. *Leaves*
opposite, short-stalked, oblong to lance-shaped, to about 8 in. (20 cm) long, thickish. *Flowers*
in woolly-stalked umbels at the summit of the stems or in the axils of the upper leaves, the
corolla lobes about ³/₈ in. (10 mm) long, pink to greenish purple, spreading outward and
downward, the inner flower with 5 pinkish or whitish hoodlike structures, the hoods tapering
to the tip and each with a short inwardly curving hornlike appendage within. *Fruit* podlike,
white woolly, sometimes somewhat spiny.
Range and Habitat: Western Canada to Kansas, New Mexico, and California. Usually found
in damp, open ground, often in valleys near streams throughout New Mexico; 5,500–8,500
ft.
Key Characters: Showy milkweed is distinguished by the often tall, unbranched stems, the
corolla with backward-spreading pinkish to greenish purple petals, and pink to whitish,
somewhat spreading hoodlike structures within the flower.
Related Species: The also widespread *A. brachystephana* differs in having shorter stems, not
more than 10 in. (25 cm) tall, purplish flowers, and the inner hoodlike structures with large
teeth on the margins.

228. **Large-fruited dodder**   *Cuscuta megalocarpa*   Morning-glory family

Parasitic herbs, the stems slender, mostly yellowish, twining or trailing, on various
herbaceous or shrubby hosts. *Flowers* in small clusters along the stem, the corolla regular,
bell-shaped, whitish, with 5 spreading triangular lobes and with 5 lobed or fringed
appendages inside the tube. *Fruit* a capsule about ³/₁₆–¹/₄ in. (4–6 mm) long.
Range and Habitat: Minnesota to Wyoming, southward to New Mexico. On various herbs
and shrubs throughout New Mexico; 4,500–7,000 ft.
Key Characters: Large-fruited dodder is distinguished by the slender, often twining,
yellowish stems and dense clusters of small bell-shaped flowers having fringed or lobed
appendages inside and toward the base of the corolla tube.
Related Species: Another widespread species on various hosts, *C. umbellata,* differs in having
the corolla lobes lance-shaped and the fringed inner appendages at least as long as the corolla
tube. This is a difficult group of plants to identify to species but delimitation of the genus is
relatively easy.

Asclepias subverticillata

Asclepias speciosa

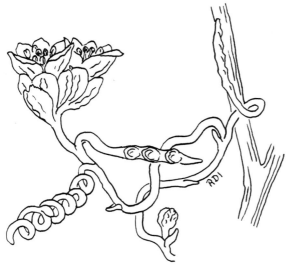

Cuscuta megalocarpa

229. **Silky evolvulus** *Evolvulus pilosus* Morning-glory family

Spreading to prostrate perennial herb, the stems to about 8 in. (20 cm) long, both stems and leaves with silky hairs. *Leaves* simple, alternate, lance-shaped to elliptic, without marginal teeth or lobes, nearly sessile, 3/8–5/8 in. (8–15 mm) long, the upper ones not appreciably smaller than the lower. *Flowers* somewhat bell-shaped or funnel-shaped, the lobes united to give the corolla face a somewhat 5-angled outline, the corolla lavender, about 3/8 in. (10–12 mm) wide.

Range and Habitat: North Dakota and Montana to Texas and Arizona. Usually on open plains or low, dry hills throughout New Mexico; 3,500–6,000 ft.

Key Characters: Silky evolvulus is easily identified by the low-growing, mostly sprawling habit with both stems and leaves densely covered with silky hairs, the small leaves sharply angled upward or appressed to the stem, and the conspicuous, solitary, lavender flowers, these similar to small morning glories.

Related Species: Similar species include *E. sericeus,* from the southern parts of the state, differing in having the leaves spreading, and *E. arizonicus,* from extreme southwestern areas, differing in having erect to ascending stems and white or blue flowers.

230. **Bush morning glory** *Ipomoea leptophylla* Morning glory family

Shrublike perennial herb, the stems numerous, smooth, ascending to somewhat trailing especially at the tip, to about 4½ ft. (1.5 m) long, from massive roots. *Leaves* alternate, linear to narrowly lance-shaped, unlobed, to about 6 in. (15 cm) long and 3/8 in. (8 mm) wide, short-stalked. *Flowers* solitary or 2–4 in a cluster, very conspicuous, funnel-shaped, not appreciably lobed, pink to rose purple, about 2–3¼ in. (5–8 cm) long, the sepals ovate, blunt, unequal in length.

Range and Habitat: South Dakota and Montana to Texas and New Mexico. Dry, open, usually very sandy ground from northern to eastern and central New Mexico; 4,500–5,500 ft.

Key Characters: Bush morning glory is easily recognized by the shrubby appearance, the narrow willowlike leaves, and the very conspicuous pinkish to purplish funnel-shaped flowers.

231. **Star glory** *Ipomoea coccinea* Morning glory family

Smooth perennial herb, the stems twining. *Leaves* alternate, entire or nearly so, mostly somewhat heart-shaped. *Flowers* in small stalked clusters in the axils of the leaves, the corolla narrowly funnel-shaped, bright scarlet, about 3/4–1 in. (20–25 mm) long, not lobed but five-angled.

Range and Habitat: Western Texas to Arizona, southward into tropical America. Usually found in moist ground in scattered locations from central to southern New Mexico; 4,000–6,500 ft.

Key Characters: Star glory is readily distinguished by the mostly heart-shaped, smooth-margined leaves and the conspicuous, bright scarlet, funnel-shaped flowers.

Related Species: A variety of star glory, having a similar range and habitat, *I. coccinea hederifolia,* differs in having at least some of the leaves deeply parted into 3 or 5 segments.

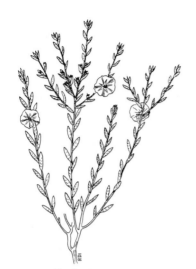

Evolvulus pilosus

Ipomoea leptophylla

Ipomoea coccinea

232. **Hedge bindweed** *Convolvulus sepium* Morning-glory family

Prostrate to twining perennial herb, the stems to 6 ft. (2 m) or more long. *Leaves* alternate, somewhat rounded-triangular, with the base of the blade extended into an angled or rounded lobe on each side. *Flowers* solitary in the leaf axils, the corolla white to pink, funnel-shaped, mostly 1¹/₂–2¹/₄ in. (4–6 cm) long, the sepals surrounded by a pair of heart-shaped bracts ³/₈–1 in. (10–25 mm) long. This plant is one of several species of bindweeds, all potentially troublesome weedy forms.

Range and Habitat: Nearly cosmopolitan. Common in open fields, in waste ground, in lawns, or along roadsides, often in saline soils, throughout New Mexico; 4,000–8,000 ft.

Key Characters: Hedge bindweed is distinguished by the prostrate or twining stems, the alternate, somewhat triangular leaves, the white or pinkish funnel-shaped flowers, and the sepals enclosed by a pair of large heart-shaped bracts.

Related Species: Two similar species include field bindweed, *C. arvensis,* and silky bindweed, *C. incanus,* these differing from hedge bindweed in having short floral bracts below the calyx and not enclosing it.

233. **Panicled ipomopsis** *Ipomopsis laxiflora* Phlox family

Erect, branching annual, the stems smooth or with minute glandular hairs on the upper part, mostly 4–16 in. (10–40 cm) tall. *Leaves* alternate, pinnately lobed, the lobes very narrow and tipped with an abrupt short point, the upper leaves sometimes without lobes. *Flowers* in an open, loose cluster, white or tinged with blue, with a narrow tube ³/₈–⁵/₈ in. (10–15 mm) long and spreading lobes about ³/₁₆ in. (3–5 mm) long, the calyx about half as long as the tube, whitish below the sinuses between the lobes, each lobe with an apical spine, the stamens not projecting beyond the flower.

Range and Habitat: Texas to Utah and Arizona. Mostly found on open plains throughout much of New Mexico; 5,500–6,500 ft.

Key Characters: Panicled ipomopsis is distinguished by the whitish flowers arranged in a loose, open cluster, the anthers not projecting beyond the flower, and the spine-tipped calyx lobes.

Related Species: Another widespread annual, *I. pumila,* differs in having somewhat woolly stems, often pink or bluish flowers, and stamens projecting from the flower.

234. **Throated trumpet** *Ipomopsis longiflora* Phlox family

Erect, branching annual, the stems smooth or sometimes with short, glandular hairs below the flower cluster. *Leaves* narrow, pinnately lobed, the upper leaves sometimes unlobed. *Flowers* in open, loose clusters, on slender stalks, whitish to blue or pink, with a slender tube 1¹/₄–2 in. (3–5 cm) long and spreading lobes, these about ³/₈ in. (8–10 mm) long, the calyx usually less than ¹/₅ as long as the corolla tube and with spine-tipped lobes, the stamens not projecting beyond the flowers.

Range and Habitat: Nebraska to Utah, southward to Texas, Arizona, and Mexico. Usually found on dry plains, slopes, or mesas, often in sandy soils, throughout New Mexico; 4,000–7,000 ft.

Key Characters: Throated trumpet is distinguished by the conspicuously long corolla tubes, these much longer than those of any other species in our area.

Related Species: A well-known perennial, *I. multiflora,* differs in having stems with numerous long, whitish hairs, and flowers in a narrow cluster, the corolla tube only ³/₁₆–³/₈ in. (5–10 mm) long.

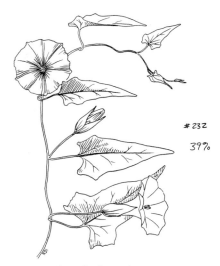

Convolvulus sepium

#232

39%

#233

43%

Ipomopsis laxiflora

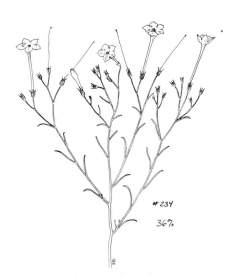

#234

36%

Ipomopsis longiflora

235. **Red rocket**   *Ipomopsis aggregata*   Phlox family

Biennial herb, the stems often solitary, to 24 in. (60 cm) tall, hairy and usually glandular.
Leaves alternate, pinnately divided into linear lobes with a short, sharp point at the tip.
Flowers in small clusters along the upper stem, red to pink or white, often spotted with
yellow, tube-shaped to narrowly funnel-shaped, the tube about ³/₄–1³/₄ in. (20–45 mm) long,
the lobes lance-shaped, spreading or somewhat recurved, the stamens sometimes projecting
from the flower. There are several very similar subspecies of this plant in our area, differing in
relatively few characters, and all with a long flowering period.
Range and Habitat: Montana to British Columbia, southward to New Mexico, California,
and Mexico. Usually associated with dry ground on open plains and slopes, often scattered in
open coniferous forests, throughout New Mexico; 5,000–9,500 ft.
Key Characters: Red rocket is easily recognized by the usually tall, slender stems, the leaves
divided into several narrow lobes, and the conspicuous, tube-shaped flowers with spreading
lobes.

236. **Stiffleaf gilia**   *Gilia rigidula*   Phlox family

Perennial herb, the stems and branches spreading, to about 10 in. (25 cm) tall, both stems
and leaves with gland-tipped hairs. *Leaves* alternate, the basal ones divided into several
flattened segments or sometimes the segments very slender and sharply pointed, the upper
leaves divided into needlelike segments or sometimes not divided. *Flowers* scattered, blue to
purple with a yellow center, the corolla funnel-shaped, ⁵/₁₆–¹/₂ in. (8–12 mm) long, the lobes
oval, spreading, longer than the corolla tube, the stamens projecting beyond the flower.
Range and Habitat: Texas to Colorado, New Mexico, and Arizona. Usually associated with
dry, sandy plains and hills in southern New Mexico; 4,500–6,500 ft.
Key Characters: Stiffleaf gilia is distinguished by the very slender, spine-tipped leaf
segments, the blue or purple flowers with a yellow eye, and the corolla lobes that are longer
than the tube.

237. **Jacob's-ladder**   *Polemonium foliosissimum*   Phlox family

Perennial herb, the stems erect, often branched, mostly 12–36 in. (30–90 cm) tall, hairy and
often glandular. *Leaves* alternate, pinnately lobed or pinnately compound, the leaflets mostly
lance-shaped and ³/₈–1 in. (10–25 mm) long. *Flowers* in somewhat open clusters, the corolla
bell-shaped, white to purple, ³/₈–³/₄ in. (10–18 mm) long, the lobes longer than the tube,
the calyx often densely glandular. *Fruits* of small pods with brown or black seeds.
Range and Habitat: Idaho to Colorado, New Mexico, and Arizona. Scattered in damp woods
or meadows in the mountains from northern to south-central and western New Mexico;
7,000–10,000 ft.
Key Characters: Jacob's-ladder is distinguished by the usually tall stems with pinnately
lobed or pinnately compound leaves and the conspicuous blue, purple, or white bell-shaped
flowers.
Related Species: Similar forms of this species occurring in New Mexico include var. *flavum*
with yellow flowers and var. *molle* with rounded instead of pointed corolla lobes and mostly
less than 20 leaflets or lobes for each leaf. Another species with blue bell-shaped flowers is
skunkleaf Jacob's-ladder (*P. delicatum*), differing in having stems mostly clustered and not
more than 8 in. (20 cm) tall. Another montane northern species is *P. brandegei*, conspicuous
for its golden yellow or sometimes whitish or straw-colored, funnel-shaped flowers, and low-
growing, clustered stems bearing sticky glands.

Ipomopsis aggregata

Gilia rigidula

Polemonium foliosissimum

238. Cushion phlox   *Phlox caespitosa*   Phlox family

Perennial herb, the stems mostly spreading, often matted, to about 4 in. (10 cm) long. *Leaves* opposite, slender, stiff, sharply pointed, 3-veined, about ³/₁₆–¹/₂ in. (5–12 mm) long. *Flowers* solitary at the tips of the branches, not or only slightly stalked, the corolla white to pale blue with lobes about ¹/₄ in. (5–6 mm) long and the tube ³/₈–⁵/₈ in. (10–15 mm) long, the calyx teeth narrow and sharply pointed, with margins fringed with stiffish hairs. *Fruits* of small, ovoid pods.

Range and Habitat: Montana to Oregon, southward to New Mexico and California. A conspicuous feature of many rocky mountain meadows in northern New Mexico; 11,000–13,000 ft.

Key Characters: Cushion phlox is easily distinguished by the usually matted, almost mosslike habit, the masses of whitish or pale bluish flowers, and the small, slender-pointed leaves.

Related Species: Two other densely clustered, often mat-forming species are woolly phlox (*P. hoodii*), differing in having often woolly hairy stems and calyx, and desert phlox (*P. austromontana*), differing in having leaves ³/₈–⁵/₈ in. (10–15 mm) long and often bluish or purplish flowers. Both of these species are found at elevations of 5,000–7,000 ft., far below the lowest elevational range of cushion phlox.

239. Santa Fe phlox   *Phlox nana*   Phlox family

Perennial herb, the stems mostly 4–10 in. (10–25 cm) long, with numerous gland-tipped hairs especially on the upper stem and in the flower cluster. *Leaves* opposite, narrowly lanceolate, ¹/₂–1⁵/₈ in. (12–40 mm) long and ¹/₈–³/₁₆ in. (2–5 mm) wide, the margins without teeth. *Flowers* scattered, pink, tube-shaped, ¹/₂–³/₄ in. (13–18 mm) long, the lobes spreading abruptly, mostly ¹/₂–³/₄ in. (12–20 mm) long, irregularly toothed on the margins. This is one of our more common phloxes in New Mexico, often occurring in dense populations.

Range and Habitat: Western Texas to Arizona and Mexico. Often associated with grassy areas of plains, hills, and mountain slopes throughout all but northern New Mexico; 5,000–7,500 ft.

Key Characters: Santa Fe phlox may be recognized by the somewhat stiffish, narrowly lance-shaped leaves, the gland-tipped hairs on the upper stems and flower bases, and the large pink flowers with irregularly toothed lobe margins.

Related Species: Several related species include *P. cluteana,* differing in having evergreen, elliptic leaves and very few glands on the upper stem; *P. mesoleuca,* differing in having linear leaves ¹/₈ in. (1–3 mm) wide and only a few gland-tipped hairs on the upper stem; and *P. triovulata,* differing in having narrowly linear leaves and no gland-tipped hairs on the upper stem.

240. Small-flowered collomia   *Collomia linearis*   Phlox family

Erect annual, the stems 2¹/₂–14 in. (6–35 cm) tall, hairy. *Leaves* alternate, linear to lance-shaped, ³/₄–2³/₈ in. (20–60 mm) long, the margins without teeth. *Flowers* in dense terminal clusters, each flower subtended by leaflike bracts, the corolla funnel-shaped, pinkish purple to white, ³/₈–⁵/₈ in. (8–15 mm) long, the calyx about half as long as the corolla tube.

Range and Habitat: Canada to Minnesota, New Mexico, Arizona, and California. Mostly found in open meadows in the mountains of northern and western New Mexico; 7,000–9,000 ft.

Key Characters: Small-flowered collomia is distinguished by the narrowly funnel-shaped or tubular, white or pinkish purple flowers in leafy bracted terminal clusters and alternate leaves with smooth margins.

Related Species: The similar big-flowered collomia (*C. grandiflora*) differs in having creamy white to pinkish flowers about ³/₄–1¹/₄ in. (20–30 mm) long.

Phlox caespitosa

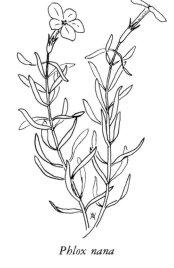

Phlox nana

Collomia linearis

201

241. **Toothed-leaf scorpionweed**   *Phacelia integrifolia*   Waterleaf family

Erect annual, the stems robust, 8–20 in. (20–50 cm) tall, leafy, with numerous hairs, many of them gland-tipped and sticky. *Leaves* alternate, somewhat oblong, 1–2¹/₂ in. (2–6 cm) long, with broad rounded teeth, never lobed. *Flowers* in dense, 1-sided, incurled spikes, the corolla funnel-shaped with small projections within, white or blue, the lobes about ³/₈ in. (8 mm) long and not toothed.

Range and Habitat: Kansas to Utah, southward to Texas, New Mexico, Arizona, and Mexico. Usually found on dry plains and hills throughout New Mexico; 5,000–7,000 ft.

Key Characters: Toothed-leafed scorpionweed is distinguished by the stout stems, the stems and calyx with sticky glands, the funnel-shaped white or blue flowers, and the leaves without lobes but with rounded marginal teeth.

Related Species: A similar species, *P. corrugata,* differs in having bell-shaped corollas and leaves often pinnately lobed or wavy in outline.

242. **New Mexico scorpionweed**   *Phacelia neomexicana*   Waterleaf family

Erect or ascending annual, the stems 8–28 in. (20–70 cm) tall, hairy and glandular, especially the upper part. *Leaves* alternate, 1–2¹/₂ in. (25–65 mm) long, irregularly pinnately lobed with each segment also lobed. *Flowers* in dense, 1-sided, curled spikes, funnel-shaped, purplish, the corolla lobes toothed, the stamens sometimes projecting from the flowers.

Range and Habitat: Colorado to New Mexico and Arizona. Locally common on wooded slopes in southern and western New Mexico; 7,000–9,000 ft.

Key Characters: New Mexico scorpionweed is distinguished by the usually robust growth habit, the pinnately lobed leaves with each segment having smaller lobes, the glandular upper stems, and the corollla lobes with toothed margins.

Related Species: Another summer-flowering species is *P. popei,* differing in having spreading, almost prostrate stems with glandular hairs absent or very few. Two varieties of New Mexico scorpionweed have been described for the state; they include the white-flowered var. *alba* and the often prostrate-stemmed var. *pseudoarizonica.*

243. **Western waterleaf**   *Hydrophyllum fendleri*   Waterleaf family

Perennial herb, the stems mostly 8–24 in. (20–60 cm) tall. *Leaves* alternate, to 12 in. (30 cm) long, pinnately divided nearly to the midrib into several coarsely toothed lobes, bell-shaped or funnel-shaped, white or pale blue, about ¹/₄–³/₈ in. (6–10 mm) long, the lobes rounded, not spreading, about half as long as the tube, each lobe with a slender projection at the base.

Range and Habitat: Wyoming to Washington, southward to New Mexico and Utah. Associated with wet areas, often along streams, in the mountains throughout New Mexico; 7,000–9,000 ft.

Key Characters: Western waterleaf is distinguished by the large, pinnately divided, coarsely toothed leaves and the somewhat bell-shaped blue or white flowers.

Phacelia integrifolia

Phacelia neomexicana

Hydrophyllum fendleri

203

244. **Narrow-leaved coldenia**   *Coldenia hispidissima*   Borage family

Prostrate perennial herb, the stems slender, about 4 in. (10 cm) long, branched, covered with stiff hairs. *Leaves* alternate, crowded, stiffly hairy, linear to lance-shaped, the base usually somewhat expanded and with soft, long hairs. *Flowers* small, mostly funnel-shaped, whitish or bluish, about 3/16 in. (5 mm) long, solitary in the leaf axils, the stamens attached at different levels on the corolla tube.

Range and Habitat: Western Texas to Utah, Nevada, New Mexico, and Arizona. Usually found on dry hills and plains in central and southern New Mexico; 3,000–5,000 ft.

Key Characters: Narrow-leaved coldenia is distinguished by the short, prostrate stems, the crowded, narrow leaves with margins rolled under, and the stems and leaves covered with stiffish hairs. Many of our plants probably belong to the var. *latior,* differing in having broader, more lance-shaped leaves.

Related Species: Other summer-flowering species include *C. greggii,* differing in having flowers in short, dense clusters and small awllike leaves; and *C. canescens,* differing in having woody stems and ovate or elliptic leaves covered with dense, whitish hairs.

245. **Bindweed heliotrope**   *Heliotropium convolvulaceum*   Borage family

Annual herb, the stems with many spreading branches, both stems and leaves stiffly hairy. *Leaves* alternate, lance-shaped or sometimes linear, not fleshy, 3/8–1 5/8 in. (10–40 mm) long, without teeth. *Flowers* in the axils of upper leaves, conspicuous, the corolla white, funnel-shaped, about 3/8–5/8 in. (10–15 mm) wide, essentially unlobed, the tube stiffly hairy. This relative of the garden heliotrope has pleasantly scented flowers which open in the afternoon.

Range and Habitat: Nebraska to Utah, southward to Mexico. Usually found in dry, sandy, open ground, often along roadsides throughout New Mexico; 4,000–6,000 ft.

Key Characters: Bindweed heliotrope is distinguished by its low-spreading growth habit and the broadly funnel-shaped white flowers with conspicuously 5-angled margins.

Related Species: A small-flowered species from southern New Mexico, *H. greggii* differs in having slender, one-sided, incurved flower clusters and slender, linear leaves. The well-known quailplant, *H. curassavicum* has fleshy stems and leaves, both without hairs, and flowers in conspicuous, incurved, one-sided spikes.

246. **Quailplant**   *Heliotropium curassavicum*   Borage family

Annual or perennial herb, the stems with many spreading branches, smooth. *Leaves* alternate, fleshy, narrowly oblong or broader toward the tip and tapering to the base, to 2 3/8 in. (6 cm) long, without hairs. *Flowers* in usually paired, incurved, one-sided spikes, the corolla white or with a tinge of blue, funnel-shaped, about 1/4–3/8 in. (6–9 mm) wide, the lobes rounded at the apex. This attractive plant is made more attractive by its pleasing fragrance.

Range and Habitat: Florida to New Mexico, southward into tropical America. Widely distributed in alkaline soils in New Mexico; 4,000–5,000 ft.

Key Characters: Quailplant is easily recognized by the smooth, fleshy leaves and the usually white, funnel-shaped flowers with the corolla having rounded lobes.

Coldenia hispidissima

Heliotropium convolvulaceum

Heliotropium curassavicum

247. Common hounds's tongue — *Cynoglossum officinale* — Borage family

Coarse biennial or perennial herb, the stems to 24 in. (60 cm) tall, hairy. *Leaves* alternate, mostly lance-shaped, to 12 in. (30 cm) long, becoming much smaller upward, the lower ones petioled, the upper ones sessile. *Flowers* in elongate terminal clusters, usually purplish, the corolla with a short tube and 5 usually spreading lobes, about $1/4$–$3/8$ in. (6–9 mm) wide. *Fruit* a cluster of 4 flattened nutlets bearing short, barbed bristles.

Range and Habitat: Although introduced from Europe, this plant is established here and there in North America. Usually associated with waste ground from northern to south-central New Mexico; 5,000–8,000 ft.

Key Characters: Common hound's tongue is easily identified by the coarse, hairy stems, the large, usually lance-shaped leaves, the purplish flowers, and the barbed fruits.

248. Many-flowered stickseed — *Hackelia floribunda* — Borage family

Coarse perennial, the stems 18–36 in. (5–10 dm) tall, with numerous stiff, often appressed hairs. *Leaves* alternate, 2–6 in. (5–15 cm) long, coarsely hairy, often widest toward the tip and tapering to the base. *Flowers* numerous, in dense, slender clusters, the lower flowers subtended by leafy bracts, the corolla white to bluish, about $3/16$–$3/8$ in. (5–10 mm) wide, the calyx covered with stiffish hairs. *Fruits* of 4 small nutlets, each with a narrow rim bearing several barbed prickles, the 4 nutlets together appearing burlike.

Range and Habitat: Manitoba to British Columbia, southward to New Mexico, Arizona, and California. Usually found on brushy slopes or in damp thickets, or occasionally in open areas, throughout New Mexico; 7,000–10,000 ft.

Key Characters: Many-flowered stickseed is distinguished by the slender, many-flowered, one-sided clusters, these tending to curve or coil at the tip.

Related Species: Two other species, also of montane habitats, are *H. grisea*, differing in having stiffer hairs with whitish, bulbous bases and flowers in loose clusters, and *H. pinetorum*, differing in having lance-shaped leaves, those of the midstem conspicuously stalked, and the flowers mostly less than $1/4$ in. (7 mm) wide.

249. Franciscan bluebells — *Mertensia franciscana* — Borage family

Erect perennial, the stems mostly 12–20 in. (30–50 cm) tall. *Leaves* alternate, elliptic to ovate, 2–4 in. (5–10 cm) long, with short, stiff hairs on the upper surface and often nearly smooth beneath, all but the upper leaves stalked. *Flowers* in loose terminal clusters, funnel-shaped, 5-lobed, bluish or whitish, the tube $3/16$–$3/8$ in. (5–9 mm) long, the calyx divided nearly to the base, and fringed with hairs on the margins.

Range and Habitat: Colorado to Utah and Nevada, southward to New Mexico and Arizona. Scattered in damp meadows or along streams in the mountains throughout New Mexico; 7,000–11,500 ft.

Key Characters: Franciscan bluebells can be recognized by the blue or white, bell-shaped or funnel-shaped flowers with small crestlike projections in the throat and the usually lance-shaped leaves with short, stiff hairs on the upper surface.

Related Species: Similar species include the several varieties of *M. lanceolata*, differing in having the calyx divided not more than two-thirds of the distance to the base; *M. ciliata*, differing in having leaves with a marginal fringe of stiff hairs; *M. viridis*, differing in having the upper leaves without hairs on both surfaces; and *M. alpina*, differing in having stems not more than 8 in. (20 cm) tall and basal leaves with winged stalks.

Cynoglossum officinale

Hackelia floribunda

Mertensia franciscana

207

250. Smooth-throated puccoon   *Lithospermum cobrense*   Borage family

Biennial or perennial herb, the stems 6–16 in. (15–40 cm) tall, stiffly hairy. *Leaves* alternate, stiffly hairy, linear to narrowly lance-shaped, ³/₄–2 in. (20–50 mm) long. *Flowers* pale yellow, the corolla funnel-shaped with the tube not more than ³/₈ in. (10 mm) long and the lobes with smooth margins, the flower about ³/₈ in. (10 mm) wide, the inner surface of the tube smooth.

Range and Habitat: Western Texas to Arizona. Scattered on wooded slopes in the mountains of central and southern New Mexico; 5,000–9,000 ft.

Key Characters: Smooth-throated puccoon is distinguished by the pale yellow, funnel-shaped flowers with the corolla tube not more than ³/₈ in. (10 mm) long and with the inner surface smooth and without crestlike appendages.

251. Large-flowered gromwell   *Macromeria viridiflora*   Borage family

Coarse, erect, perennial bearing bristly hairs, the stems mostly 15–32 in. (40–80 cm) tall. *Leaves* alternate, lance-shaped, without marginal teeth, 2–4¹/₂ in. (5–12 cm) long, strongly veined. *Flowers* in terminal, recurved, bracteate, loose clusters, greenish yellow, tubular-funnelform, mostly ³/₄–1⁵/₈ in. (20–40 mm) long, much longer than the calyx, with 5 short lobes.

Range and Habitat: New Mexico and Arizona to Mexico. Usually found on rocky, often wooded slopes in the mountains of southern New Mexico; 6,500–9,000 ft.

Key Characters: Large-flowered gromwell is easily recognized by the coarse stems and leaves bearing bristly hairs, the strongly veined leaf blades, and the elongate, tubular, greenish yellow flowers.

Related Species: A similar species in another genus, *Onosmodium occidentale* (false gromwell), differs in having much smaller flowers and the stamens not projecting beyond the corolla.

252. Longleaf cryptantha   *Cryptantha flavoculata*   Borage family

Perennial herb, the stems mostly 4–12 in. (10–30 cm) tall, covered with stiffish hairs. *Leaves* alternate, spatula-shaped, ³/₄–4 in. (2–10 cm) long, with both soft and stiff hairs, those of the lower surface enlarged at the base. *Flowers* in narrow, usually recurved or coiled, 1-sided clusters, the corolla white to pale yellow, with the tube ¹/₄–³/₈ in. (7–10 mm) long, and spreading to ¹/₄–³/₈ in. (7–10 mm) at the top, funnel-shaped. *Fruits* of small, minutely warty nutlets.

Range and Habitat: Wyoming to California, southward to Mexico. Dry open areas from north-central to south-central and western New Mexico; 5,000–6,500 ft.

Key Characters: Longleaf cryptantha is distinguished by the long, narrow leaves, these often 2¹/₂–4 in. (6–10 cm) long, and the conspicuous white or yellowish, funnel-shaped flowers.

Related Species: The widespread and similar *C. jamesii* and its complex of several varieties differs in having only white flowers with a corolla tube only about ¹/₈ in. (3 mm) long and conspicuous appendages (crests) in the throat.

Lithospermum cobrense

Macromeria viridiflora

Cryptantha flavoculata

| 253. **Lemon verbena** | *Aloysia lycioides* | Vervain family |

Aromatic shrub, the stems branched, to 5 ft. (1 1/2 m) tall, often densely covered with minute hairs. *Leaves* on very short stalks, lance-shaped to elliptic, to 1 1/4 in. (30 mm) long, without teeth or rarely with a few minute teeth, with hairs on the upper surface, densely short hairy and glandular dotted beneath. *Flowers* in dense spikes, in opposite pairs in the axils of the leaves, the calyx densely hairy and with lobes unequal in length, the corolla tubelike, white or blue, about 1/8 in. (3 mm) wide, with soft hairs in the throat, and 4 stamens. *Fruit* a pair of nutlets enclosed in the calyx.

Range and Habitat: Western Texas to Arizona, southward to South America. Usually found on dry, rocky slopes, often associated with limestone deposits, in southern New Mexico; 3,000–4,000 ft.

Key Characters: Lemon verbena is easily recognized by its shrubby habit and pleasant aroma, the leaves opposite and without teeth, and the flowers in dense spikes on opposite sides of the stems.

Related Species: The only related species in New Mexico is the also shrubby *A. wrightii,* from central and southern areas, differing in having leaves regularly toothed and with the lower surfaces finely woolly.

| 254. **Wedgeleaf phyla** | *Phyla cuneifolia* | Vervain family |

Creeping perennial herb, the stems to about 3 ft. (1 m) long, variously hairy. *Leaves* narrowly wedge-shaped, 1/2–1 1/4 in. (12–30 mm) long, with 1–4 pairs of teeth above the middle on the margins. *Flowers* in small rounded heads subtended by bracts, the corolla white or purple, 2-lipped, the upper lip notched, the lower lip 3-toothed. *Fruits* of a pair of nutlets enclosed in the calyx.

Range and Habitat: South Dakota and Wyoming to Mexico. Mostly found in dry stream beds and playas throughout New Mexico; 4,000–6,000 ft.

Key Characters: Wedgeleaf phyla is distinguished by the narrowly wedge-shaped, toothed leaves, the whitish or purplish flowers about 3/16 in. (5 mm) long, and the slender, creeping stems.

Related Species: The somewhat similar *P. incisa,* from central and southern areas, differs in having the flower heads on stalks extending much beyond the leaves.

| 255. **Creeping vervain** | *Verbena ciliata* | Vervain family |

Low, branching herb, the stems often creeping or sometimes slightly ascending, to 20 in. (50 cm) long, hairy. *Leaves* opposite, cleft into narrow lobes or teeth and rolled under on the margins. *Flowers* in somewhat flattened, headlike clusters, rose purple, subtended by lance-shaped bracts fringed with conspicuous hairs, the corolla tubular but with the lobes turned abruptly outward, the tube about 3/8 in. (10 mm) long, the limb about 1/4 in. (7 mm) wide.

Range and Habitat: Western Texas to Arizona and Mexico. Usually found on open plains or on open or wooded slopes from central to southern and western New Mexico; 3,500–7,500 ft.

Key Characters: Creeping vervain is distinguished by the often creeping stems, the dense, somewhat headlike clusters of rose purple flowers subtended by bracts conspicuously fringed with hairs, and the opposite leaves divided into at least 3 narrow lobes.

Related Species: The similar *V. bipinnatifida* differs in having the stems ascending and the floral bracts without a conspicuous fringe of marginal hairs.

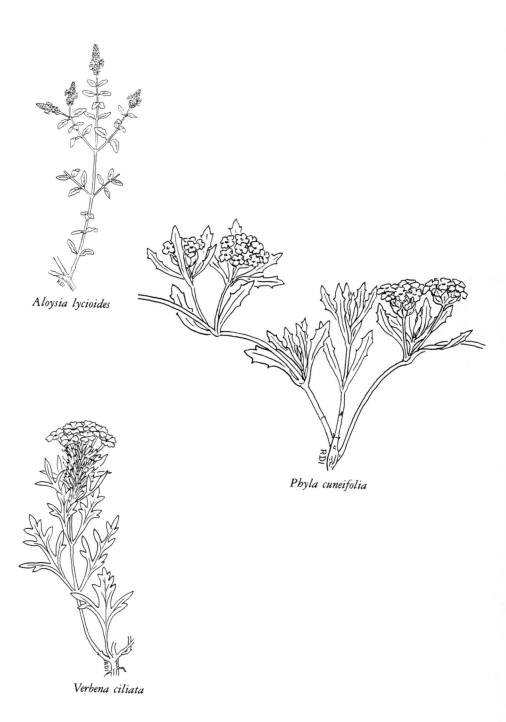

Aloysia lycioides

Phyla cuneifolia

Verbena ciliata

256. **Western vervain**   *Verbena ambrosiaefolia*   Vervain family

Prostrate to spreading herb, the stems 8–18 in. (20–45 cm) long, hairy. *Leaves* opposite, hairy, to about 2 1/2 in. (60 mm) long, pinnately divided into several segments, with each segment further divided into lance-shaped lobes. *Flowers* in somewhat flattened, headlike clusters, the flowers subtended by hairy, lance-shaped floral bracts, these shorter than the glandular calyx, the corolla pinkish or purplish, longer than the calyx, about 1/4 in. (6–8 mm) wide at the summit. *Fruits* of 4 small nutlets.

Range and Habitat: Oklahoma and Colorado to Texas, Arizona, and Mexico. Locally common on dry plains and slopes throughout New Mexico; 4,000–6,000 ft.

Key Characters: Western vervain is distinguished by the pinkish or purplish flowers in dense, relatively broad, headlike clusters with the corolla tube about 3/8 in. (10 mm) or more long and the ultimate leaf segments lance-shaped.

Related Species: The also relatively common *V. wrightii* differs in having the stems mostly erect or ascending and the calyx teeth not more than 1/8 in. (2 mm) in length.

257. **New Mexico vervain**   *Verbena neomexicana*   Vervain family

Erect herb, the stems mostly 12–32 in. (30–80 cm) tall. *Leaves* opposite, mostly 1 1/4–3 1/2 in. (30–84 mm) long, sharply toothed to somewhat pinnately lobed. *Flowers* bluish or purplish, in slender, elongate, interrupted spikes, the fruiting calyx longer than the floral bracts, the corolla about 3/16–3/8 in. (4–8 mm) wide. *Fruits* of 4 small nutlets.

Range and Habitat: Western Texas to Arizona and Mexico. Found in many habitats, especially in open, often sandy areas in southern New Mexico; 3,000–8,000 ft.

Key Characters: New Mexico vervain is distinguished by the sharply toothed or lobed leaves, the mostly upright stems, and the small, pinkish or purplish flowers in slender, interrupted spikes.

Related Species: A species of dry plains of eastern and southern New Mexico, *V. plicata,* differs in having the leaves usually folded into pleats and the veins whitish near the margins of the leaves.

258. **Western spike vervain**   *Verbena macdougalii*   Vervain family

Stout, erect herb, the stems to 3 ft. (1 m) tall, sometimes with branches near the summit. *Leaves* opposite, hairy, somewhat elliptic to broadly lance-shaped, 2 3/8–4 1/2 in. (6–12 cm) long, short-stalked, irregularly and often coarsely toothed, wrinkled. *Flowers* numerous, in one or several cylindrical spikes subtended by leaves at the base, the floral bracts longer than the calyx, the corolla blue or purple, about 1/4 in. (5–7 mm) long and as wide. *Fruits* of 4 small nutlets.

Range and Habitat: Wyoming to western Texas, New Mexico, and Arizona. Usually associated with open meadows or high valleys in the mountains throughout New Mexico; 7,000–8,500 ft.

Key Characters: Western spike vervain is easily recognized by the tall, stout, sparingly branched stem, the toothed, thickened, somewhat wrinkled leaves, and the small flowers in cylindrical spikes.

Verbena ambrosiaefolia

Verbena neomexicana

Verbena macdougalii

213

259. **Bigbract vervain**   *Verbena bracteata*   Vervain family

Diffusely branched herb, the stems decumbent to spreading upward, to about 16 in. (40 cm) long, hairy. *Leaves* opposite, to about 1⅝ in. (40 mm) long, divided into 3 main divisions, with each division sharply toothed or cleft, the middle division larger than the laterals. *Flowers* in robust, elongate spikes ⅜ in. (10 mm) or more wide, the floral bracts usually at least twice as long as the calyx, hairy, usually recurved in age, the corolla pale blue to purple, slightly longer than the calyx and ⅛ in. (3 mm) wide at the summit. *Fruits* of 4 small nutlets.

Range and Habitat: Widely distributed in North America. Mostly on open plains or in fields or waste ground throughout New Mexico; 3,500–7,500 ft.

Key Characters: Bigbract vervain is distinguished by the leaves divided into 3 main divisions, the flowers in thick, elongated spikes, and the conspicuous floral bracts, these much longer than the calyces.

260. **Wild bergamot**   *Monarda menthaefolia*   Mint family

Perennial herb, the stems usually unbranched, to about 32 in. (80 cm) tall, variously hairy. *Leaves* opposite, ovate to lance-shaped, toothed, 1⅝–3¼ in. (4–8 cm) long. *Flowers* in terminal, solitary, conspicuous headlike clusters subtended by large, leaflike, often pinkish bracts, the calyx mostly ⅜ in. (8–10 mm) long, with slenderly pointed teeth, the corolla purplish, about 1¼ in. (30 mm) long, much longer than the calyx, conspicuously 2-lipped, the upper lip arched, the lower lip 3-lobed, the 2 stamens somewhat projecting from the corolla. *Fruits* of 4 small, smooth nutlets.

Range and Habitat: Western Canada to Texas, New Mexico, and Arizona. Usually found on open or wooded slopes in the mountains throughout New Mexico; 5,000–8,500 ft.

Key Characters: Wild bergamot is distinguished by the large, opposite, toothed leaves and the conspicuous terminal heads of purplish 2-lipped flowers.

Related Species: A smaller species from southern New Mexico and occupying about the same elevational range, *M. austromontana* differs in having the leaf margins without teeth or sometimes with minute teeth, the floral bracts strongly reflexed, and the corolla whitish or tinged with purple.

261. **Plains beebalm**   *Monarda pectinata*   Mint family

Slender annual herb, the stems branched from the base, 5–12 in. (12–30 cm) tall, with backward-pointing hairs. *Leaves* opposite, oblong to lance-shaped, to 2 in. (5 cm) long, sometimes toothed. *Flowers* in dense, headlike clusters in the axils of the leaves, the clusters subtended by leaflike, spine-pointed bracts with a fringe of hairs on the margins, the corolla pink or white, tubular, 2-lipped, the lower lip 3-lobed, the corolla tube about 3/16–⅜ in. (5–10 mm) long. *Fruits* of 4 small, smooth nutlets.

Range and Habitat: Nebraska to Utah, southward to Texas, New Mexico, and Arizona. Typically found in open ground of dry plains and hills throughout New Mexico; 5,000–8,000 ft.

Key Characters: Plains beebalm is distinguished by its annual habit, the stems branched from the base, the spine-pointed floral bracts, and the pink or white flowers in small axillary clusters.

Related Species: Another widespread species of about the same elevational range, *M. punctata* (purple-dotted beebalm), differs in having a pale yellowish corolla with purplish spots and recurved floral bracts.

Verbena bracteata

Monarda menthaefolia

Monarda pectinata

215

262. False pennyroyal   *Hedeoma nana*   Mint family

Small perennial herb, the stems erect, branching, mostly 4–12 in. (10–30 cm) tall, with the grayish hairs usually pointing downward. *Leaves* oblong to ovate, ¼–⅜ in. (6–10 mm) long, not stalked, sometimes with minute marginal teeth. *Flowers* small, in clusters in the axils of the upper leaves, the calyx tubelike, conspicuously swollen at the base at maturity, the teeth spreading, 2-lipped, those of the lower lip much longer than those of the upper lip, the corolla purplish, about ¼–⅜ in. (6–8 mm) long, 2-lipped, the upper lip 3-lobed, the lower lip 2-lobed and usually marked with white, with 2 stamens. *Fruits* of 4 smooth nutlets.
Range and Habitat: Western Texas to California, southward into Mexico. Often abundant on dry hills and rocky slopes in central and southern New Mexico; 3,500–5,500 ft.
Key Characters: False pennyroyal is distinguished by the slender stems with recurved hairs, the small, opposite, usually toothless leaves, the calyx lobes of the lower lip much longer than those of the upper lip, and the purplish corolla marked with white on the lower lip.
Related Species: A widespread also perennial species found on dry hills and plains, *H. drummondii*, differs in having the teeth of the calyx converging and essentially closing the orifice of the floral tube.

263. **Davidson sage**   *Salvia davidsonii*   Mint family

Square-stemmed perennial herb, the stems to 16 in. (40 cm) tall. *Leaves* opposite, pinnately compound, to about 3 in. (7 cm) long, the 3 leaflets usually rounded or triangular and coarsely toothed, the terminal leaflet larger than the others. *Flowers* conspicuous, somewhat tubular, 1–1⅜ in. (25–35 mm) long, red, 2-lipped, the upper lip arched.
Range and Habitat: New Mexico and Arizona. Associated with rocky slopes in extreme southwestern New Mexico; 5,000–7,000 ft.
Key Characters: Davidson sage is characterized by the pinnately compound leaves with 3 coarsely toothed leaflets and the conspicuous, red, tubular, 2-lipped flowers.
Related Species: Another spectacular red-flowered sage, *S. henryi*, differs in having mostly 3–5 leaflets, with the terminal leaflet much larger than the laterals and strongly irregularly toothed or lobed.

264. **Mealycup sage**   *Salvia farinosa*   Mint family

Large perennial herb, the stems about 24–40 in. (60–100 cm) tall, covered with very short hairs. *Leaves* linear to narrowly oblong, mostly 1¼–3¼ in. (3–8 cm) long and ⅛–¾ in. (3–20 mm) wide, at least the lower ones irregularly toothed. *Flowers* in dense, often woolly clusters at the upper nodes, bluish or purplish, somewhat tubular, ¾–1 in. (20–25 mm) long, 2-lipped, the calyx with whitish or bluish hairs and squared off at the top.
Range and Habitat: Western Texas and New Mexico. Usually found in limestone soils of plains, slopes, and canyons of southern New Mexico; 3,500–7,000 ft.
Key Characters: Mealycup sage may be recognized by the long, narrow leaves, the dense clusters of bluish or purplish flowers, and the whitish or bluish, hairy calyx.
Related Species: The lovely blue sage, *S. azurea*, differs in having the calyx sparingly marked with minute hairs and in the conspicuous calyx teeth.

Hedeoma nana

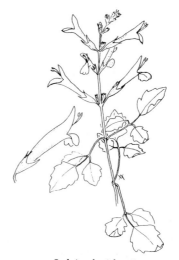

Salvia davidsonii

Salvia farinosa

217

265. **Cutleaf germander** *Teucrium laciniatum* Mint family

Square-stemmed perennial herb, the stems hairy, leafy, to about 8 in. (20 cm) tall, branched at the base. *Leaves* opposite, pinnately divided to the middle into narrow lobes. *Flowers* scattered, somewhat funnel-shaped, bluish or purplish, 1/2–3/4 in. (12–20 mm) long, 2-lipped, with the upper lip much shorter than the lower, the calyx with 10 ribs.
Range and Habitat: Oklahoma to Texas, westward to Colorado and New Mexico. Associated with open plains and meadows in all but western New Mexico; 4,000–7,500 ft.
Key Characters: Cutleaf germander is characterized by the leaves deeply divided into narrow lateral lobes and by the flowers with the upper lip much shorter than the lower one.
Related Species: The less common western germander, *T. canadense*, differs in having the leaves merely toothed and hairy beneath and the calyx toothed rather than deeply lobed.

266. **Woundwort** *Stachys palustris* Mint family

Perennial herb, the stems mostly 10–24 in. (25–60 cm) tall, both stems and leaves covered with spreading hairs. *Leaves* opposite, oblong to lance-shaped, 5/8–2 1/2 in. (15–65 mm) long, 3/8–5/8 in. (8–15 mm) wide, sessile or on short stalks, squarish or often heart-shaped at the base, toothed. *Flowers* in clusters at the upper nodes, subtended by leaflike bracts, the corolla somewhat tubular, 2-lipped, pinkish purple, about 3/8–5/8 in. (10–15 mm) long, the calyx nearly as long as the corolla tube, with 5 nearly equal, slender-pointed teeth and a ring of soft hairs inside and below the middle of the tube.
Range and Habitat: Alberta to New Mexico and Arizona, also in Europe and Asia. Usually associated with moist, shady places throughout New Mexico; 6,500–9,000 ft.
Key Characters: Woundwort may be recognized by the stems and leaves with spreading hairs, the opposite, nearly sessile leaves, and the pinkish purple flowers with the corolla tube about as long as the calyx.
Related Species: Scarlet hedge nettle, *S. coccinea*, one of our showiest wildflowers but southern and western in distribution, differs in having leaves on stalks at least 1/2 in. (12 mm) long, and conspicuous bright red flowers, these much longer than the calyx.

267. **Common selfheal** *Prunella vulgaris* Mint family

Square-stemmed perennial, the stems erect to somewhat creeping, mostly 4–20 in. (10–50 cm) long. *Leaves* oblong to lance-shaped, opposite, obscurely toothed, 3/4–2 5/8 in. (20–65 mm) long, on stalks at least 3/8 in. (10 mm) long. *Flowers* in dense terminal spikes, each flower subtended by a broad bract, the corolla violet, somewhat tubular, 2-lipped, the upper lip 3-toothed and arched, the stamens 4, under the upper lip, the calyx reddish purple, 2-lipped, 10-ribbed.
Range and Habitat: Throughout cooler areas of North America and Eurasia. Mostly found in moist ground throughout New Mexico; 5,500–9,500 ft.
Key Characters: Selfheal is easily recognized by the violet flowers in dense, conspicuously bracted spikes, the corollas and calyces 2-lipped, and the reddish purple calyx tube.

Teucrium laciniatum

Stachys palustris

Prunella vulgaris

268. **Pallid giant hyssop**   *Agastache pallidiflora*   Mint family

Square-stemmed perennial herb, the stems erect, minutely hairy, mostly 12–24 in. (30–60 cm) tall. *Leaves* triangular-ovate or triangular, coarsely toothed, ³/₄–2 in. (2–5 cm) long, stalked, opposite. *Flowers* in cylindrical, spikelike clusters 1¹/₄–3 in. (3–8 cm) long, the corolla 2-lipped, whitish, the tube ³/₁₆–³/₈ in. (5–8 mm) long, the calyx 15-nerved, often tinged with pink, with slender triangular teeth about ¹/₈ in. (3 mm) long.
Range and Habitat: Colorado to New Mexico and Arizona. Mostly found on wooded slopes throughout all but eastern New Mexico; 7,000–10,000 ft.
Key Characters: Pallid giant hyssop can be recognized by the opposite, triangular, coarsely toothed leaves and the whitish, 2-lipped flowers with 4 projecting stamens, the flowers in terminal, spikelike clusters.
Related Species: A variety of pallid giant hyssop and possibly more widespread, var. *neomexicana,* differs only in having deeply rose purple flowers and calyces. A similar plant having a more southern distribution, *A. wrightii,* also has purplish corollas but with calyx only about half as long as that of the pallid giant hyssop.

269. **Field mint**   *Mentha arvensis*   Mint family

Aromatic perennial herb from creeping rootstocks, the stems 6–30 in. (15–80 cm) tall, often branched, 4-angled. *Leaves* opposite, oblong to ovate, ³/₄–2³/₈ in. (20–60 mm) long, toothed on the margins, distinctly stalked. *Flowers* in clusters in the axils of the upper leaves, the corolla pink to violet or white, tubular, about ¹/₄ in. (4–6 mm) long, with 5 nearly equal lobes, the calyx ¹/₈ in. (3 mm) long, 10-ribbed, with 5 narrowly triangular teeth. *Fruits* of 4 smooth nutlets.
Range and Habitat: Widespread in North America. Mostly found in damp ground throughout New Mexico; 4,500–9,000 ft.
Key Characters: Field mint is characterized by the square stems, the opposite, toothed leaves, the flowers in dense clusters in the axils of the upper leaves, and the nearly regular corollas.
Related Species: The introduced but widespread roundleaf mint, *M. rotundifolia,* differs in having nearly sessile, heart-shaped leaves and flowers in slender, terminal spikes.

270. **Horehound**   *Marrubium vulgare*   Mint family

Coarse perennial herb, the stems erect, square in cross section, densely white-woolly, to 3 ft. (1 m) tall. *Leaves* opposite, mostly ovate to somewhat rounded, ³/₄–1⁵/₈ in. (20–40 mm) long and nearly as wide, with wrinkled surface and margins with rounded teeth, at least the lower surface woolly. *Flowers* in dense clusters in the axils of the upper leaves, white to purplish, the corolla somewhat tubular, about ³/₈ in. (10 mm) long, 2-lipped, the notched upper lip erect, the 3-lobed lower lip spreading, the 4 stamens included in the corolla, the calyx with 10 ribs and spreading, hooked teeth. *Fruits* of 4 roughened, black nutlets.
Range and Habitat: Introduced from Europe and Asia, now widely distributed in North America, especially in temperate areas. Mostly associated with damp ground throughout New Mexico; 5,000–7,500 ft.
Key Characters: Horehound is easily recognized by the often somewhat rounded, opposite leaves with rounded marginal teeth, the whitish to purplish flowers in clusters in the axils of the leaves, and the calyces with 10 rigid, hooked teeth.

Agastache pallidiflora

Mentha arvensis

Marrubium vulgare

221

271. **Jimsonweed**   *Datura meteloides*   Nightshade family

Coarse, spreading, foul-smelling annual or perennial herb, the stems branching, to about 4 1/2 ft. (1.5 m) tall. *Leaves* ovate, stalked, 2–8 in. (5–20 cm) long, often irregularly wavy-toothed on the margins. *Flowers* large, solitary, the corolla white to violet, somewhat fragrant, funnel-shaped, 6–8 in. (15–20 cm) long, 5-toothed, the calyx about half as long as the corolla tube, 5-lobed. *Fruit* nodding, globe-shaped, 1 1/4–1 5/8 in. (3–4 cm) in diameter, spiny, opening irregularly. This plant is also known as thorn apple or Indian apple.
Range and Habitat: Colorado and Texas to southern California and Mexico. Usually scattered on open, often waste ground throughout New Mexico; 3,000–6,500 ft
Key Characters: Jimsonweed may be recognized by the large, foul-smelling, ovate leaves and the conspicuous funnel-shaped flowers, these unlobed but with 5 slender teeth.
Related Species: The also widespread but probably less common *D. stramonium* differs in having the corolla only 2–3 1/4 in. (5–8 cm) long and the capsule erect, ovoid, and regularly dehiscent.

272. **Desert tobacco**   *Nicotiana trigonophylla*   Nightshade family

Stout herb with few branches, the stems to about 32 in. (80 cm) tall, sticky with gland-tipped hairs. *Leaves* scattered, the basal leaves stalked, the stem leaves usually sessile, clasping the stem by earlike lobes at the base, 3/4–2 3/8 in. (2–8 cm) long, the margins usually without teeth. *Flowers* in loose clusters, the corolla greenish white, tubular, about 3/4 in. (20 mm) long, constricted at the base of the lobes, about 3/8 in. (8–10 mm) wide at the top. *Fruit* a many-seeded capsule about 3/8 in. (10 mm) long.
Range and Habitat: Western Texas to California and Mexico. Found mostly in canyons and gravelly washes, often in partial shade, in southern New Mexico; 3,500–6,000 ft.
Key Characters: Desert tobacco may be recognized by the stems with sticky hairs, the upper leaves clasping the stem, and the greenish white, tubular flowers.
Related Species: The less common tree tobacco, *N. glauca,* differs in having smooth stems, oval leaves, and a longer, yellowish corolla. The coyote tobacco, *N. attenuata,* differs in having stalked, never clasping leaves and flowers that open only at night.

273. **Blue-flowered wolfberry**   *Lycium berlandieri*   Nightshade family

Stout, much branched shrub, the stems to 6 ft. (2 m) tall, the branches grayish, often ending in slender spines. *Leaves* often in clusters, otherwise alternate, linear to spatula-shaped, 3/8–1 in. (10–25 mm) long and about 1/8 in. (2–3 mm) wide, rounded to acute at the tip. *Flowers* solitary or clustered, about 1/4 in. (5–7 mm) long, somewhat funnel-shaped, the short lobes pinkish. *Fruit* red, berrylike, about 1/4 in. (5–8 mm) long.
Range and Habitat: Texas to Arizona and Mexico. Locally common on dry plains in southern New Mexico; 3,500–5,500 ft.
Key Characters: Blue-flowered wolfberry can be recognized by the numerous branches, often ending in spines, the often clustered, mostly narrowly spatula-shaped leaves, and the bluish, funnel-shaped flowers.
Related Species: There are several other species of wolfberries having a similar growth habit, but these are spring-flowering forms, typically with whitish or greenish flowers.

Datura meteloides

Nicotiana trigonophylla

Lycium berlandieri

223

274. **Purple groundcherry**   *Physalis lobata*   Nightshade family

Perennial herb, the stems branching from the base, 4–8 in. (10–20 cm) tall, with small, bladderlike structures on the surface. *Leaves* lance-shaped in outline, 1⅛–4 in. (4–10 cm) long, wavy or lobed on the margins, tapering to a winged stalk at the base. *Flowers* axillary, wheel-shaped, mostly blue, ⅝–¾ in. (15–20 mm) wide, the 5 stamens with clusters of hairs between the filaments, the anthers yellow and conspicuous, the calyx, in fruit greatly inflated, resembling a small Japanese lantern, 5-angled. *Fruit* a globose berry surrounded by the large, persistent calyx.

Range and Habitat: Kansas and Texas to Colorado, Nevada, and Arizona. Usually found in waste ground, on open prairies, or in foothills throughout New Mexico; 4,000–6,000 ft.

Key Characters: Purple groundcherry is easily recognized by the low, spreading habit, the stems covered with minute bladderlike structures, the often pinnately lobed leaves, and the greatly enlarged, inflated, 5-angled calyx.

275. **New Mexico groundcherry**   *Physalis foetens*   Nightshade family

Branching annual, the stems to about 24 in. (60 cm) tall, both stems and leaves densely hairy with glandular hairs. *Leaves* alternate, the blades ovate, 1¼–2 in. (30–65 mm) long, toothed on the margins, on stalks about one-half to three-fourths as long as the blade. *Flowers* solitary or clustered, the corolla yellow with bluish basal spots, about ¼ in. (7 mm) long, the 5 anthers bluish, the calyx greatly inflated and conspicuously angled in fruit, ¾–1¼ in. (20–30 mm) long. *Fruit* a fleshy, globose berry, completely surrounded by the inflated calyx.

Range and Habitat: Colorado to New Mexico and Arizona. Usually found on mountain slopes among junipers or pines but sometimes seen in waste or cultivated ground, throughout New Mexico; 5,000–7,500 ft.

Key Characters: New Mexico groundcherry can be recognized by the annual habit, the stems and leaves with dense glandular hairs, and the yellow corolla with bluish basal spots.

Related Species: The similar *P. virginiana*, represented in New Mexico by several varieties, differs in having a perennial growth habit, flowers on stalks less than ⅜ in. (10 mm) long, usually erect rather than incurved corolla lobes, and stems and leaves with nonglandular hairs. The groundcherries comprise a very complex assemblage of similar taxa, the delimitation of which is beyond the scope of this book.

276. **Buffalo bur**   *Solanum rostratum*   Nightshade family

Much branched annual, the stems to about 24 in. (60 cm) high, both stems and leaves densely covered with stellate hairs and armed with numerous slender, yellowish prickles. *Leaves* simple, alternate, stalked, 1⅛–4¾ in. (4–12 cm) long, irregularly pinnately or bipinnately lobed. *Flowers* in terminal or axillary clusters, the corolla yellow, with 5 angular lobes, ¾–1¼ in. (20–30 mm) wide, 5 yellow stamens with 1 of them larger than the other 4, the calyx prickly and persistently and closely surrounding the fruit. *Fruit* a many-seeded berry, appearing prickly because of the surrounding calyx.

Range and Habitat: North Dakota to New Mexico, Arizona, and Mexico. Associated with open disturbed or waste ground throughout New Mexico; 4,000–7,000 ft.

Key Characters: Buffalo bur is easily recognized by the annual habit, the strongly lobed leaves, the herbage and calyx bearing numerous slender spines, and the yellow flowers with angulate lobes.

Related Species: The similar and also widespread melonleaf nightshade, *S. heterodoxum*, differs in having purple flowers and greenish brown prickles. Several other summer-flowering species include the wild potatoes, *S. jamesii*, with white, deeply lobed flowers, and *S. fendleri*, with purplish, angulately lobed flowers, both with underground tubers similar to small potatoes.

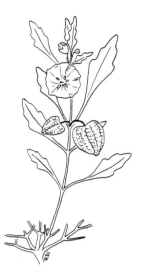

Physalis lobata

Physalis foetens

Solanum rostratum

225

277. **Horse-nettle**   *Solanum elaeagnifolium*   Nightshade family

Perennial herb, the stems to nearly 3 ft. (1 m) tall, both stems and leaves covered with silvery, star-shaped hairs and often bearing slender, sharp spines. *Leaves* scattered, oblong to lance-shaped, 1½–4 in. (4–10 cm) long, the margins often wavy-toothed. *Flowers* in small clusters, usually purple, 5-lobed, about ¾–1¼ in. (20–30 mm) wide, with 5 conspicuous yellow anthers about 5/16 in. (8 mm) long. *Fruit* a globelike berry about 5/16–5/8 in. (8–15 mm) in diameter. This is a weedy but attractive plant.

Range and Habitat: Kansas to California, southward to tropical America. Typically associated with waste ground throughout New Mexico; 3,500–6,500 ft.

Key Characters: Horse-nettle is characterized by the upright, spiny stems with numerous star-shaped hairs, the usually wavy-margined leaves, and the loose clusters of conspicuous, purplish flowers with large yellow anthers.

278. **Arizona nightshade**   *Solanum douglasii*   Nightshade family

Large perennial herb, the stems angled, to about 3 ft. (1 m) tall. *Leaves* alternate, stalked, ovate, to about 4 in. (10 cm) long, smooth-margined or coarsely toothed. *Flowers* in small clusters, the corolla white with greenish spots at the base, about 3/8–3/4 in. (10–18 mm) wide, deeply 5-lobed, the stamens with hairy stalks. *Fruit* a black berry.

Range and Habitat: Oregon to Nevada, New Mexico, and southern California. Usually associated with canyons and rocky slopes from central to south-central and western New Mexico; 4,500–7,500 ft.

Key Characters: Arizona nightshade can be distinguished by the simple, unlobed leaves and the white flowers with greenish basal spots.

Related Species: A species found throughout much of western North America, *S. triflorum* differs mostly in its annual habit and the deeply pinnately lobed leaves.

279. **Black nightshade**   *Solanum nigrum*   Nightshade family

Branching annual, the stems to 32 in. (80 cm) long, often without hairs. *Leaves* lance-shaped to ovate, stalked, 1¼–3¼ in. (3–8 cm) long, without marginal teeth or sometimes irregularly toothed. *Flowers* in small clusters, about ¼–3/8 in. (5–10 mm) wide, white with small yellowish basal spots, deeply lobed. *Fruit* a dull black berry about ¼–3/8 in. (5–8 mm) in diameter.

Range and Habitat: Introduced from Europe, now widespread in North America. Usually scattered in waste ground or sometimes in partially shaded areas in New Mexico; 4,500–7,000 ft.

Key Characters: Black nightshade may be distinguished by the nearly hairless stems and leaves, the leaves without teeth or sometimes irregularly toothed, and the white flowers with minute yellowish basal spots.

Related Species: The similar, widespread, common nightshade, *S. americanum,* differs in having thin, translucent leaves and lustrous black berries.

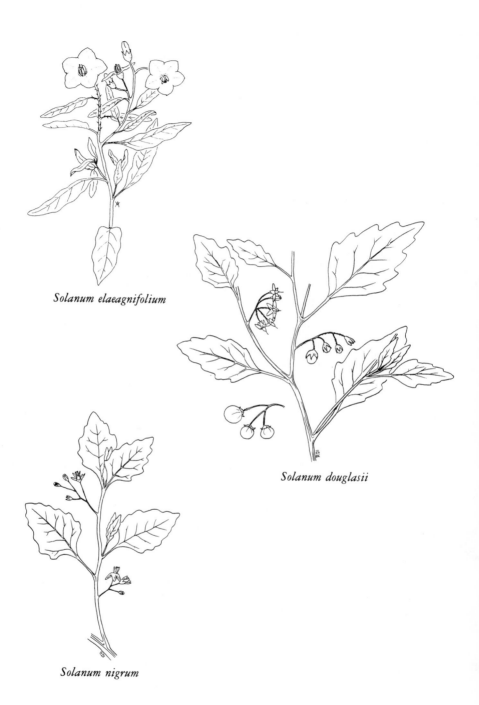

Solanum elaeagnifolium

Solanum douglasii

Solanum nigrum

227

280.　**Scurfy groundcherry**　　*Chamaesaracha coronopus*　　Nightshade family

Low, often prostrate perennial herb, the stems branching, mostly 4–8 in. (10–20 cm) long, covered with small, scalelike, star-shaped hairs as well as longer hairs. *Leaves* linear to lance-shaped or sometimes broader toward the tip, usually with wavy lobes or teeth, about 2–2³/₈ in. (5–6 cm) long. *Flowers* solitary or few in a cluster, yellow or greenish, sometimes tinged with purple, about ³/₈ in. (10 mm) wide, 5-angled, the calyx hairy with often branched hairs. *Fruit* a whitish berry about ¹/₄ in. (6–8 mm) in diameter.
Range and Habitat: Kansas to Utah, southward to Mexico. Mostly scattered on open, dry plains or low hills, or in valleys throughout New Mexico; 3,500–7,000 ft.
Key Characters: Scurfy groundcherry can be distinguished by the low, spreading habit, the stems and leaves covered with scalelike hairs, the narrow leaves with usually wavy margins, and the yellowish or greenish flowers.
Related Species: The widespread, locally abundant *C. conioides* differs in having the stems and leaves sticky and covered with short hairs and often some long hairs and lance-shaped to ovate, often deeply lobed leaves.

281.　**Miner's candle**　　*Verbascum thapsus*　　Figwort family

Coarse biennial herb, the stems to about 6 ft. (2 m) tall, both stems and leaves densely covered by soft, branched hairs, giving the surfaces a flannellike appearance. *Leaves* alternate, elliptic to lance-shaped, to about 16 in. (40 cm) long, the base extending down the stem for a distance below the point of attachment. *Flowers* in dense terminal or lateral spikes, the corolla yellow, nearly regular, about ⁵/₈–1 in. (15–25 mm) wide, the 5 lobes rounded, the 5 stamens projecting from the corolla. *Fruit* a woolly capsule with many roughened seeds.
Range and Habitat: Introduced from Europe, now widespread in temperate North America. Typically found in waste ground throughout New Mexico; 6,000–8,500 ft.
Key Characters: Miner's candle is easily recognized by the stiffly erect stems, the woolly herbage, and the yellow flowers in dense spikes.

282.　**Dalmatian toadflax**　　*Linaria dalmatica*　　Figwort family

Perennial herb, the stems erect, coarse, to about 3 ft. (1 m) tall. *Leaves* alternate or opposite, mostly ovate to lance-shaped, ⁵/₈–1⁵/₈ in. (15–40 mm) long, without teeth or lobes, clasping the stem at the point of attachment. *Flowers* in terminal racemes, yellow, strongly 2-lipped, 1¹/₄–1⁵/₈ in. (30–40 mm) long, the corolla tube bearing a spurlike projection about ⁵/₈ in. (15 mm) long, the base of the lower lip with a prominent inner projection, the 4 stamens not projecting beyond the corolla. *Fruit* a nearly globe-shaped, many-seeded capsule, opening at the apex.
Range and Habitat: Introduced from Europe, now widespread but seldom abundant in temperate North America. Usually associated with waste ground, often along roadsides in central and south-central New Mexico, probably elsewhere; 4,000–6,000 ft.
Key Characters: Dalmatian toadflax can be recognized by the conspicuous yellow, spurred flowers and the alternate or opposite leaves with the base clasping the stem.
Related Species: The also introduced butter-and-eggs, *L. vulgaris,* from northern counties above 6,000 ft. differs in having the yellow flowers with an orange projection in the throat and narrowly linear leaves. The typically spring-blooming blue toadflax, *L. texana,* sometimes blooms in early summer and differs in having blue flowers.

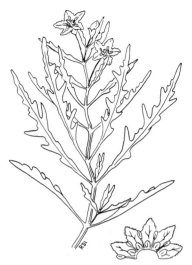

Chamaesaracha coronopus

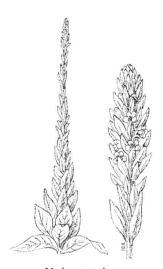

Verbascum thapsus

Linaria dalmatica

229

283.   **Vining snapdragon**   *Maurandya antirrhiniflora*   Figwort family

Vining or prostrate perennial herb, the stems slender, often elongate. *Leaves* scattered, with petioles about as long as the triangular blades, the blades about ³/₈–1 in. (10–25 mm) long, the base broadly notched and spreading into a pair of pointed lobes. *Flowers* conspicuous, solitary, the corolla pink or purple, irregularly funnelform, 5-lobed, 1–1¹/₄ in. (25–30 mm) long, bearing within a yellowish, hairy projection which nearly closes the throat. *Fruit* a globe-shaped capsule about ⁵/₁₆ in. (7–8 mm) in diameter. This attractive plant is a conspicuous part of the flora of sandy slopes.

Range and Habitat: Texas to California and Mexico. Mostly associated with sandy slopes and rocky hills of central and southern New Mexico; 4,000–7,000 ft.

Key Characters: Vining snapdragon is easily recognized by the elongate vining or creeping stems, the triangular leaves, and the conspicuous snapdragonlike flowers.

Related Species: A species with similar appearance, habitat, and distribution, *M. wislizenii,* differs in having often larger leaves, a conspicuously reticulately veined calyx, and a corolla without a hairy projection in the throat.

284.   **Needleleaf beardtongue**   *Penstemon pinifolius*   Figwort family

Perennial herb, the stems clustered, to about 16 in. (40 cm) tall. *Leaves* opposite, more numerous on the lower stem, very slender, somewhat needlelike, less than ¹/₁₆ in. (1 mm) wide. *Flowers* in 1-sided clusters, scarlet, about 1–1¹/₄ in. (25–30 mm) long, with long yellow hairs in the throat, with 4 functional stamens, the fifth stamen represented by an elongate filament bearded with bright yellow hairs for most of its length. *Fruit* a small, ovoid capsule with numerous angular seeds.

Range and Habitat: New Mexico to southwestern Arizona and Mexico. Mostly restricted to rocky slopes and ridges in southwestern New Mexico; 6,000–8,500 ft.

Key Characters: Needleleaf beardtongue is easily distinguished by the markedly slender leaves crowded mostly on the lower part of the stem, the flowers in 1-sided clusters, and the scarlet corollas with conspicuous yellow hairs in the throat.

Related Species: Cardinal beardtongue, *P. cardinalis,* differs in having mostly elliptic to ovate leaves, the flowers dull red or crimson, and the sterile filament bearded only at the tip.

285.   **Virgate beardtongue**   *Penstemon virgatus*   Figwort family

Slender perennial herb, the stems to about 32 in. (80 cm) tall. *Leaves* opposite, linear to narrowly lance-shaped. *Flowers* in narrow, 1-sided clusters, mostly blue or white, rarely pinkish, ⁵/₈–1 in. (15–25 mm) long, usually marked with purplish lines in the broadly expanded throat, sometimes with a few hairs on the lower lip, with 4 functional stamens, the sterile filament without hairs. *Fruit* a small ovoid capsule with numerous angulate seeds.

Range and Habitat: New Mexico and Arizona. Scattered in meadows and woodlands from north-central to southern and western New Mexico; 7,000–8,500 ft.

Key Characters: Virgate beardtongue is distinguished by the slender, often tall, wandlike stems, the blue, white, or pink, tubular, 2-lipped flowers in 1-sided clusters, and the sterile staminal filament without hairs.

Related Species: Often locally abundant in the mountains in most of New Mexico is scarlet beardtongue, *P. barbatus* and its varieties, differing from virgate beardtongue in the conspicuous, scarlet flowers with the lower lip of the corolla strongly bent backward and the flower cluster not 1-sided.

Maurandya antirrhiniflora

Penstemon pinifolius

Penstemon virgatus

286. **Pink plains penstemon**   *Penstemon ambiguus*   Figwort family

Much-branched perennial herb, the stems to about 24 in. (60 cm) tall, covered with minute hairs. *Leaves* opposite, linear, usually inrolled. *Flowers* numerous, in loose clusters, pinkish or purplish, tube-shaped, 5/8–1 in. (15–25 mm) long, somewhat 2-lipped, with rounded lobes, the upper lobes reflexed and the lower ones projecting forward, the 4 stamens not projecting from the corolla, the sterile staminal filament without hairs. *Fruit* a small, many-seeded capsule.

Range and Habitat: Nevada, southward to western Texas and eastern Colorado, New Mexico, and Arizona. Typically found on sandy hills and plains from eastern to central and western New Mexico; 4,500–6,000 ft.

Key Characters: Pink plains penstemon is distinguished by the linear leaves and the pinkish or purplish flowers with rounded, reflexed upper lobes.

287. **Crandall's beardtongue**   *Penstemon crandallii*   Figwort family

Low perennial herb, the stems to about 10 in. (25 cm) tall, often with the lower part of the stem lying down and rooting at the nodes. *Leaves* opposite, linear, about 1/8 in. (1–3 mm) wide, with short hairs along the midvein beneath. *Flowers* in 1-sided, glandular clusters with leaflike floral bracts, the corolla tube-shaped, 2-lipped, 5/8–1 in. (15–25 mm) long, with purplish tube and blue lobes, usually with dark lines in the throat, with 4 functional stamens, the sterile staminal filament bearing bright golden hairs along most of its length. *Fruit* a small capsule with numerous angular seeds.

Range and Habitat: Colorado and New Mexico. Usually found in dry, open areas and associated with pinyons, junipers, and yellow pines in northern New Mexico; 6,000–8,000 ft.

Key Characters: Crandall's beardtongue is recognized by the linear leaves, the bluish purple flowers in 1-sided clusters, the calyx lobes with eroded margins, and the sterile staminal filament with conspicuous bright golden hairs.

Related Species: A species of somewhat lower elevations and usually more open habitats, *P. jamesii* differs in having broader, often toothed leaves, the lower lobes of the corolla prominently bearded at the base with long whitish hairs, and the sterile staminal filament bearing pale yellow hairs at the tip and golden yellow hairs for a distance below the apical cluster.

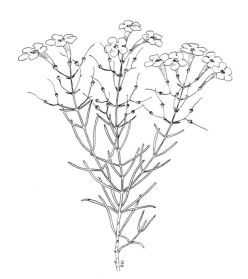

Penstemon ambiguus

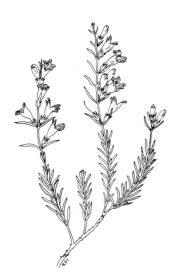

Penstemon crandallii

233

288. **Mountain beardtongue**   *Penstemon oliganthus*   Figwort family

Erect perennial herb, the stems to about 24 in. (60 cm) tall, covered with minute hairs. *Leaves* opposite, the basal ones in a rosette, elliptic to ovate, stalked, the upper leaves linear to lance-shaped, mostly erect. *Flowers* on erect stalks, arranged in small clusters, bluish to reddish purple, about 5/8–1 in. (15–25 mm) long, glandular on the outer surface, the throat much paler than the tube and with 2 prominent ridges, the lower lobes bearded at the base, with 4 functional stamens, the sterile staminal filament bearing numerous yellow hairs. *Fruit* a small capsule with numerous angular seeds.

Range and Habitat: Colorado and New Mexico to Arizona. Usually found in open meadows or on rocky slopes, but sometimes in open woods, from northern to central and western New Mexico; 8,000–9,500 ft.

Key Characters: Mountain beardtongue is distinguished by the basal leaves stalked and in rosettes, the relatively few flowers on mostly erect stalks, the bluish or purplish flowers with the paler throat strongly 2-ridged, and the sterile staminal filament bearing numerous yellowish hairs.

Related Species: Two other montane species with bluish or purplish flowers are Whipple's beardtongue, *P. whippleanus,* often found above 10,000 ft., differing in having a dull purplish corolla and a sterile staminal filament with no hairs or sometimes with a few yellowish hairs at the tip, and stiff beardtongue, *P. strictus,* differing in having flowers in 1-sided clusters, the anthers bearing long, soft, white hairs, and the sterile filament expanded at the tip and usually without hairs.

289. **Purslane speedwell**   *Veronica peregrina*   Figwort family

Small annual, the stems usually erect, bearing gland-tipped hairs. Lower *leaves* often opposite, oblong or broadest above the middle, 3/8–3/4 in. (10–20 mm) long, sometimes toothed, the upper leaves much smaller, alternate, linear or narrowly lance-shaped. *Flowers* solitary in the axils of the upper leaves, white, less than 1/8 in. (2–3 mm) wide, with 4 sepals and petals. *Fruit* a flattened, notched capsule bearing short, gland-tipped hairs.

Range and Habitat: Widespread in North America. Typically found in moist waste ground throughout New Mexico; 6,500–8,000 ft.

Key Characters: Purslane speedwell is characterized by the erect stems, the tiny white flowers, and the notched, glandular fruits.

Related Species: The American brooklime, *V. americana,* mostly found in shallow water of streams, differs in having prostrate, purplish stems and larger bluish flowers with white centers.

Penstemon oliganthus

Veronica peregrina

235

290. Spotted monkeyflower   *Mimulus guttatus*   Figwort family

Perennial herb, the stems erect to creeping. *Leaves* opposite, ovate to oblong, coarsely and irregularly toothed, the lower ones stalked, the upper sessile. *Flowers* solitary in the leaf axils or in racemes, somewhat 2-lipped but 5-lobed, yellow with reddish spots, ³/₄–1⁵/₈ in. (20–40 mm) long, the throat nearly closed by a projection, the calyx about half as long as the corolla, becoming enlarged in fruit, 5-toothed, the upper tooth about twice as long as the others. *Fruit* a capsule enclosed by the persistent calyx.

Range and Habitat: Alaska to New Mexico, California, and Mexico. Usually associated with shallow water or with muddy areas near streams or springs from northern to south-central and western New Mexico; 5,000–10,000 ft.

Key Characters: Spotted monkeyflower is distinguished by the large, yellow, red-spotted flowers, these mostly more than ³/₄ in. (20 mm) long, and the irregular, much enlarged calyx with a strongly projecting upper tooth.

Related Species: Two annual species, both with red-spotted flowers, include *M. cordatus,* differing in having leaves broadly ovate to nearly orbicular and nearly as broad as long and a corolla only ³/₈–³/₄ in. (10–20 mm) long, and *M. floribundus,* differing in having flowers only ³/₈–⁵/₈ in. (8–15 mm) long, the throat not at all obstructed by a projection, and the calyx with all teeth equal in length.

291. Kittentails   *Besseya plantaginea*   Figwort family

Perennial herb, the flowering stems with numerous bractlike leaves, to about 12 in. (30 cm) tall. Basal *leaves* elliptic to ovate, short-stalked, 2–6 in. (5–15 cm) long, with rounded teeth on the margins. *Flowers* in dense, conspicuously bracteate spikes, the floral bracts broadly ovate, the corolla whitish or purplish, somewhat bell-shaped but moderately 2-lipped. *Fruit* a compressed capsule about ¹/₄ in. (6 mm) long.

Range and Habitat: Wyoming to New Mexico and Arizona. Usually found in meadows or on moist wooded slopes from northern to central and western New Mexico; 7,000–10,000 ft.

Key Characters: Kittentails is easily distinguished by the primary leaves in basal clusters, the leafy bracted stems, and the flowers in dense terminal spikes.

Related Species: Arizona kittentails, *B. arizonica,* from similar habitats in northwestern counties, differs in having the basal leaves rounded to heart-shaped at the base, the floral bracts white-fringed, and the flowers with white corollas.

292. Alpine kittentails   *Besseya alpina*   Figwort family

Perennial herb, the flowering stems to about 6 in. (15 cm) tall, with 4–6 leafy bracts bearing soft white hairs, the young stems and leaves woolly. Basal *leaves* with blades mostly ³/₄–2 in. (2–5 cm) long, elliptic to oval, on slender stalks, with rounded teeth on the margins. *Flowers* in dense terminal spikes, violet or purplish, about ¹/₄ in. (6–8 mm) long, 2-lipped, the margin of the upper lip irregularly toothed, and 2 stamens. *Fruit* a compressed capsule.

Range and Habitat: Wyoming to Utah and New Mexico. Usually found in mountain meadows in northern New Mexico; 11,000–13,000 ft.

Key Characters: Alpine kittentails is easily recognized by the short flowering stems with white-fringed bracts and purplish flowers.

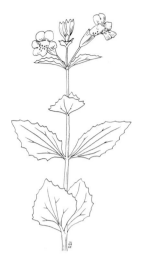

Mimulus guttatus

Besseya alpina

Besseya plantaginea

237

293. **Clubflower**   *Cordylanthus wrightii*   Figwort family

Annual herb, the stems erect, to about 18 in. (45 cm) tall. *Leaves* alternate, divided into several linear, almost threadlike divisions. *Flowers* in dense terminal clusters, each flower subtended by leaflike floral bracts, the corolla yellowish or purplish, tubular, the lobes equal or slightly 2-lipped with the upper lip unlobed and the lower lip 3-toothed, the 4 stamens usually fringed or hairy, the style of the ovary hooked at the tip, the calyx about as long as the corolla, split nearly to the base on both sides. *Fruit* a flattened capsule.
Range and Habitat: Colorado and Utah to Texas, Arizona, and Mexico. Usually found on open, dry plains and hills in the mountains of New Mexico; 5,000–8,000 ft.
Key Characters: Clubflower is distinguished by the leaves divided into mostly 3–5 narrowly linear divisions, the yellowish or purplish tubular flowers, and the conspicuous calyx cleft on both sides nearly to the base.

294. **Elephanthead**   *Pedicularis groenlandica*   Figwort family

Perennial herb, the stems to about 24 in. (60 cm) tall, both leaves and stems mostly without hairs. *Leaves* roughly lance-shaped in outline, parted nearly to the middle into several to many segments, each segment toothed or divided into smaller segments, the larger leaves about 2–4 1/2 in. (5–12 cm) long. *Flowers* in dense terminal spikes, reddish purple, about 3/8 in. (10 mm) long, conspicuously 2-lipped, the upper lip arched and curved downward and projecting into a slender beak which then curves upward, the whole resembling an elephant's head, and 4 stamens. *Fruit* a flattened capsule about 1/4 in. (7 mm) long.
Range and Habitat: Greenland to Alaska, southward in the mountains to New Mexico and California. Typically associated with bogs or wet meadows in the mountains of northern New Mexico; 8,500–12,000 ft.
Key Characters: Elephanthead is easily recognized by the leaves dissected into numerous divisions and the reddish purple flowers resembling a miniature elephant's head.

295. **Gray's lousewort**   *Pedicularis grayi*   Figwort family

Coarse perennial herb, the stems leafy, to 3 ft. (1 m) or more tall. *Leaves* numerous, to about 22 in. (55 cm) long, pinnately divided nearly to the midrib into lance-shaped, toothed or incised segments. *Flowers* numerous, in an elongate, spikelike cluster to 20 in. (50 cm) in length, the lower flowers subtended by pinnately lobed floral bracts, the corolla 1–1 1/4 in. (25–30 mm) long, dull yellowish green and often streaked with red, 2-lipped, the upper lip arching and curved downward but squared off and with 2 teeth at the apex, the lower lip 3-lobed. *Fruit* a flattened capsule.
Range and Habitat: Wyoming to New Mexico and Arizona. Mostly found in damp woods, often along streams in the mountains throughout New Mexico; 7,500–10,000 ft.
Key Characters: Gray's lousewort is distinguished by the pinnately divided, somewhat fernlike, often very large leaves and the dull yellowish green, often red-streaked flowers with the upper lip of the corolla squarish and 2-toothed at the tip.
Related Species: A smaller but similar species, *P. parryi*, differs in having stems usually not more than 16 in. (40 cm) tall, corollas with the upper lip incurved and projecting into a slender beak, and the calyx marked with 5 dark lines.

Cordylanthus wrightii

Pedicularis groenlandica

Pedicularis grayi

296. **Colorado paintbrush**   *Castilleja confusa*   Figwort family

Perennial herb, the stems to 20 in. (60 cm) tall. *Leaves* alternate, sessile, narrowly lance-shaped or sometimes wider toward the tip, 1½–3 in. (4–8 cm) long, usually without teeth but the upper ones sometimes with 1 or 2 lobes. *Flowers* in dense, hairy spikes, the conspicuous, scarlet floral bracts with 1 or 2 pairs of lateral lobes, the corolla strongly projecting but inconspicuous, greenish with some red markings, 2-lipped, the upper lip densely hairy, the lower lip with incurved lobes, the calyx cleft on both upper and lower sides to about half the length of the tube.

Range and Habitat: Colorado and New Mexico. Scattered on wooded slopes in the mountains of northern, central, and south-central New Mexico; 7,000–12,000 ft.

Key Characters: Colorado paintbrush is distinguished by the glabrous leaves, the scarlet-tipped, lobed floral bracts, and the usually hairy flower parts.

Related Species: There are many similar species in the Indian paintbrush genus, but a smiliar species of the higher mountains of northern New Mexico, *C. rhexifolia,* may be confused sometimes with *C. confusa,* from which it differs in having glandular hairs on the flower parts, and the floral bracts without teeth or with a single pair of lateral lobes.

297. **Narrow-leaved paintbrush**   *Castilleja linariaefolia*   Figwort family

Perennial herb, the stems often purplish, to about 30 in. (75 cm) tall. *Leaves* alternate, linear, glabrous, the upper ones pinnately lobed. *Flowers* in a dense, hairy, spikelike raceme, the floral bracts shorter than the flowers, bright red above the middle, cleft into slender lobes, hairy, the corolla inconspicuous, about 1½ in. (35 mm) long, 2-lipped, the lower lip with incurved lobes, the calyx tube pink to yellowish green but red at the tip, hairy on the veins, cleft about half the length of the tube on the upper side but only about one-fourth the length of the tube on the lower side.

Range and Habitat: Wyoming to California, southward to Mexico. Usually found in open woods or on brushy slopes from north-central to central and western New Mexico; 7,000–12,000 ft.

Key Characters: Narrow-leaved paintbrush is distinguished by the narrow, hairless, linear leaves with the upper ones pinnately lobed, the soft hairs on the flower cluster, and the calyx with the tube greenish yellow, red-tipped, and the upper side cleft about twice as far as the lower side.

Related Species: A species of the higher mountains of western New Mexico, *C. austromontana,* differs in having the floral bracts unlobed but sometimes with a few teeth, the leaves hairy on the lower surface, and the calyx cleft about the same amount on both the upper and lower sides. Two other species of the higher mountains include the short-stemmed {to about 8 in. (20 cm) tall} western paintbrush, *C. occidentalis,* having floral bracts yellow but tinged with purple and the much larger but possibly less attractive sulfur paintbrush, *C. septentrionalis,* with stems mostly 10–20 in. (25–50 cm) tall and the floral bracts yellow or yellowish green but not tinged with purple.

Castilleja confusa

Castilleja linariaefolia

298. **Wholeleaf paintbrush**   *Castilleja integra*   Figwort family

Perennial herb, the stems mostly erect, to 16 in. (40 cm) tall. *Leaves* alternate, narrow, to about 2³/₄ in. (7 cm) long, smooth above but hairy beneath, the margins without teeth. *Flowers* in a dense spike, inconspicuous but subtended by showy, red floral bracts, the individual flowers greenish, tubular, 2-lipped, about 1–1³/₈ in. (25–35 mm) long, the tubular calyx yellowish except scarlet at the tip, hairy, cleft about the same amount on both upper and lower sides.
Range and Habitat: Texas to Colorado, Arizona, and Mexico. Usually scattered on dry, often rocky slopes throughout New Mexico; 4,500–10,000 ft.
Key Characters: Wholeleaf paintbrush is distinguished by the thickish, narrow, unlobed leaves and the variously red floral bracts which are mostly without teeth or lobes.
Related Species: The closely related woolly paintbrush, *C. lanata,* from canyon areas of southern New Mexico, differs in having densely woolly stems and leaves and the usually lobed floral bracts. A spectacular species of open meadows above 11,000 ft. is Hayden's paintbrush, *C. haydenii,* differing in the rose-colored or lilac floral bracts with 3–7 linear lobes, and the calyx tube deeply rose-colored. This is one of our loveliest alpine wildflowers.

299. **Yellow owl-clover**   *Orthocarpus luteus*   Figwort family

Erect, leafy annual, the stems hairy, to 12 in. (30 cm) tall. *Leaves* alternate, linear to narrowly lance-shaped, to about 1⁵/₈ in. (40 mm) long, almost always unlobed. *Flowers* in dense, bracteate clusters, the floral bracts about as long as the flowers, cleft into 3–5 narrow divisions, the corolla tubular, strongly 2-lipped, yellow, the upper lip straight, the lower lip somewhat expanded to form a saclike structure. *Fruit* a capsule with numerous seeds.
Range and Habitat: Western Canada to Nebraska, New Mexico, and California. Scattered on dryish plains, hills, and mountain slopes in northern and western New Mexico; 6,000–9,000 ft.
Key Characters: Yellow owl-clover can be distinguished by the typically unlobed linear or narrowly lanceolate leaves, the narrowly lobed floral bracts, and the yellow, 2-lipped flowers, with the lower lip rounded and saclike, curving up under the upper lip.
Related Species: The purple-white owl-clover, *O. purpureo-albus,* also of dry plains and slopes, differs in having the corolla purple and white and the flowers arranged in loose spikes.

300. **Desert willow**   *Chilopsis linearis*   Catalpa family

Large shrub or small tree to about 12 ft. (4 m) or more tall, the twigs slender and spreading or drooping. *Leaves* alternate, linear to narrowly lance-shaped, without teeth, about 4–6 in. (10–15 cm) long, narrowly tapering to a point. *Flowers* showy, in short terminal clusters, irregularly funnel-shaped, strongly 2-lipped, 1–1³/₈ in. (25–35 mm) long, variously lavender to whitish, often with purple markings, the lobes irregularly toothed or wavy. *Fruit* a slender pod to 12 in. (30 cm) long, with numerous fringe-margined seeds. The desert willow is often cultivated in the Southwest for the willowlike foliage and somewhat orchidlike flowers.
Range and Habitat: Western Texas to Califonia, southward into Mexico. Scattered or sometimes common in gravelly soils along water courses in central or southern New Mexico; 3,500–5,500 ft.
Key Characters: Desert willow may be recognized by the narrow, willowlike leaves, the conspicuous, somewhat orchidlike flowers, and the elongate, slender, drooping pods.
Related Species: Another large shrub, the spectacular yellow elder, *Tecoma stans,* differs in having opposite, pinnately compound leaves and bright yellow flowers.

Castilleja integra

Orthocarpus luteus

Chilopsis linearis

301. **Small-flowered unicorn-plant**   *Proboscidea parviflora*   Unicorn-plant family

Spreading annual, the stems to about 32 in. (80 cm) long, densely covered with gland-tipped hairs, as are the leaves and fruits. *Leaves* broadly triangular to somewhat rounded, shallowly wavy on the margins, about 3–6 in. (8–15 cm) wide. *Flowers* few, showy, to about 1³/₈ in. (35 mm) long, and 1 in. (25 mm) wide at the top, irregularly funnel-shaped, the 5 lobes flaring, reddish purple or sometimes whitish, often with streaks of yellow. *Fruit* a capsule with an elongate curved beak which splits into two curved parts at maturity. This plant, in flower, is attractive. The young pods reputedly have been used as food by certain Indian tribes.

Range and Habitat: Western Texas to California and Mexico. Usually found on dry, often sandy slopes in central and southern New Mexico; 4,000–5,500 ft.

Key Characters: This unicorn-plant is distinguished by the sticky, glandular stems and leaves, the rounded-triangular leaf blades, and the showy, irregular, funnel-shaped flowers.

Related Species: The strongly similar proboscis flower, *P. louisianica,* of sandy areas of southern and eastern New Mexico, differs in having flowers with the corolla about 1⁵/₈ in. (4 cm) long and the calyx about ³/₄ in. (20 mm) long.

302. **Desert cancerroot**   *Orobanche multiflora*   Broomrape family

Parasitic perennial herb, the stems mostly 4–12 in. (10–30 cm) long, with several scalelike bracts and covered with sticky gland-tipped hairs. *Leaves* reduced to alternate, scalelike, nongreen bracts. *Flowers* in terminal spikes, brownish purple, the corolla about ⁵/₈–1³/₈ in. (15–35 mm) long, tubular, curved, the lobes 2-lipped and rounded, the calyx about ³/₈–⁵/₈ in. (10–15 mm) long, the lobes about equal in length. *Fruit* a 1-celled capsule with numerous seeds. There are several similar varieties of this species in New Mexico. Members of this genus have been used in the treatment of ulcers.

Range and Habitat: Texas and New Mexico to Washington and California. Mostly found in sandy soils on open plains throughout New Mexico; 3,500–7,00 ft.

Key Characters: Desert cancerroot is characterized by the sticky, scaly stems, and the spikes of brownish purple, curved, tubular flowers.

Related Species: Two similar species include the plains cancerroot, *O. ludoviciana,* and its varieties, differing in having pointed corolla lobes, and *O. fasciculata,* differing in having the flowers in a loose raceme, each flower on an unbracted stalk.

303. **Desert honeysuckle**   *Anisacanthus thurberi*   Acanthus family

Stiff shrub, to about 3 ft. (1 m) tall, the bark whitish and scaling off. *Leaves* opposite, lance-shaped, about ³/₄–2 in. (20–50 mm) long, often narrowly tapering to a point at the tip. *Flowers* orange to purplish red, about 1¹/₄–2 in. (30–50 mm) long, with the corolla irregularly funnel-shaped and 2-lipped, the upper lip notched, the lower lip 3-lobed, and 2 stamens. *Fruit* a flattened capsule about ³/₄ in. (20 mm) long. This is one of our most conspicuous shrubs in flower but is often heavily browsed by livestock.

Range and Habitat: New Mexico and Arizona to Mexico. Usually found on dry, open, often gravelly or rocky slopes or mesas in southwestern New Mexico; 4,000–5,000 ft.

Key Characters: Desert honeysuckle may be identified by the stiffly shrubby habit, the whitish scaly bark, and the showy, honeysucklelike flowers.

Prosboscidea parviflora

Orobanche multiflora

Anisacanthus thurberi

304. Bigleaf plantain   *Plantago major*   Plantain family

Annual or biennial herb with flowering stems to 16 in. (40 cm) tall. *Leaves* in basal rosettes, broadly ovate or elliptic, sometimes somewhat heart-shaped, to about 6 in. (15 cm) long, the blades strongly ribbed, often toothed, and on a channeled stalk. *Flowers* in dense terminal spikes, the corolla very small, whitish, with 4 pointed lobes and 4 stamens, the floral bracts membranaceous on the margins. *Fruit* a small capsule with several brownish seeds.
Range and Habitat: Introduced from Europe, now widespread and common in North America. Usually associated with waste ground or lawns throughout New Mexico; 4,000–7,000 ft.
Key Characters: Bigleaf plantain may be recognized by the broadly ovate or elliptic basal leaves, the perennial habit, and the dense, slender spike of small, whitish, 4-parted flowers.
Related Species: Another very common species of waste ground or grassy areas is buckhorn plantain, *P. lanceolata,* differing mostly in having lance-shaped leaves, gradually narrowing to the base. A common species of dry plains and hills, *P. purshii* differs in having linear leaves, these gradually tapering to the base, mostly not more than ¼ in. (5 mm) wide, and covered with soft hairs.

305. Northern bedstraw   *Galium boreale*   Madder family

Perennial herb, the stems erect, very leafy, to about 32 in. (80 cm) tall, usually glabrous. *Leaves* in whorls of 4, linear to narrowly lance-shaped, mostly ¾–2 in. (20–50 mm) long, with 3 longitudinal veins. *Flowers* numerous, small, in dense terminal clusters, the corolla white, about ³⁄₁₆ in. (4 mm) in diameter, 4-lobed, and 4 stamens. *Fruit* a pair of rounded, 1-seeded pods.
Range and Habitat: Widely distributed in cooler areas throughout North America and Eurasia. Commonly found in meadows and on damp slopes throughout New Mexico; 6,500–10,000 ft.
Key Characters: Northern bedstraw is distinguished by the nearly glabrous stems and leaves and the 3-veined leaves in whorls of 4.
Related Species: Two similar species include *G. fendleri,* differing in having 1-nerved, often reflexed leaves, and the sweet-scented bedstraw, *G. triflorum,* differing in having weak, reclining stems, 5 or 6 leaves in each whorl, and flowers often greenish or yellowish.

306. Goosegrass   *Galium aparine*   Madder family

Weak annual, often reclining on other plants, the stems to about 32 in. (80 cm) long, with small hooked hairs on the angles. *Leaves* in whorls of 6–8, mostly narrowly oblong, ¾–2³⁄₈ in. (20–60 mm) long, 1-nerved, with a minute point at the apex, with short, rough hairs on margins and midvein. *Flowers* solitary or in axillary clusters of 2 or 3, white or greenish white. *Fruit* of a pair of rounded, 1-seeded pods covered with short hooked bristles.
Range and Habitat: Introduced from Europe, now widespread in North America. Usually found in damp ground, often near streams or in shady places from north-central to south-central New Mexico; 6,000–10,000 ft.
Key Characters: Goosegrass is distinguished by the short, stiff hairs on the angles of the stems and on the margins and midvein of the leaves, the leaves in whorls of 6–8, the flowers in small clusters or solitary, and the hooked bristles on the fruit.

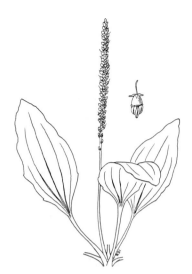

Plantago major

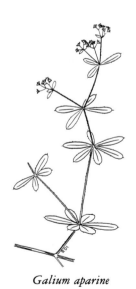

Galium aparine

Galium boreale

247

307. **Bluets**   *Hedyotis nigricans*   Madder family

Perennial herb, the stems mostly erect or ascending, 4–12 in. (10–30 cm) tall, both stems and leaves glabrous. *Leaves* opposite, linear or narrowly lance-shaped. *Flowers* in crowded clusters, the flower stalks erect or ascending, the corolla white, about ³/₁₆ in. (5 mm) long, the lobes spreading at right angles with the tube and hairy on the inner surface. *Fruit* an oblong, 2-lobed capsule.

Range and Habitat: Michigan to Florida, Texas, and Arizona. Usually associated with open, dry slopes in eastern and southern New Mexico; 5,000–7,000 ft.

Key Characters: Bluets can be distinguished by the glabrous stems and leaves, the linear or lance-shaped leaves, and the white flowers on erect or ascending stalks.

Related Species: A locally abundant species, especially in eastern New Mexico, is needleleaf bluets, *H. acerosa,* differing in having needlelike, often clustered leaves and a perennial habit.

308. **Desert innocence**   *Hedyotis rubra*   Madder family

Perennial herb, the stems clustered, to 4 in. (10 cm) tall. *Leaves* opposite or in basal clusters, stiff, linear to narrowly lance-shaped. *Flowers* deep rose pink or, rarely, white, with a slender tube ³/₄–1¹/₄ in. (20–30 mm) long and 4 lobes projecting at right angles to the top, the flower about ³/₈ in. (10 mm) wide, with 4 purplish stamens. *Fruit* of small, usually nodding, 2-lobed capsules. This is a very pretty little desert plant, among the smallest members of the genus.

Range and Habitat: New Mexico to Arizona and Mexico. Found on dry, sandy plains and slopes throughout New Mexico; 4,000–6,500 ft.

Key Characters: Desert innocence is distinguished by the short, tufted stems with stiffish, erect leaves and conspicuous, long-tubed deep pink flowers.

309. **Rocky Mountain red elder**   *Sambucus microbotrys*   Honeysuckle family

Spreading shrub, the stems to about 6 ft. (2 m) tall. *Leaves* opposite, pinnately compound, the 5 or 7 leaflets broadly lance-shaped, mostly 2¹/₄–4³/₄ in. (6–12 cm) long, glabrous, rounded at the base, pointed at the tip, coarsely toothed on the margins. *Flowers* in dense, somewhat pyramid-shaped clusters, with 3–5 yellow petals, and with 5 stamens attached at the base of the petals. *Fruit* berrylike, bright red, about ³/₁₆ in. (5 mm) in diameter.

Range and Habitat: Wyoming to New Mexico, westward to California. Usually found in scattered populations in moist woods in the mountains of northern, central, south-central, and western New Mexico; 8,000–12,000 ft.

Key Characters: Rocky Mountain red elder can be identified by the pinnately compound leaves with smooth, coarsely toothed leaflets, the large clusters of pale yellow flowers, and the bright red berries.

Related Species: Blackbead elder, *S. melanocarpa,* a large shrub of similar habitats in northern New Mexico, differs in having leaflets hairy on the lower surface, white flowers, and black fruits.

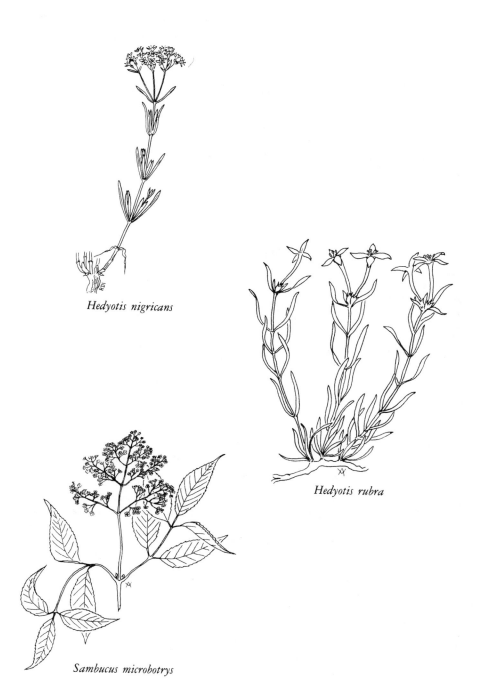

Hedyotis nigricans

Hedyotis rubra

Sambucus microbotrys

310. **New Mexican elder**   *Sambucus neomexicana*   Honeysuckle family

Shrub or small tree, the stems to 18 ft. (6 m) tall, the pith of the older branches white, both stems and leaves glabrous. *Leaves* opposite, the 5 or 7 or occasionally 9 leaflets lance-shaped or elliptic, to about 4 in. (10 cm) long, obliquely angled at the base, toothed on the margins. *Flowers* in an open, flat-topped cluster as much as 10 in. (25 cm) wide, the corolla white, with 3–5 lobes and 5 stamens attached at the base of the corolla. *Fruit* a dark blue berry about 1/4 in. (6 mm) in diameter.

Range and Habitat: New Mexico and Arizona, possibly northern Mexico. Usually found along streams in central and southern New Mexico; 7,000–9,500 ft.

Key Characters: New Mexican elder is easily distinguished by the leaflets glabrous and often obliquely angled at the base, the often treelike aspect, and the white flowers in a flat-topped, open cluster.

Related Species: A variety of this species, var. *vestita,* from southern New Mexico, differs in having the leaves and younger branches persistently covered with short or matted hairs. The similar Mexican elder, *S. mexicana,* differs in having leaflets 3/4–2 3/8 in. (2–6 cm) long and often somewhat hairy, and pale yellow flowers.

311. **American twinflower**   *Lonicera borealis americana*   Honeysuckle family

Creeping evergreen perennial herb, the stems to 3 ft. (1 m) long. *Leaves* simple, opposite, often somewhat rounded, 3/8–3/4 in. (10–20 mm) long, usually toothed above the middle, hairy, short-stalked. *Flowers* regular, nodding, in pairs at the summit of elongated flower stalks, the funnel-shaped corolla pink, 5-lobed, about 3/8 in. (10 mm) long, with 4 stamens, the calyx subtended by densely glandular bracts. *Fruit* dry, 1-seeded. This is a very pretty little plant, a favorite of many wildflower enthusiasts.

Range and Habitat: Greenland to Michigan, southward to New Mexico and Arizona. Found in occasional populations in damp woods in the mountains of northern New Mexico; 9,000–11,000 ft.

Key Characters: American twinflower is distinguished by the creeping stems with opposite evergreen leaves toothed above the middle and the nodding, 5-lobed, pink flowers arranged in pairs at the summit of flower stalks.

312. **Mountain snowberry**   *Symphoricarpos oreophilus*   Honeysuckle family

Erect, much branched shrub, the stems to 3 ft. (1 m) or more tall, the young twigs glabrous, the bark often splitting off in shreds. *Leaves* opposite, oval, glabrous, sometimes toothed, to 1 1/4 in. (3 cm) long, on short stalks. *Flowers* in pairs in the axils of the leaves or in terminal clusters, subtended by oval floral bracts, the pink corolla tubular to funnel-shaped, 3/8–5/8 in. (10–15 mm) long, the tube much longer than the lobes. *Fruit* a white, ellipsoid berry about 3/8 in. (9 mm) long.

Range and Habitat: Colorado to Nevada, southward to Texas and Arizona. Usually associated with wooded slopes in the mountains throughout New Mexico; 6,500–9,000 ft.

Key Characters: Mountain snowberry is distinguished by the shrubby aspect, the oval, usually glabrous leaves, and the pink, tubular or narrowly funnel-shaped flowers in pairs in the leaf axils or in clusters at the summit of the branches.

Related Species: Similar species flowering in the summer include Western snowberry, *S. occidentalis,* differing in having leaves often toothed or lobed, on stalks 3/16–3/8 in. (5–10 mm) long, and bell-shaped flowers; desert snowberry, *S. longiflorus,* differing in the flowers with lobes turned outward at right angles and the anthers without filaments; and Utah snowberry, *S. utahensis,* differing in having leaves with short hairs on both surfaces and the young twigs hairy.

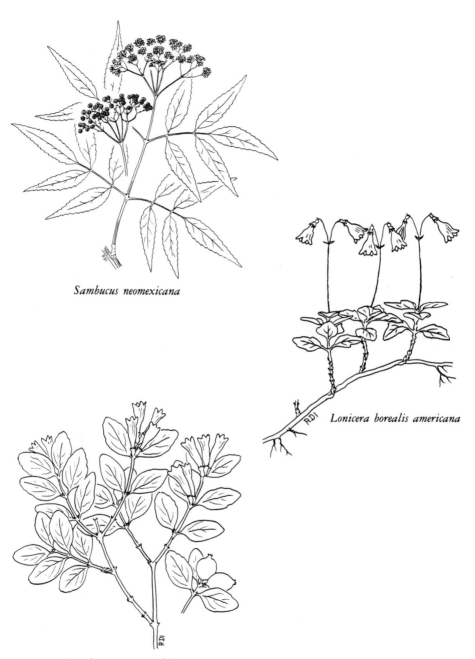

Sambucus neomexicana

Lonicera borealis americana

Symphoricarpos oreophilus

251

313. **Inkberry** *Lonicera involucrata* Honeysuckle family

Erect to ascending shrub, the stems to 9 ft. (3 m) tall, the 4-angled twigs glabrous, the older bark often splitting off in shreds. *Leaves* opposite, simple, ovate to elliptic, to about 4 in. (10 cm) long, smooth above but hairy on the veins beneath. *Flowers* mostly axillary, in clusters of 2 or 3, on stalks to about 1¹/₄ in. (3 cm) long, subtended by closely arranged series of conspicuous, often leaflike bracts, these eventually becoming reflexed, the corolla yellow, funnel-shaped, about ³/₈ in. (10 mm) long, the lobes about half as long as the tube, spreading, bearing glandular hairs. *Fruit* a conspicuous, lustrous, purplish black berry about ³/₈ in. (10 mm) long.

Range and Habitat: Quebec to Alaska, southward to Michigan, New Mexico, California, and Mexico. Locally common in open woods near streams from north-central to central and western New Mexico; 7,500–10,000 ft.

Key Characters: Inkberry is easily distinguished by the shrubby aspect, the shreddy older bark, the mostly ovate to elliptic leaves hairy on the veins beneath, the yellow, funnel-shaped flowers, and the shiny, purplish black berries cradled in floral bracts.

Related Species: Other summer-flowering species include Arizona honeysuckle, *L. arizonica,* of south-central and western New Mexico, differing in having trailing or climbing stems, sessile, red to orange flowers, and red fruit, and Utah fly-honeysuckle, *L. utahensis,* differing in having the leaves rounded or obtusely angled at the tip, the floral bracts absent or minute, and the fruit orange, yellow, or red.

314. **Thickleaf valerian** *Valeriana edulis* Valerian family

Perennial herb, the stems mostly 6–24 in. (15–60 cm) tall, glabrous. *Leaves* opposite and basal, thickish, with conspicuous lateral veins, the basal leaves spatula-shaped, tapering to an elongate stalk, sometimes pinnately parted, the stem leaves in 1–3 pairs, mostly sessile, usually pinnately lobed. *Flowers* in usually open, terminal clusters, the corolla 4- or 5-lobed, about ¹/₈ in. (3 mm) long, yellowish, the tube swollen on 1 side, the calyx represented by a series of bristles, these persisting on the 1-seeded fruit.

Range and Habitat: British Columbia to New Mexico and Arizona. Usually found in meadows or woods in the mountains throughout New Mexico; 7,000–11,000 ft.

Key Characters: Thickleaf valerian can be distinguished by the basal cluster of narrow, often pinnately lobed leaves, the few pairs of pinnately lobed stem leaves, and the small yellowish flowers not more than ¹/₈ in. (3 mm) long.

Related Species: Two other species, blooming in early summer, include Arizona valerian, *V. arizonica,* differing in having ovate to nearly round basal leaves and white or pink tubular flowers about ³/₈ in. (8–12 mm) long, and *V. capitata acutiloba,* differing in having relatively thin, narrow, almost always unlobed basal leaves and white or pink, tubular flowers about ¹/₄ in. (5–7 mm) long.

315. **Cutleaf globeberry** *Ibervillea tenuisecta* Melon family

Perennial, herbaceous vine from a somewhat globe-shaped root, the stems slender, prostrate or climbing, to 10 ft. (3 m) or more long, bearing unbranched tendrils at the nodes. *Leaves* alternate, stalked, deeply 3- to 5-lobed, ³/₄–1⁵/₈ in. (2–4 cm) wide, the lobes deeply cleft into narrow segments. *Flowers* unisexual, the male and female flowers on different plants, yellow, the tube about ³/₁₆ in. (3–4 mm) long, the lobes spreading at right angles from the tube, and 3 stamens. *Fruit* a red, globe-shaped, modified berry with swollen, wrinkled seeds.

Range and Habitat: Western Texas to New Mexico and Mexico. Usually associated with sandy ground in southern New Mexico; 3,000–5,000 ft.

Key Characters: Cutleaf globeberry is easily recognized by the slender, often climbing, tendrilled stems, the leaves cleft into several narrow lobes, the small, yellow, unisexual flowers, and the round, red fruits.

252

Lonicera involucrata

Valeriana edulis

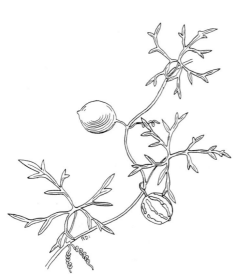

Ibervillea tenuisecta

253

316. **Melon-loco**   *Apodanthera undulata*   Melon family

Stiffly hairy, odoriferous, coarse vine from a thick root, the stems creeping or climbing, bearing tendrils. *Leaves* alternate, rounded or somewhat kidney-shaped, with a rounded notch at the base of the blade, sometimes lobed. *Flowers* large, unisexual, with both sexes on the same plant, yellow, 5-lobed, the calyx tube cylindrical and ⅝–1 in. (15–25 mm) long, with 3 stamens. *Fruit* a longitudinally ridged, ovoid modified berry with a tough rind and numerous seeds.

Range and Habitat: Western Texas to Arizona and Mexico. Rarely or occasionally found on dry plains or mesas in southern New Mexico; 3,500–5,500 ft.

Key Characters: Melon-loco is distinguished by the tendrilled vines bearing stiff, appressed hairs, the rounded, somewhat kidney-shaped leaves, and the slender-tubed yellow flowers.

Related Species: The spiny cucumber, *Echinopepon wrightii,* also occasional in southern New Mexico on the lower slopes of the mountains, differs in having leaves roughly heart-shaped in outline but with angular, shallow lobes and fruit often densely spiny.

317. **Buffalo gourd**   *Cucurbita foetidissima*   Melon family

Herbaceous perennial vine, the stems prostrate, harshly pubescent, with branched tendrils opposite the leaves. *Leaves* alternate, coarse, stalked, roughly triangular, with shallow angled lobes, flattened or notched at the base, 4–10 in. (10–25 cm) long, ill-smelling. *Flowers* large, solitary, yellow, unisexual, with both male and female flowers on the same plant, the staminate (male) flowers with 3 stamens, the pistillate (female) flowers ridged, harshly pubescent, the corolla mostly 3–6 in. (8–15 cm) long, funnel-shaped. *Fruit* globe-shaped, about 2½–4 in. (5–10 cm) in diameter, smooth, striped or mottled in different shades of green. This plant is rapidly spreading in roadside areas throughout the Southwest.

Range and Habitat: Western Missouri to California, southward to Mexico. Usually found on open plains or in waste ground throughout New Mexico; 4,000–6,500 ft.

Key Characters: Buffalo gourd is distinguished by the harshly pubescent, ill-smelling stems and leaves, the large, coarse, somewhat triangular leaves, and the conspicuous funnel-shaped yellow flowers.

Related Species: The cutleaf gourd, *C. digitata,* occurring in southwestern New Mexico, differs mostly in having palmately deeply 5-lobed leaves.

318. **Western cardinal flower**   *Lobelia cardinalis*   Bluebell family

Erect perennial herb, the stems mostly unbranched, to about 3 ft. (1 m) tall. *Leaves* alternate, narrowly oblong to broadly lance-shaped, to 6 in. (15 cm) long, toothed, sessile or on very short stalks. *Flowers* in terminal racemes, tubular, red, conspicuously 2-lipped, the upper lip 2-lobed, the lower lip 3-lobed, the corolla about ¾–1⅜ in. (20–35 mm) long, the 5 stamens with filaments united into a tube toward the top, the calyx with 5 slender, pointed sepals. *Fruit* a many-seeded capsule about ⅜–¾ in. (6–10 mm) long.

Range and Habitat: Widespread in North America and Central America. Usually found in wet ground, especially along streams throughout New Mexico; 5,500–7,500 ft.

Key Characters: Western cardinal flower is distinguished by the often tall, mostly unbranched stems, the alternate, toothed, nearly sessile leaves, and the slender, spikelike raceme of conspicuous, 2-lipped, red flowers.

Related Species: Bluebell lobelia, *L. anatina,* a species of wet habitats in southern and western New Mexico, differs in having a blue flower with a whitish eye and 2 of the stamens bearing a tuft of white hairs.

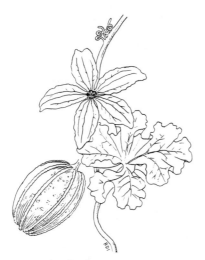

Apodanthera undulata

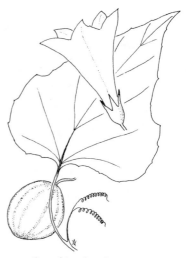

Cucurbita foetidissima

Lobelia cardinalis

255

319. **Harebell**   *Campanula rotundifolia*   Bluebell family

Perennial herb, the stems erect or spreading, to 20 in. (50 cm) tall, mostly glabrous. *Leaves* alternate, simple, the lower ones stalked, ovate to elliptic or somewhat heart-shaped, often falling from the plant before flowering occurs, the upper leaves linear to narrowly lance-shaped, glabrous, sessile, without teeth or lobes. *Flowers* several, often nodding, blue, bell-shaped, ³/₈–³/₄ in. (10–20 mm) long, the calyx lobes slender. *Fruit* a nodding capsule containing numerous seeds.
Range and Habitat: Canada to New Mexico, California, and Mexico; also Eurasia. Typically found in montane meadows throughout New Mexico; 7,000–13,000 ft.
Key Characters: Harebell is easily recognized by the basal leaves, when present, heart-shaped at the base, and the often nodding, blue, conspicuously bell-shaped flowers.
RelatedSpecies: Parry's bellflower, *C.parryi,* occasional in northern New Mexico, differs in having leaf margins with small teeth and a single erect flower at the summit of the stem or sometimes on 1 or more lateral branches.

320. **Slender-leaved wire-lettuce**   *Stephanomeria tenuifolia*   Sunflower family

Slender, branching perennial, the stems to 2 ft. (60 cm) tall, smooth, the branches usually marked with narrow longitudinal lines. *Leaves* linear or broader at the tip and tapering to the base, the basal leaves pinnately lobed, the upper ones much reduced and usually without teeth or lobes. *Flower heads* pinkish, all raylike, ¹/₄–³/₈ in. (7–9 mm) high, mostly 5-flowered, the subtending bracts usually 5, but with a few smaller bracts at the base. *Fruits* of slender, nearly smooth achenes, these usually marked with longitudinal lines and with a crown of white, feathery bristles.
Range and Habitat: Montana to Washington, southward to Texas, New Mexico, Arizona, and California. Mostly found on dry plains and mountain slopes throughout New Mexico; 3,000–8,000 ft.
Key Characters: Slender-leaved wire-lettuce is distinguished by the slender, smooth, pinnately lobed lower leaves, the small pinkish flower heads, and the fruit crowned with white, feathery bristles.
Related Species: The similar *S. thurberi* differs in having larger heads with 10–20 flowers, and *S. exigua* differs in its annual habit and the bristles on the fruit expanded at the base.

321. **Meadow goatsbeard**   *Tragopogon pratensis*   Sunflower family

Erect perennial, the stems often branching, to 3 ft. (1 m) tall. *Leaves* slender and somewhat grasslike, tapering to the apex and often recurved, smooth throughout and without teeth. *Flower heads* yellow, the flowers all raylike and longer than the subtending bracts, the flower head bracts usually 8 or 9, about equal in length, in a single series, and united at the base. *Fruits* of longitudinally ribbed achenes, these abruptly tapering to a slender, elongated beak crowned by a ring of feathery, webbed, white bristles resembling a kind of parachute.
Range and Habitat: Widespread in Canada and the United States; introduced from Europe. Usually found in waste ground throughout New Mexico; 4,000–7,000 ft.
Key Characters: Meadow goatsbeard is distinguished by the conspicuous yellow flower heads, the grasslike leaves, and the long-beaked fruit crowned by parachutelike white bristles.
Related Species: The closely related *T. porrifolius* differs in having purplish flowers and brownish bristles on the fruit, and *T. dubius* is characterized by having 10–13 flower head bracts and flower head stalks strongly expanded just below the heads.

Campanula rotundifolia

Stephanomeria tenuifolia

Tragopogon pratensis

322. Chicory *Cichorium intybus* Sunflower family

Erect perennial, the stems branching, with a few stiff hairs, to about 32 in. (80 cm) tall. *Leaves* alternate, to about 6 in. (15 cm) long, the basal ones usually broader above the middle and becoming somewhat narrower toward the base, and often clasping the stem, the margins usually lobed or toothed but sometimes without teeth or lobes. *Flower heads* blue or occasionally white, 1–1½ in. (25–38 mm) wide, the flowers all raylike and 5-toothed at the apex, the flower head bracts in 2 series, the inner ones linear and much longer than the ovate outer ones. *Fruits* of 5-angled achenes, these flattened at the summit and with a crown of short scales.
Range and Habitat: Widely established in North America; introduced from Europe. Mostly found in waste ground, especially along roadsides in northern and central New Mexico; 4,000–6,500 ft.
Key Characters: Chicory is distinguished by the relatively large heads of usually blue flowers with the rays flattened and 5-toothed at the tip.

323. Chicory-lettuce *Lactuca pulchella* Sunflower family

Smooth perennial with milky juice, the stems leafy, to 6 ft. (2 m) tall. *Leaves* alternate, linear to narrowly lance-shaped, to about 8 in. (20 cm) long, entire to toothed on the margins, or the lower leaves somewhat pinnately lobed, the teeth and veins without prickles. *Flower heads* in a loose cluster, ¾–1¼ in. (20–30 mm) wide when fully expanded, blue or purple, the flower head bracts in 3 or 4 unequal series. *Fruits* of flattish, black achenes, tapering to a slender beak less than half as long as the expanded part of the fruit and crowned by soft white bristles.
Range and Habitat: Quebec to Alaska, southward to Missouri, New Mexico, and California. Mostly found in waste ground throughout New Mexico; 4,500–8,000 ft.
Key Characters: Chicory-lettuce is distinguished by the mostly lobed or toothed, nonprickly leaves, the bluish or purplish flowers, and the strongly flattened fruits.
Related Species: The closely related *L. serriola* differs in having irregularly distributed spiny teeth as well as lobes on most leaves and yellow flowers, and *L. graminifolia* differs in having leaves without teeth or else the lobes very slender, and fruits transversely wrinkled.

324. False dandelion *Pyrrhopappus multicaulis* Sunflower family

Branching perennial, the stems minutely hairy or nearly smooth, to 16 in. (40 cm) long. *Leaves* mostly basal, to about 6 in. (15 cm) long, the lower ones with wavy teeth or pinnate lobes, the upper leaves smaller. *Flower heads* golden yellow, ⅜–⅝ in. (10–15 mm) high, the rays ⅝–¾ in. (15–20 mm) long, the flower head bracts in 2 series, those of the inner series linear and much longer than those of the outer series. *Fruits* of slender, 5-ribbed, reddish, transversely wrinkled achenes, these tapering to a slender beak longer than the expanded portion of the fruit and crowned by slender, soft, reddish brown bristles.
Range and Habitat: Texas to New Mexico, Arizona, and Mexico. Mostly found in damp ground throughout New Mexico; 3,500–7,000 ft.
Key Characters: False dandelion is distinguished by the conspicuous golden yellow heads and the reddish, 5-ribbed, wrinkled, beaked achenes crowned with soft brownish bristles.

Cichorium intybus

Lactuca pulchella

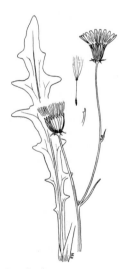

Pyrrhopappus multicaulis

259

325. **Dandelion**   *Taraxacum officinale*   Sunflower family

Perennial herb, without true stems but with slender, naked flower head stalks (scapes) to about 12 in. (30 cm) tall. *Leaves* basal, broader toward the tip, to about 12 in. (30 cm) long, with somewhat triangular lobes, the lobes often toothed. *Flower* heads (including rays) about 3/4–2 in. (20–50 mm) wide, yellow, many-flowered, all raylike, the subtending bracts narrowly lance-shaped, usually reflexed (recurved). *Fruits* of slender, grayish or greenish achenes with roughened surfaces near the tips and tapering to slender beaks at the top and crowned with numerous soft, slender bristles.

Range and Habitat: Cosmopolitan. Mostly found in open fields, lawns, and waste ground throughout New Mexico; 3,000–10,000 ft.

Key Characters: Common dandelion is distinguished by the leaves with somewhat triangular lobes and the conspicuous yellow flower heads on naked flowering stalks.

Related Species: All species of *Taraxacum* are rather closely related, differing primarily in such characters as the presence of wings on the margins of the petioles, arrangement of the subtending bracts of the flower heads, and fruit color.

326. **Orange-flowered mountain-dandelion**   *Agoseris aurantiaca*   Sunflower family

Perennial herb, smooth or with a few long, soft hairs, without a true stem but flower head stalks (scapes) about 4–20 in. (10–50 cm) tall. *Leaves* somewhat lance-shaped and blunt at the tip, 2–10 in. (5–25 cm) long, the margins without teeth but sometimes with a few lobes. *Flower heads* solitary at the apex of the scapes, the flowers all raylike, burnt orange in color or becoming purplish in age, the flower head bracts in about 2 series, the inner bracts about twice as long as the broader outer ones, the outer bracts with hairs on the margins and often on the back. *Fruits* of slender, conspicuously ribbed achenes, these tapering into a narrow beak and crowned by numerous slender white bristles.

Range and Habitat: Western Canada to New Mexico, Arizona, and California. Usually found in meadows and open coniferous forests in northern New Mexico; 6,500–11,000 ft.

Key Characters: Orange-flowered mountain-dandelion is distinguished by the burnt orange dandelionlike flower heads on slender stalks, the basal leaves, and the usually reddish purple leaf stalks.

Related Species: The closely related *A. glauca* differs in having yellow flowers and green leaf stalks, and *A. graminifolia* differs in having pale yellow flowers and narrowly linear, grasslike leaves, these without teeth or lobes and tapering to the tip.

327. **Fendler hawkweed**   *Hieracium fendleri*   Sunflower family

Perennial herb, the stems hairy, to 12 in. (30 cm) tall. Basal leaves broadest above the middle and tapering to the base, to about 3 1/4 in. (8 cm) long and 3/4 in. (18 mm) wide, the margins with minute teeth or none, the upper leaves ranging from lance-shaped to very small and linear. *Flower heads* dandelionlike, yellow, in loose clusters, the flower head bracts in 2 series, the inner bracts slender and about 1/2–5/8 in. (12–14 mm) long, the outermost bracts much shorter. *Fruits* of reddish or blackish achenes with 10 or more longitudinal ridges and a crown of slender whitish or brownish bristles.

Range and Habitat: South Dakota to Mexico. Mostly associated with open or wooded slopes in the mountains of New Mexico; 6,000–10,000 ft.

Key Characters: Fendler hawkweed is distinguished by the hairy stems, the lower leaves unlobed and tapering to the base, the yellowish dandelionlike flower heads, and the usually reddish fruits.

Related Species: A variety of this species from the Mogollon Mountains differs in having the inner flower head bracts only 3/8 in. (10 mm) long.

Taraxacum officinale

Agoseris aurantiaca

Hieracium fendleri

261

328. Stiff skeleton plant   *Lygodesmia juncea*   Sunflower family

Smooth perennial, the stems much branched, stiff, with longitudinal lines or angles, to 2 ft. (60 cm) tall. *Leaves* rigid, linear to lance-shaped, to 2 in. (5 cm) long, the margins without teeth or lobes, the upper leaves usually very small. *Flower heads* solitary on the flowering stalks, pink or white, usually 5-flowered, the flower head bracts in 2 series, the inner bracts usually gland-tipped and much longer than the very small outer ones. *Fruits* of slender, mostly smooth achenes, these not beaked and with a crown of numerous unequal, dirty white bristles.
Range and Habitat: Southern Canada to Missouri, Colorado, and New Mexico. Usually found on open plains and hills throughout New Mexico; 5,000–7,000 ft.
Key Characters: Stiff skeleton weed is distinguished by the rigid stems and leaves, the stems with longitudinal lines or angles, and the mostly 5-flowered heads.

329. Dwarf-dandelion   *Krigia biflora*   Sunflower family

Erect perennial, the stems smooth, branched above, to 2 ft. (60 cm) tall. *Leaves* mostly basal, the lower ones to 6 in. (15 cm) long, broadest above the middle and tapering to the base, often toothed or pinnately lobed and with an enlarged terminal lobe, 1–3 upper leaves clasping the stem, much smaller than the basal ones. *Flower heads* dandelionlike, yellow or orange, on slender, smooth stalks or branches. *Fruits* of short achenes, these 15- to 20-ribbed, flattened at the top and crowned by numerous delicate, slender bristles subtended by an outer series of blunt, narrow scales.
Range and Habitat: Widespread in North America except in extreme southeastern, south-central, and far western regions. Occasionally found in meadows, prairies, and open woods in New Mexico; 7,000–8,000 ft.
Key Characters: Dwarf-dandelion is distinguished by the dandelionlike yellow or orange heads and the clasping stem leaves.

330. Fendler desert dandelion   *Malacothrix fendleri*   Sunflower family

Annual, the stems smooth, somewhat branched, to about 12 in. (30 cm) tall. *Leaves* mostly glabrous, with coarse, wavy teeth or lobes, roughly oblong in outline, the basal leaves to 3 1/8 in. (8 cm) long, often with woolly hairs at the base, the upper leaves smaller than the basal ones, sometimes without teeth or lobes. *Flower heads* (including rays) 3/4–1 1/8 in. (20–30 mm) wide, all flowers raylike as in dandelions, the rays yellow but tinged with purple beneath, 1/4–3/8 in. (7–10 mm) long, the flower head bracts in two lengths, the inner bracts membranelike, purplish-tipped, and much longer than the outer series. *Fruits* of cylindrical achenes with 15 prominent longitudinal ribs and crowned with soft, slender bristles.
Range and Habitat: Western Texas to southern Arizona and northern Mexico. Occurring on sandy or rocky slopes, flats, or plains in New Mexico; 4,000–6,000 ft.
Key Characters: Fendler desert dandelion is characterized by the basal cluster of usually wavy-toothed or lobed leaves and reduced upper leaves, the dandelionlike yellow flower heads, and the 15-ribbed fruits.
Related Species: The closely related *M. sonchoides* differs mostly in having longer rays, 3/8–1/2 in. (10–12 mm) long and fruits with only 5 prominent longitudinal ribs.

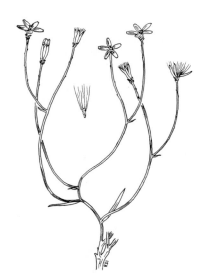

Lygodesmia juncea

Krigia biflora

Malacothrix fendleri

331. **Brownfoot** *Perezia wrightii* Sunflower family

Perennial herb, the stems erect, branching, to about 3 ft. (1 m) or more tall. *Leaves* lance-shaped to ovate, to 4³/4 in. (12 cm) long and 2 in. (5 cm) wide, somewhat rough to the touch, usually lobed at the base and often clasping the stem, spiny toothed. *Flower heads* in dense clusters, 8- to 12-flowered, pinkish purple or white, individual flowers 2-lobed, the upper lobe with 2 teeth, the lower with 3, the flower head bracts in 2 or 3 series, usually lance-shaped. *Fruits* of slender achenes, crowned by numerous white bristles.
Range and Habitat: Western Texas to southern Utah, Arizona, and Mexico. Mostly found in canyons and on rocky slopes in southern New Mexico; 4,000–6,500 ft.
Key Characters: Brownfoot is distinguished by the 8- to 12-flowered, pinkish heads and the spiny-toothed leaves with brownish hairs at the base of the stem.
Related Species: The similar *P. thurberi* differs in having smaller heads with only 4–6 flowers and the stems, leaves, and flower head bracts with conspicuous gland-tipped hairs.

332. **Yellow thistle** *Cirsium pallidum* Sunflower family

Coarse perennial, the stems very leafy, to 6 ft. (2 m) tall, with tangled, cobwebby hairs. *Leaves* alternate, oblong to lance-shaped in outline, greenish and without hairs on the upper surface, often with cobwebby hairs beneath, the margins with irregular, spine-tipped teeth or lobes. *Flower heads* greenish yellow, about 1 in. (25 mm) wide, clustered on stems or branches having numerous small spiny leaves, the flower head bracts in many series, each tapering to a long spine at the tip, covered with numerous cobwebby hairs. *Fruits* of smooth, compressed achenes crowned by numerous bristles.
Range and Habitat: Colorado and New Mexico. Mostly found in moist ground near streams from northern to south-central New Mexico; 7,000–10,000 ft.
Key Characters: Yellow thistle is distinguished by the greenish yellow flower heads, the herbage with cobwebby hairs, especially on the stems, lower surface of the leaves, and flower head bracts, and the inner bracts conspicuously fringed.

333. **New Mexico thistle** *Cirsium neomexicanum* Sunflower family

Coarse biennial, the stems to about 3 ft. (1 m) tall, with woolly hairs. *Leaves* oblong to lance-shaped in outline, wavy-toothed or pinnately lobed, the teeth or lobes tipped with spines about ³/16–³/8 in. (5–10 mm) long. *Flower heads* solitary on stems or branches, 1³/16–2³/8 in. (3–6 cm) in diameter, white to pinkish purple, the flowers all tubelike, the flower head bracts covered with woolly hairs, each bract tipped with a conspicuous spine, the outer bracts usually bent outward. *Fruits* of compressed, smooth achenes crowned by numerous bristles, these united at the base.
Range and Habitat: Colorado and New Mexico to California. Mostly found on plains or dry hills from northern to south-central and southwestern New Mexico; 4,000–7,000 ft.
Key Characters: New Mexico thistle may be recognized by the woolly-hairy stems, the flower heads solitary on stems or branches, white to pinkish purple, with tubelike flowers, and the flower head bracts bearing woolly hairs and tipped with a conspicuous spine, the outer bracts usually bent outward.
Related Species: The related *C. megacephalum* differs in having leaf spines mostly shorter than ³/16 in. (5 mm) and the flower head bracts not bent outward.

Perezia wrightii

Cirsium pallidum

Cirsium neomexicanum

334. **Wavyleaf thistle**   *Cirsium undulatum*   Sunflower family

Coarse, erect biennial, the stems to about 3 ft. (1 m) tall, persistently white-woolly. *Leaves* lance-shaped in outline, wavy-toothed, spiny, usually bearing woolly hairs on both surfaces. *Flower heads* 3/4–1 1/4 in. (2–3 cm) wide, rose purple, solitary or in small clusters, the flowers all tubelike, the flower head bracts lance-shaped, with woolly, cobwebby hairs on the margins, the outer bracts spine-tipped, the inner bracts irregluarly notched on the margins and often twisted. *Fruits* of compressed, smooth achenes crowned by numerous bristles.
Range and Habitat: Michigan to British Columbia, southward to Texas, New Mexico, and Arizona. Usually found on dry slopes in hills and mountains throughout New Mexico; 7,000–9,500 ft.
Key Characters: Wavyleaf thistle is distinguished by the permanently white, woolly stems and leaves, the wavy, spiny leaf margins, and the twisted inner flower head bracts.
Related Species: The less common *C. drummondii* differs in having flowers mostly whitish or slightly tinged with purple and the leaves and stems without hairs or sometimes with cobwebby hairs.

335. **American basketflower**   *Centaurea americana*   Sunflower family

Coarse annual, the stems unbranched, to 4 1/2 ft. (1.5 m) tall, smooth. *Leaves* lance-shaped, smooth, to about 4 in. (10 cm) long, the margins minutely toothed or without teeth. *Flower heads* at the apex of the stems and branches, 3/4–1 5/8 in. (2–4 cm) wide, the flowers purple or pink, all tubelike but the outer flowers with conspicuous, elongate linear lobes, the flower head bracts conspicuously fringed on the margins, the outer bracts spreading outward. *Fruits* of compressed, smooth achenes, these with an elevated margin at the summit and crowned by several series of unequal bristles.
Range and Habitat: Missouri to Kansas, southward to Louisiana, New Mexico, eastern Arizona, and northern Mexico. Mostly found in moist ground in southern New Mexico; 5,000–7,500 ft.
Key Characters: American basketflower is distinguished by the conspicuous purple to pink heads having outer flowers each with 5 slender, elongate lobes and flower head bracts fringed with 4–6 pairs of slender appendages.
Related Species: The similar *C. rothrockii* differs in having yellowish central flowers in the flower head and the flower head bracts fringed with 8–12 pairs of slender appendages.

336. **Pussytoes**   *Antennaria parvifolia*   Sunflower family

Low, woolly perennial, the stems usually densely matted, to about 6 in. (15 cm) tall. *Leaves* broadest above the middle and tapering to the base, obtuse or rounded at the apex, 3/8–1 in. (10–25 mm) long, bearing woolly hairs on both surfaces. *Flowering heads* in small, dense, rounded clusters, the flowers inconspicuous, narrowly tubular, the flower head bracts dry, paperlike, white to pink, sometimes with a brownish spot in the center. *Fruits* of small, smooth achenes crowned by numerous slender white bristles.
Range and Habitat: Manitoba to British Columbia, southward to New Mexico and Arizona. Mostly found on dry, open hills or in open woods from northern to south-central and western New Mexico; 7,000–11,000 ft.
Key Characters: Pussytoes is distinguished by the low matted habit, the stems and leaves with woolly hairs throughout, and the papery flower head bracts.
Related Species: At about the same range of elevation, one may find *A. rosea,* which differs in having smaller heads, mostly 3/16–1/4 in. (4–7 mm) high, and pinkish flowers head bracts, and *A. rosulata* which differs in its stemless habit and the flower heads nestled among the leaves.

Cirsium undulatum

Centaurea americana

Antennaria parvifolia

337. **Cottony everlasting**   *Gnaphalium chilense*   Sunflower family

Annual or biennial herb, the stems to about 24 in. (60 cm) tall, usually aromatic, both stems and leaves loosely covered with cobwebby hairs. *Leaves* broadest toward the tip and narrowed at the base, to about 2 in. (5 cm) long and ³/₈ in. (10 mm) wide, the base somewhat clasping the stem and extended for a distance downward. *Flower heads* in dense, often somewhat rounded clusters, woolly, about ³/₁₆ in. (5 mm) high, the flowers yellow but never raylike, the flower head bracts whitish when young, becoming yellowish in age. *Fruits* of small cylindrical achenes, crowned by a single series of slender bristles.
Range and Habitat: Montana to Washington, southward to Texas, New Mexico, and California. Usually found in damp ground throughout New Mexico; 4,000–7,000 ft.
Key Characters: Cottony everlasting is distinguished by the stems and leaves covered with loose, woolly hairs, the small whitish heads without rays flowers, and the leaf bases which extend for a distance down the stem.
Related Species: The similar *G. wrightii* differs in the leaves neither clasping nor extending down the stem at the base and in the loosely arranged flower heads.

338. **Western ironweed**   *Vernonia marginata*   Sunflower family

Coarse, leafy perennial, the stems smooth or nearly so, to 30 in. (75 cm) tall. *Leaves* linear or narrowly lance-shaped, alternate, to about 2 in. (5 cm) long and 1 in. (25 mm) wide, smooth, the margins sometimes with tiny teeth. *Flower heads* in loose clusters, about ³/₈ in. (10 mm) high, rarely more than 25-flowered, the flower head bracts in several series. *Fruits* of slender, ribbed achenes crowned by a ring of slender, often brownish bristles with an outer series of scalelike bristles.
Range and Habitat: Kansas and Colorado, southward to Texas and New Mexico. Mostly found in open plains and prairies in eastern New Mexico; 4,000–5,000 ft.
Key Characters: Western ironweed is distinguished by the smooth, linear or narrowly lance-shaped leaves and the loose clusters of small rayless heads with rose-colored or purplish flowers.

339. **Western throughwort**   *Eupatorium herbaceum*   Sunflower family

Perennial herb, the stems minutely hairy, often rough to the touch, to about 32 in. (80 cm) tall. *Leaves* opposite, more or less triangular in shape, ³/₄–2 in. (2–5 cm) long, often somewhat flattened at the base, with small rounded teeth on the margins. *Flower heads* in dense clusters, white, the flowers tubular, 5-toothed, never raylike, the flower head bracts nearly equal, lance-shaped, dryish, with narrow, longitudinal lines. *Fruits* of cylindric, 5-ribbed achenes crowned by a single series of numerous slender bristles.
Range and Habitat: Colorado to California, southward to New Mexico and Arizona. Mostly found on forested slopes or shaded canyon walls throughout New Mexico; 6,500–9,000 ft.
Key Characters: Western throughwort is distinguished by the triangular, minutely toothed leaves and the small, white, densely clustered flower heads.
Related Species: The less common *E. greggii* differs in having deeply divided leaves with narrow lobes and purplish flower heads.

Gnaphalium chilense

Vernonia marginata

Eupatorium herbaceum

340. **False boneset**   *Kuhnia chlorolepis*   Sunflower family

Branched perennial, the stems minutely hairy, to about 28 in. (70 cm) tall. *Leaves* alternate, very narrow, to 1⅝ in. (4 cm) long, the margins usually without teeth and revolute or rolled under, the blades glandular-dotted. *Flower heads* in open panicles, about ⅜ in. (10 mm) high, the flowers tubular, yellowish white, 5-lobed, none of them raylike, the flower head bracts in several series, linear to narrowly lance-shaped, usually with longitudinal lines. *Fruits* of 10-ribbed achenes crowned by a single series of feathery bristles.

Range and Habitat: Colorado to Texas, New Mexico, Arizona, and Mexico. Mostly found on mesas, open slopes, or openings in pine forests throughout New Mexico; 4,000–7,500 ft.

Key Characters: False boneset is distinguished by the slender, mostly toothless leaves, the yellowish white flowers, and the fruits with feathery bristles at the summit.

341. **Gumweed**   *Grindelia aphanactis*   Sunflower family

Erect biennial, the stems usually branched, smooth, to about 16 in. (40 cm) tall. *Leaves* oblong or broadest above the middle and tapering to the base, to 3¼ in. (8 cm) long and ⅜ in. (10 mm) wide, usually at least 5 times as long as wide, without hairs but with resinous dots, with or without teeth, the basal ones sometimes lobed. *Flower heads* solitary on stems and branches, ⅜–1 in. (10–25 mm) wide, individual flowers tubular and 5-toothed, none of them raylike, the flower head bracts in several series, somewhat resinous, the slender tips loosely spreading outward. *Fruits* of strongly angled and furrowed brownish black achenes crowned by 2 or 3 awns.

Range and Habitat: Colorado and Utah to Texas, New Mexico, and Arizona. Mostly found along roadsides or on open plains or slopes throughout New Mexico; 4,000–7,000 ft.

Key Characters: Gumweed is distinguished by the resinous-dotted leaves, the conspicuous yellowish heads without ray flowers, the resinous flower head bracts, and the strongly angled and furrowed fruits.

342. **Snakeweed**   *Gutierrezia sarothrae*   Sunflower family

Perennial herb, sometimes woody at the base, the stems mostly erect, to about 24 in. (60 cm) tall, with resinous dots on the surface. *Leaves* alternate, often with clusters of smaller leaves in the leaf axils, linear, gland-dotted, to about 2¾ in. (7 cm) long and ⅛ in. (1–3 mm) wide, the margins not toothed. *Flower heads* (including rays) ¼–½ in. (6–12 mm) wide, numerous, with 4–6 yellow rays ⅛–³/₁₆ in. (2–5 mm) long, and with 4 or 5 disk flowers, the flower head bracts yellowish with greenish tips. *Fruits* of hairy achenes crowned with several scales. This plant is a common invader after habitats have been disturbed, as in overgrazing, and often occurs in dense populations.

Range and Habitat: Manitoba and Minnesota to California, southward to Mexico. Common on dry plains and slopes in heavier soils throughout New Mexico; 3,000–8,000 ft.

Key Characters: Snakeweed is distinguished by the slender, gland-dotted leaves, the clusters of axillary leaves, and the numerous small yellow flower heads with only 4–6 rays.

Related Species: Other species of snakeweed flowering at the same time include the similar *G. microcephala* with smaller flower heads having only 1 or 2 ray flowers, and *G. glutinosa* with its annual habit and smooth stems and leaves.

Kuhnia chlorolepis

Grindelia aphanactis

Gutierrezia sarothrae

271

343. **Western goldenrod**   *Solidago sparsiflora*   Sunflower family

Perennial herb, the stems 12–24 in. (30–60 cm) tall, grayish, rough to the touch. *Leaves* alternate, narrowly lance-shaped to elliptic, sparingly toothed or without teeth, 3-nerved, covered with minute hairs. *Flower heads* very numerous, in a pyramidal cluster, arranged on one side of recurved branches, the flowers of both ray and disk types, the rays only about ⅛ in. (3 mm) long, the flower head bracts linear to narrowly lance-shaped. *Fruits* of achenes with minute, stiffish hairs, and crowned at the summit with numerous, very slender, whitish bristles.

Range and Habitat: South Dakota to Texas, New Mexico, and Arizona. Mostly found on brushy slopes, open meadows, or pine forests in the mountains throughout New Mexico; 6,000–8,000 ft.

Key Characters: Western goldenrod is distinguished by the grayish, somewhat roughened stems and the small yellowish flower heads arranged on one side of recurved branches.

Related Species: The similar *S. missouriensis* differs in having leaves with hairs only on the margins.

344. **Dwarf alpine goldenrod**   *Solidago spathulata*   Sunflower family

Dwarf perennial, usually decumbent at the base, the stems 4–6 in. (10–15 cm) tall, often reddish brown, mostly smooth. *Leaves* alternate, stalked, with 1 main vein, smooth on both sides, the basal leaves toothed and rounded or blunt at the tip, the upper stem leaves smaller. *Flower heads* in a narrow, interrupted cluster, yellow, with both ray and disk flowers, the flower head bracts oblong and blunt at the tip. *Fruits* of achenes covered with minute hairs and crowned with numerous, very slender, whitish bristles.

Range and Habitat: British Columbia to Colorado, New Mexico, and Arizona. Mostly found in montane meadows in both subalpine and alpine regions of northern New Mexico; 10,000–13,000 ft.

Key Characters: Dwarf alpine goldenrod is distinguished by the short, stout, decumbent stems and the smooth, toothed leaves having a single main vein.

Related Species: The closely related *S. rigida* differs in having stems at least twice as tall and leaves hairy on both surfaces.

345. **Spinyleaf goldenweed**   *Haplopappus spinulosus*   Sunflower family

Perennial herb, the stems leafy, branching, 8–24 in. (20–60 cm) tall. *Leaves* alternate, sometimes woolly, narrow, broadest above the middle and tapering to the base, to about 2⅜ in. (6 cm) long and ⅜ in. (10 mm) wide, with bristle-tipped teeth or lobes. *Flower heads* (including rays) 1–1¼ in. (25–30 mm) wide, borne at the tips of the branches, the flower head bracts in several series, linear, usually bristle-tipped, greenish in the center, the flowers of both ray and disk types, the rays yellow, 5/16–⅜ in. (8–10 mm) long. *Fruits* of hairy achenes covered with numerous slender, brownish bristles.

Range and Habitat: Southern Canada to Texas, New Mexico, Arizona, and Mexico. Usually found on dry plains, prairies, and open slopes throughout New Mexico; 3,500–6,500 ft.

Key Characters: Spinyleaf goldenweed is distinguished by the leaves with spiny-tipped teeth or lobes, the usually many flowered yellow-rayed flower heads, and the green-centered flower head bracts.

Related Species: Several varieties of this species occur in New Mexico, differing from the typical form in one or more relatively small features. A close relative, *H. gracilis,* differs in being annual or biennial and having a conspicuous green spot at the tip of the flower head bracts.

Solidago sparsiflora

Solidago spathulata

Haplopappus spinulosus

273

346. **Parry goldenweed**   *Haplopappus parryi*   Sunflower family

Perennial herb, the stems erect, to about 20 in. (50 cm) tall, covered with minute hairs. *Leaves* alternate, somewhat spatula-shaped, to about 8 in. (20 cm) long. *Flower heads* often numerous, with both ray and disk flowers, the rays pale yellow, $^3/_{16}$–$^1/_4$ in. (5–8 mm) long, the flower head bracts in about 3 series, oblong, often blunt at the tip. *Fruits* of smooth or sparsely hairy achenes crowned with slender, white or tawny bristles.
Range and Habitat: Wyoming to New Mexico and Arizona. Usually found on wooded slopes in the mountains of New Mexico; 8,000–11,500 ft.
Key Characters: Parry goldenweed is distinguished by the spatula-shaped leaves, the leaf margins without teeth or sometimes sparingly toothed, and the pale yellow flower heads.
Related Species: Another conspicuous species is *H. croceus* which differs in the much larger, solitary flower heads and golden yellow rays, these $^5/_8$–$1^1/_4$ in. (15–30 mm) long.

347. **Arizona lazy-daisy**   *Aphanostephus arizonicus*   Sunflower family

Annual or perennial herb, the stems to 14 in. (35 cm) tall, often branched, both stems and leaves softly pubescent. *Leaves* alternate, linear to spatula-shaped, the lower leaves withering early, to $1^5/_8$ in. (4 cm) long and $^3/_4$ in. (20 mm) wide, narrowed to a petiole at the base, usually with scattered teeth or lobes. *Flower heads* solitary on stems and branches, daisylike, with yellow disk flowers and white ray flowers, the rays white, often tinged with pink or violet on the back, about $^3/_8$ in. (8 mm) long, the flower head bracts hairy, with a greenish or brownish centerline, a pale, membranaceous margin, and a fringe of marginal hairs. *Fruits* of sparsely hairy, distinctly ridged achenes crowned by a series of small bristles.
Range and Habitat: Western Texas to Arizona and Mexico. Mostly found in sandy or silty soils of dry stream beds and washes in central, southern, and western New Mexico; 3,500–5,500 ft.
Key Characters: Arizona lazy-daisy is distinguished by the grayish, softly hairy stems and leaves, the daisylike heads with white rays, these often tinged with pink or violet, and the flower head bracts with greenish centers and pale margins.

348. **Dwarf Townsend's aster**   *Townsendia exscapa*   Sunflower family

Dwarf perennial, often tufted, to about 2 in. (5 cm) tall. *Leaves* alternate, linear to spatula-shaped, crowded, to $2^3/_8$ in. (6 cm) long and $^1/_8$–$^1/_4$ in. (3–6 mm) wide, variously hairy, without teeth. *Flower heads* about 1–$1^1/_2$ in. (25–35 mm) wide (including rays), nestled among the leaves, the disk flowers yellow, the rays white or tinged with pink or purple, $^3/_8$–$^3/_4$ in. (10–20 mm) long, the flower head bracts narrowly lance-shaped, the margins membranaceous and with a fringe of hairs. *Fruits* of somewhat compressed, 2-ribbed, hairy achenes crowned by small scales or barbed bristles.
Range and Habitat: Saskatchewan to Texas, Arizona, and Mexico. Mostly on open slopes and plains throughout New Mexico; 4,500–8,000 ft.
Key Characters: Dwarf Townsend's aster is distinguished by the dwarf habit, the crowded, often matted leaves, and the conspicuous flower heads nestled among the leaves.

Haplopappus parryi

Aphanostephus arizonicus

Townsendia exscapa

349. **Smooth Townsend's aster**   *Townsendia formosa*   Sunflower family

Erect perennial, the stems unbranched, nearly smooth, to 16 in. (40 cm) tall. *Leaves* alternate, the lower ones spatula-shaped, to 3¹/₄ in. (8 cm) long and ³/₄ in. (20 mm) wide, blunt at the tip, smooth on both surfaces but with a fringe of minute hairs on the margins. *Flower heads* solitary on the stems, 1⁵/₈–2 in. (4–5 cm) wide (including rays), daisylike, the disk flowers yellow, the rays purplish or sometimes with white margins, the flower head bracts hairy. *Fruits* of smooth achenes crowned with a few small scales.

Range and Habitat: New Mexico and eastern Arizona. Usually found on open, often damp mountain slopes from central to southwestern New Mexico; 7,000–9,000 ft.

Key Characters: Smooth Townsend's aster is distinguished by the erect habit, the smooth stems and leaves, and the conspicuous flower heads with purplish rays ⁵/₈–1 in. (15–25 mm) long.

Related Species: Two other species which flower at about the same time are *T. incana,* with shorter, pubescent stems and ray flowers ¹/₄–¹/₂ in. (7–12 mm) long, and *T. fendleri,* with spreading stems bearing grayish hairs and shorter, whitish or pinkish rays.

350. **Naked-headed spreading fleabane**   *Erigeron nudiflorus*   Sunflower family

Biennial herb, the stems to 20 in. (50 cm) tall, leafy, terminating in a naked flower head stalk, the base forming elongate, leafy, creeping laterals (stolons) late in the growing season. *Leaves* narrow, tapering to the base from near the tip, spatula-shaped, densely hairy, ³/₈–³/₄ in. (10–20 mm) long, the margins with or without teeth. *Flower heads* (including rays) ¹/₂–1 in. (12–25 mm) wide, with usually 75–100 white or pinkish rays about ³/₁₆–³/₈ in. (5–10 mm) long. *Fruits* of sparsely hairy achenes crowned with an outer series of scales and an inner series of slender bristles. This plant often forms large populations but individually is not among the most conspicuous of our wildflowers.

Range and Habitat: Kansas to Nevada, southward to Texas, New Mexico, and Arizona. Most common on dry slopes, often in sandy soils from north-central and northwestern to south-central and southwestern New Mexico; 5,500–8,000 ft.

Key Characters: Naked-headed spreading fleabane is distinguished by the stout, naked flower head stalks, the whitish or pinkish rays, and the leafy, creeping lateral branches produced after midseason.

Related Species: The closely related spreading fleabane, *E. divergens,* differs in lacking the late-season lateral creeping branches.

351. **Common fleabane**   *Erigeron philadelphicus*   Sunflower family

Biennial herb, the stems to 39 in. (1 m) tall, with short offsets at the base. *Leaves* alternate, the basal ones broadest above the middle and tapering to the base, to 6 in. (15 cm) long and 1¹/₄ in. (30 mm) wide, the margins usually toothed, the upper leaves usually oblong, their bases rounded and often clasping the stems. *Flower heads* (including rays) ⁵/₈–1³/₈ in. (15–35 mm) wide, usually numerous, nodding before opening fully, the flower head bracts linear and often purplish, the rays of the marginal flowers very slender, 150–200 or more, white to pinkish or purplish, ¹/₄–³/₈ in. (5–10 mm) long. *Fruits* of sparsely hairy achenes with a pair of longitudinal ridges and crowned with a single series of threadlike bristles. This plant is a conspicuous member of our summer flora.

Range and Habitat: Much of North America except Mexico. Usually found in open fields and openings in woods in all except eastern New Mexico; 6,000–8,500 ft.

Key Characters: Common fleabane is distinguished by the tall, robust stems with short offset branches at the base, the large basal leaves tapering to the base, and the conspicuous flower heads, with yellow centers and numerous slender white to purplish rays.

Related Species: The widespread but less conspicuous bushy fleabane, *E. bellidiastrum,* differs in having shorter, much-branched stems, mostly linear leaves, and smaller heads with only 30–70 ray flowers.

Townsendia formosa

Erigeron nudiflorus

Erigeron philadelphicus

352. **White aster**   *Leucelene ericoides*   Sunflower family

Low, much-branched perennial, the stems leafy, to about 6 in. (15 cm) long. *Leaves* alternate, linear, fringed on the margins with stiff hairs, to ¹/₂ in. (12 mm) long, bristle-tipped. *Flower heads* small, solitary on slender branches or stems, daisylike, with yellow centers and whitish rays, the rays about ³/₁₆ in. (5 mm) long, the flower head bracts in about 3 series, greenish in the center but pale and membranaceous on the margins. *Fruits* of slender, somewhat compressed achenes crowned by a single series of white bristles.

Range and Habitat: Nebraska to Texas and California. Usually found on dry, often rocky slopes throughout New Mexico; 3,500–7,500 ft.

Key Characters: White aster is distinguished by the dwarf, much-branched habit, the short, very narrow leaves, these fringed and bristle-tipped, and the small, white, daisylike flower heads.

353. **Tahoka daisy**   *Machaeranthera tanacetifolia*   Sunflower family

Annual, the stems often branched, to 20 in. (50 cm) tall, with long, soft hairs and short, glandular hairs. *Leaves* alternate, to about 1⁵/₈ in. (4 cm) long, pinnately lobed, the lobes often again divided into narrow, bristle-tipped segments. *Flower heads* in loose clusters or solitary, daisylike, with yellow disks and 15–25 purple rays ³/₈–⁵/₈ in. (10–15 mm) long, the flower head bracts slender, greenish and spreading somewhat at the tip, and whitish at the base. *Fruits* of compressed achenes, these covered with appressed hairs and crowned with numerous threadlike bristles.

Range and Habitat: Alberta to Texas, New Mexico, Arizona, and Mexico. Usually found in dry, sandy ground throughout New Mexico; 3,500–6,000 ft.

Key Characters: Tahoka daisy is distinguished by the variously dissected leaves with bristle-tipped lobes and the purple flower heads.

Related Species: The related *M. parviflora* differs in having leaves not glandular and merely pinnately lobed without additional lobing, and ray flowers with rays only about ¹/₄ in. (5–6 mm) long.

354. **Streambank aster**   *Machaeranthera aquifolia*   Sunflower family

Erect biennial, the stems to 32 in. (80 cm) tall, hairy but with glands on the flowering branches. *Leaves* alternate, lance-shaped to somewhat spatula-shaped, not stalked, with a few spine-tipped teeth on the margins. *Flower heads* few, about ¹/₂ in. (10–12 mm) high, with yellow disks and purple or violet rays, the flower head bracts very unequal, finely glandular, the upper half and the tip green and spreading. *Fruits* of compressed achenes crowned by numerous threadlike bristles.

Range and Habitat: New Mexico and Arizona. Mostly found along streams, often in gravelly soils in southern and western New Mexico; 5,000–9,000 ft.

Key Characters: Streambank aster is distinguished by the often lance-shaped, sparingly toothed leaves, the conspicuous flower heads with purple or violet rays, and the glandular, spreading flower head bracts.

Related Species: The widespread *M. canescens* differs in having smaller heads, these only about ³/₈ in. (10 mm) high, and leaves with grayish hairs, the lower ones often broadest above the middle and tapering to the base.

Leucelene ericoides

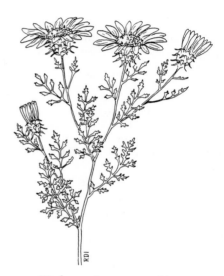

Machaeranthera tanacetifolia

Machaeranthera aquifolia

279

355. **Small-flowered aster**   *Aster pauciflorus*   Sunflower family

Perennial, the stems to 20 in. (50 cm) tall, branching above the middle, mostly smooth. *Leaves* alternate, linear to narrowly spatula-shaped, to about 4 in. (10 cm) long, smooth, the margins without teeth. *Flower heads* in clusters, the supporting branches conspicuously glandular, daisylike, with yellowish disks and white or bluish rays 3/16–1/4 in. (4–6 mm) long, the flower head bracts in 2 or 3 series, narrowly lance-shaped, greenish. *Fruits* of compressed achenes crowned with numerous threadlike bristles.
Range and Habitat: Saskatchewan to New Mexico, Arizona, and Mexico. Found mostly in damp, often saline soils in much of New Mexico; 4,000–7,000 ft.
Key Characters: Small-flowered aster is distinguished by the erect, smooth stems, the narrow, smooth leaves without marginal teeth, and the clusters of small heads with white or bluish rays.
Related Species: Although not closely related, the spiny aster, *A. spinosus,* is also found in saline soils. It differs in having stout spines at the nodes and often scalelike leaves.

356. **Leafy arnica**   *Arnica chamissonis*   Sunflower family

Erect perennial, the stems hairy, to about 3 ft. (1 m) tall. *Leaves* opposite, lance-shaped or broadest above the middle and tapering to the base, sometimes with minute teeth, the stem leaves in 5 or more pairs, not stalked, to about 12 in. (30 cm) long and 3 1/4 in. (8 cm) wide, the lower leaves often sheathing at the base. *Flowering heads* large, somewhat sunflowerlike, the disk flowers yellow, the rays pale yellow, 1/2–3/4 in. (12–20 mm) long, the flower head bracts lance-shaped, covered with soft hairs. *Fruits* of slender, minutely hairy, several-nerved achenes crowned by numerous whitish or brownish, threadlike bristles.
Range and Habitat: Western Canada to New Mexico, Arizona, and California. Mostly found in wet meadows and other moist places in northern New Mexico; 7,500–10,000 ft.
Key Characters: Leafy arnica is distinguished by the opposite leaves, the conspicuous pale yellow heads, and the slender fruits with 5 or more nerves.

357. **Bigelow butterweed**   *Senecio bigelovii*   Sunflower family

Stout perennial, the stems mostly 12–36 in. (30–100 cm) tall, usually smooth. Lower *leaves* 4–8 in. (10–20 cm) long, tapering to the winged base, toothed on the margins, the upper leaves lance-shaped and clasping the stem at the base with enlarged, often toothed lobes. *Flower heads* nodding, 3/8–3/4 in. (10–20 mm) high, yellow, the rays absent, the flower head bracts linear, smooth. *Fruits* of achenes crowned by numerous soft, threadlike bristles.
Range and Habitat: Wyoming to New Mexico and Arizona. Mostly found on grassy slopes or in coniferous forests from northern to south-central and western New Mexico; 7,000–11,000 ft.
Key Characters: Bigelow butterweed is distinguished by the large flower heads without ray flowers, the clasping upper leaves, and tiny bracts at the base of the primary flower head bracts.
Related Species: Other relatively large butterweeds, blooming at about the same time are *S. sanguisorboides,* differing in the mostly pinnately divided leaves, and the flower heads with 8–10 ray flowers.

Aster pauciflorus

Arnica chamissonis

Senecio bigelovii

358. **Groundsel** *Senecio multicapitatus* Sunflower family

Large perennial, the stems several, much branched, leafy, somewhat woody at the base, mostly 16–44 in. (40–110 cm) tall, without hairs. *Leaves* irregularly pinnately divided into linear segments. *Flower heads* numerous, with yellow disk and ray flowers, the flower head bracts about 8, smooth, subtended at the base by an outer series of small bractlets, the rays about 1/4 in. (7 mm) long. *Fruits* of hairy achenes crowned by numerous soft, threadlike bristles.

Range and Habitat: Colorado and Utah to Mexico. Mostly found on plains, in canyons, or in open woods throughout New Mexico; 4,000–7,500 ft.

Key Characters: Groundsel is distinguished by the small heads with yellow rays, the stems and leaves without hairs, and the leaves irregularly divided into narrow segments.

Related Species: The closely related threadleaf groundsel, *S. douglasii,* differs in having woolly stems and leaves and 21 flower head bracts.

359. **Wooton's butterweed** *Senecio wootonii* Sunflower family

Erect perennial, the stems without hairs, 8–20 in. (20–50 cm) tall. Lower *leaves* broadest above the middle and tapering to the base, to about 10 in. (25 cm) long and 1 3/4 in. (45 mm) wide, sometimes with minute teeth, rounded at the apex, upper stem leaves few, narrower than the basal ones, without teeth. *Flower heads* not nodding, mostly 3/8–1/2 in. (10–12 mm) high, with yellow disk flowers and yellow rays, the rays about 3/8 in. (8 mm) long, the flower head bracts about 13. *Fruits* of smooth achenes crowned with numerous soft, threadlike bristles.

Range and Habitat: Colorado to New Mexico, Arizona, and Mexico. Mostly found in dry or damp meadows throughout New Mexico; 6,500–9,500 ft.

Key Characters: Wooton's butterweed is distinguished by the hairless stems and leaves, the basal leaves broadest above the middle, and the flower heads with 6–10 yellow rays and about 13 subtending bracts.

Related Species: Two species growing at about the same elevations are *S. pseudoaureus,* differing in having the lower leaf bases heart-shaped or flattened and the ray flowers about 10–13, and *S. spartioides,* differing in having narrowly linear, toothless leaves, the ray flowers 3/8–1/2 in. (8–12 mm) long, and the fruits with silky hairs.

360. **Western yarrow** *Achillea lanulosa* Sunflower family

Perennial herb, the stems mostly 10–26 in. (25–65 cm) tall. *Leaves* alternate, mostly 2–4 in. (5–10 cm) long, finely divided into very slender spine-tipped segments, strongly aromatic. *Flower heads* (including rays) small, 5/16–3/8 in. (8–10 mm) wide, the flower head bracts blunt at the tip, yellowish brown on the margins, the 2–6 whitish or slightly pinkish rays about 1/8 in. (3–4 mm) long. *Fruits* of flattened, smooth achenes with thickish margins. This plant is valued for its reputed healing properties and has been used by certain Indian tribes in ceremonial functions.

Range and Habitat: Western Canada to New Mexico, California, and Mexico. Scattered or abundant in meadows or in wet ground in the mountains throughout most of New Mexico; 6,000–10,500 ft.

Key Characters: Western yarrow is distinguished by the numerous flower heads arranged in flattish clusters, small whitish or pinkish rays, and the pleasantly aromatic, finely divided leaves. (This plant is sometimes confused with Queen Anne's lace in the carrot family.)

Related Species: A rare species of northern New Mexico, *A. laxiflora,* differs in having the leaves coarsely divided with segments merely acute, not spine-tipped, and the flower branches often drooping.

Senecio multicapitatus

Senecio wootonii

Achillea lanulosa

283

361. **Ox-eye daisy**   *Chrysanthemum leucanthemum*   Sunflower family

Perennial herb, the stems to about 32 in. (80 cm) tall, smooth or with scattered hairs. *Leaves* alternate, the basal ones 1⁵/₈–4 in. (4–10 cm) long, on stalks longer than the blades, toothed or deeply cut, the upper leaves smaller, not stalked, sharply toothed or lobed. *Flower heads* daisylike, with yellow disk flowers and white ray flowers, the rays ³/₈–³/₄ in. (10–20 mm) long, the flower head bracts brownish on the margins, rounded and unevenly toothed at the tip. *Fruits* of achenes having 8–10 longitudinal ribs but without a crown of bristles.
Range and Habitat: Widely established in the United States, introduced from Europe. Locally established at scattered locations in New Mexico, mostly in waste ground; 5,500–7,000 ft.
Key Characters: Ox-eye daisy is distinguished by the leaves with strongly toothed or deeply cut margins and the conspicuous flower hads with yellowish disks and large white rays.

362. **Needleleaf dogweed**   *Dyssodia acerosa*   Sunflower family

Low perennial herb, the stems branched, somewhat woody at the base, to 8 in. (20 cm) tall. *Leaves* opposite or alternate, narrowly linear to needlelike, to ³/₄ in. (20 mm) long, without teeth, often with clusters of smaller leaves in the leaf axils, the leaf surfaces marked with scattered glands. *Flower heads* (including rays) about ³/₈–¹/₂ in. (8–14 mm) wide, both disk and ray flowers yellow, the flower head bracts linear, united nearly to the apex, marked by conspicuous glandular dots. *Fruits* of sparsely hairy achenes crowned by about 20 scales, each divided at the apex into 3 or more bristles.
Range and Habitat: Texas to southern Nevada and Mexico. Scattered or abundant on rocky slopes and hills throughout New Mexico; 3,500–6,500 ft.
Key Characters: Needleleaf dogweed is distinguished by the low habit, the needlelike, glandular leaves, the small yellow flower heads, and the conspicuously glandular flower head bracts.
Related Species: Two other species, blooming at the same time as *D. acerosa* include *D. thurberi* and *D. pentachaeta*. Both differ in having compound leaves pinnately divided into very slender segments and flower heads on slender, elongated stalks. In addition, the scales crowning the achenes of *D. thurberi* are all spine-tipped; those of *D. pentachaeta* are spine-tipped only on the inner series.

363. **Desert marigold**   *Baileya multiradiata*   Sunflower family

Biennial or perennial herb, the stems branching from the base, to about 16 in. (40 cm) long. *Leaves* alternate, densely woolly, to 2 in. (5 cm) long, mostly 3-lobed with each lobe again lobed or toothed, the upper leaves sometimes unlobed. *Flower heads* on stalks 4–12 in. (10–30 cm) long, conspicuous, bright yellow, with both disk and ray flowers, the rays ³/₈–⁵/₈ in. (10–15 mm) long, 7-nerved, often fading in age, the flower head bracts woolly, forming an involucre ³/₈–⁵/₈ in. (10–15 mm) wide. *Fruits* of whitish, striate achenes.
Range and Habitat: Western Texas to Nevada and California, southward to Mexico. Mostly found on dry plains, mesas, roadsides, or sandy arroyos throughout New Mexico; 3,500–6,500 ft.
Key Characters: Desert marigold is distinguished by the stems and leaves with conspicuous whitish, woolly hairs, and the large, bright yellow heads with rays becoming somewhat papery in age.

Chrysanthemum leucanthemum

Dyssodia acerosa

Baileya multiradiata

Perennial herb, the stems to 16 in. (40 cm) tall, sparsely or densely hairy, often twisted. *Leaves* alternate, linear to spatula-shaped, to about 4 in. (10 cm) long and 5/8 in. (15 mm) wide, bearing loose, soft hairs, without teeth but occasionally lobed. *Flower heads* in loose clusters, daisylike, yellow, the rays only 3, about 3/8 in. (7 mm) long, shallowly 3-lobed at the apex, the flower head bracts woolly. *Fruits* of slender, smooth achenes crowned by several lance-shaped, papery scales.

Range and Habitat: New Mexico to southern Utah and northern Arizona. Usually found on dry slopes, often in open woods from east-central to western New Mexico; 5,000–7,500 ft.

Key Characters: Paperdaisy is distinguished by the small, yellow flower heads with persistent, papery rays and the achenes crowned by several unequal scales.

Related Species: Several similar species include *P. tagetina* and its varieties, differing mostly in the leaves and often the stems densely pubescent, and *P. villosa* with rays lobed for about half their length.

Perennial herb, the stems covered with silvery silky hairs, to about 12 in. (30 cm) tall. *Leaves* usually crowded toward the base but a few upper stem leaves usually present, linear to spatula-shaped, to about 4 in. (10 cm) long, usually covered with silvery silky hairs and conspicuously dotted with impressed glands. *Flower heads* on slender stalks, about 3/8 in. (8–10 mm) high, daisylike, with both disk and ray flowers yellow, the rays 1/4–1/2 in. (6–12 mm) long, conspicuously veined, the flower head bracts with silky hairs. *Fruits* of 5-angled, hairy achenes crowned with several lance-shaped scales, each bearing an elongate spine at the apex.

Range and Habitat: New Mexico and eastern Arizona. Mostly found on dry plains and hills in all but eastern New Mexico; 5,000–7,000 ft.

Key Characters: Silvery bitterweed is distinguished by having both basal and upper stem leaves, dense silvery pubescence, and fruits crowned by conspicuous spined scales.

Related Species: Several similar species occur, including *H. acaulis,* differing in having leaves in only a basal rosette and achenes crowned by awnless or short-awned scales, and *H. ivesiana,* differing in having the hairs of the stem spreading and the scales crowning the achenes merely pointed or with short awns.

Perennial herb, the stems usually several, to about 16 in. (40 cm) tall, sparsely hairy. *Leaves* alternate, to about 6 in. (15 cm) long, usually divided into 3–7 slender segments, the basal leaves represented by persistent dead leaf bases, these conspicuously woolly in the axils. *Flower heads* in flat-topped clusters, with both disk and ray flowers, the rays yellow, the flower head bracts in two series, the outer bracts united to about half their length. *Fruits* of 5-angled, hairy achenes crowned at the summit by several acuminate or short-awned scales.

Range and Habitat: Southern Canada to Texas, New Mexico, and Arizona. Often common on rocky slopes throughout New Mexico; 5,000–10,000 ft.

Key Characters: Pinque is distinguished by having both basal and stem leaves, flower heads often many, in flat-topped clusters, and leaves divided into several slender segments.

Related Species: *H. richardsonii* consists of two varieties in our area, the typical variety with stems less than 8 in. (20 cm) tall and no more than 5 flower heads per stem, and var. *floribunda* with stems usually 10–18 in. (25–45 cm) tall and with 6 or more flower heads per stem.

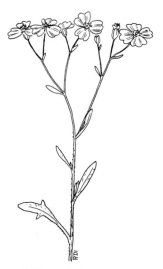

Psilostrophe sparsiflora

Hymenoxys argentea

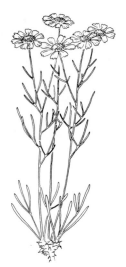

Hymenoxys richardsonii

287

367. Arrowweed — *Pericome caudata* — Sunflower family

Strongly scented perennial, the stems to 3 ft. (1 m) or more tall, with minute hairs. *Leaves* opposite, long-stalked, to about 6 in. (10 cm) long, more or less triangular, with usually pointed, spreading lobes at the base, long-pointed at the tip, glandular-dotted. *Flower heads* in loose clusters, 3/8–1/2 in. (10–12 mm) high, yellow, ray flowers absent, the flower head bracts narrow, in one series, united at the base to form a cup, without hairs. *Fruits* of slender, dark brown achenes crowned by low, irregularly cut scales.

Range and Habitat: Colorado to California, southward to Mexico. Mostly found in canyons, in washes, or on rocky hills in all except eastern New Mexico; 6,000–9,000 ft.

Key Characters: Arrowweed is distinguished by the elongated-triangular leaves with pointed, spreading lobes at the base and the flower heads without rays.

368. Pink palafoxia — *Palafoxia rosea* — Sunflower family

Annual herb, the stems branched, to 2 ft. (60 cm) tall, finely hairy. *Leaves* alternate, lance-shaped or oblong, to about 3 in. (8 cm) long and 1 in. (25 mm) wide, 3-nerved, sometimes with wavy margins. *Flower heads* rose colored, with disk flowers only, the rays absent, the flower head bracts somewhat spatula-shaped, about 8–12, rose colored at the tip, the disk flower corolla lobes about 3/16 in. (4–5 mm) long. *Fruits* of obpyramidal achenes, broadened toward the summit and crowned by conspicuous lance-shaped, membranaceous scales.

Range and Habitat: Wyoming to Texas and New Mexico. Usually found on open plains in eastern New Mexico; 4,500–6,000 ft.

Key Characters: Pink palafoxia is distinguished by the rose-colored flower heads without ray flowers, the disk corollas with corolla lobes conspicuous, about 3/16 in. (4–5 mm) long, and the pink-tipped flower head bracts.

Related Species: A related species, flowering during the latter part of the summer season, the spectacular *P. sphacelata* differs in having conspicuous ray flowers, the rays 3/8–3/4 in. (10–20 mm) long and rose purple.

369. Threadleaf white ragweed — *Hymenopappus filifolius* — Sunflower family

Perennial herb, the stems sparsely to densely woolly, to 16 in. (40 cm) tall. *Leaves* alternate, clustered at the base and with reduced upper leaves, to 5 1/2 in. (14 cm) long, dissected into narrowly linear or threadlike segments. *Flower heads* in open clusters, discoid, yellow, about 3/8–1/2 in. (8–12 mm) high, without ray flowers, the flower head bracts smooth to variously hairy, yellowish to reddish or whitish at the tip. *Fruits* of 4- or 5-angled, hairy achenes crowned by 14–18 narrow scales.

Range and Habitat: Colorado to Texas, New Mexico, and California. Usually found in rocky or sandy areas, often among conifers or oaks, in New Mexico; 5,000–10,000 ft.

Key Characters: Threadleaf white ragweed is distinguished by the considerably dissected leaves with narrowly linear or threadlike lobes, the yellowish or sometimes whitish flower heads without ray flowers, and the hairy fruits crowned by many narrow scales.

Related Species: Similar species include *H. flavescens*, differing in having fruits hairy only on the angles and crowned by 18–20 narrow scales, and *H. tenuifolius*, differing in having flower heads always white and leaves marked by conspicuous glandular dots.

Pericome caudata

Palafoxia rosea

Hymenopappus filifolius

289

370. **Newberry white ragweed**   *Hymenopappus newberryi*   Sunflower family

Perennial herb, the stems sparsely woolly or nearly without hairs, to 24 in. (60 cm) tall. *Leaves* alternate, mostly clustered at the base but a few much reduced upper stem leaves also present, the basal leaves to 10 in. (25 cm) long, much divided into linear, flattened segments, with inconspicuous glandular dots. *Flower heads* 3–8 per stem, about ¹/₂ in. (12–14 mm) high, with yellow disks and white or rarely pink rays, the rays ⁵/₈–³/₄ in. (15–18 mm) long and ³/₈–⁵/₈ in. (10–14 mm) wide, 3-lobed at the tip. *Fruits* of smooth, strongly curved achenes, without a crown of scales at the summit or sometimes with a very minute crown.
Range and Habitat: Colorado and New Mexico. Mostly found in open areas on wooded slopes in northern New Mexico; 7,000–9,000 ft.
Key Characters: Newberry white ragweed is distinguished by the extensively dissected leaves with linear segments, the flower heads with yellow disks and broad, white rays, and the fruits without a crown of scales at the summit.

371. **Firewheel**   *Gaillardia pulchella*   Sunflower family

Annual herb, the stems with appressed hairs, to 20 in. (50 cm) tall. *Leaves* alternate, dispersed along the stem, linear to oblong to spatula-shaped, to 4 in. (10 cm) long, the margins coarsely toothed, wavy-lobed, or without teeth, the surface marked by resinous dots. *Flower heads* very conspicuous, mostly 1–1¹/₂ in. (25–35 mm) wide, with purplish disks and rays with usually yellowish apex and purplish base or occasionally entirely purplish or yellowish, the rays ³/₈–³/₄ in. (10–20 mm) long. *Fruits* of hairy, 5-ribbed achenes crowned by several scales, each tipped by a conspicuous apical awn.
Range and Habitat: Virginia to Nebraska and Colorado, southward to Florida, Texas, and Arizona. Mostly found on open plains and hills throughout New Mexico; 4,000–6,500 ft.
Key Characters: Firewheel is easily recognized, especially when in flower, by the conspicuous yellowish, purplish, or yellowish and purplish ray flowers on a relatively large head, the resinous-dotted leaves, and the 5-ribbed achenes crowned by conspicuous awn-tipped scales.
Related Species: The similar *G. pinnatifida* differs in having leaves pinnately divided into narrow segments and ray flowers mostly yellow throughout except sometimes purplish at the base.

372. **Orange sneezeweed**   *Helenium hoopesii*   Sunflower family

Perennial herb, the stems longitudinally lined, to 3 ft. (1 m) tall, nearly without hairs at maturity. *Leaves* alternate, to about 12 in. (30 cm) long, broadest toward the tip and long-tapering to the usually clasping base, the upper leaves gradually reduced and becoming lance-shaped. *Flower heads* solitary or few, large, stalked, yellow, the disks about ³/₄ in. (2 cm) or more wide, the rays yellow or orange, ⁵/₈–1¹/₄ in. (15–30 mm) long, the flower head bracts linear, in 2 series, becoming reflexed in age. *Fruits* of hairy, 4- or 5-ribbed achenes crowned by lance-shaped, awned scales.
Range and Habitat: Wyoming to Oregon, southward to New Mexico and California. Characteristically found in mountain meadows in all except eastern New Mexico; 7,000–11,000 ft.
Key Characters: Orange sneezeweed is distinguished by the large, yellow to orange flower heads and the large basal leaves, these thickish, broadest above the middle, and tapering to the base.
Related Species: The less common *H. autumnale* differs in having leaf bases extending down the stem and smaller heads with ray flowers only ¹/₄–³/₈ in. (6–10 mm) long.

Hymenopappus newberryi

Gaillardia pulchella

Helenium hoopesii

373. **Woodhouse bahia**   *Bahia woodhousei*   Sunflower family

Low perennial, the stems to about 8 in. (20 cm) tall, covered with appressed hairs. *Leaves* mostly opposite, divided into 3 linear segments, covered with stiff, appressed hairs and with impressed glandular dots. *Flower heads* several, stalked, yellow or straw colored, daisylike, with both disk and ray flowers, the rays about ¹/₈ in. (3 mm) long, the flower head bracts oblong, obtuse at the tip, the outer bracts with 3 nerves. *Fruits* of slender, 4-angled, hairy achenes crowned by lance-shaped, often awn-tipped scales.
Range and Habitat: Colorado to Texas, New Mexico, and Arizona. Usually found on open plains, sometimes in brushy areas or among pinyons in northern and central New Mexico; 4,500–6,000 ft.
Key Characters: Woodhouse bahia is distinguished by the leaves divided into 3 narrow lobes and in opposite arrangement, the small, yellowish heads with short rays, and the hairy fruits.
Related Species: A species with southern distribution is *B. absinthifolia*, this differing in the stems and leaves conspicuously whitish and the ray flowers with rays ¹/₄–¹/₂ in. (6–12 mm) long.

374. **Plains blackfoot**   *Melampodium leucanthum*   Sunflower family

Low perennial herb, the stems to 12 in. (30 cm) high, covered with appressed hairs. *Leaves* opposite, narrow, sometimes broadest toward the apex, mostly without teeth but sometimes with wavy lobes, to 2³/₈ in. (6 cm) long and ¹/₄ in. (7 mm) wide, with appressed hairs. *Flower heads* on long stalks, with yellow disks and white rays, the rays ¹/₄–¹/₂ in. (6–12 mm) long, often purple-veined beneath, the flower head bracts in 2 series, the inner ones somewhat cuplike and each surrounding an achene. *Fruits* of curved achenes.
Range and Habitat: Kansas and Colorado to Texas, New Mexico, and Arizona. Commonly found on dry plains and hills throughout New Mexico; 3,500–6,500 ft.
Key Characters: Plains blackfoot is distinguished by the low, spreading growth habit, the flower heads with conspicuous white rays, these often with purplish veins, and opposite leaves.

375. **Lyrate rubberbush**   *Parthenium lyratum*   Sunflower family

Perennial herb, the stems branching, hairy, to about 16 in. (40 cm) tall. *Leaves* alternate, pinnately lobed with the apical lobe larger than the lateral ones, hairy but not woolly, at least the lower ones stalked. *Flower heads* small, numerous, with both disk and ray flowers but the rays very small and white, the flower head bracts of two kinds, the inner ones mostly wider than long and notched, the outer ones oval and blunt at the tip. *Fruits* of compressed, keeled achenes crowned by a pair of rounded-ovate scales.
Range and Habitat: Western Texas to New Mexico and Mexico. Mostly found on dry slopes and in canyons in southern New Mexico; 3,000–6,000 ft.
Key Characters: Lyrate rubberbush is distinguished by the leaves pinnately lobed and with a large terminal lobe, the flower heads with minute rays, and the flower head bracts conspicuous, the inner ones notched.
Related Species: A larger, shrubby species, *P. incanum,* commonly called mariola, differs in having woody stems, usually densely woolly leaves, and fruits crowned by minute scales.

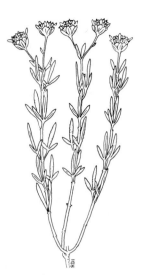

Bahia woodhousei

Melampodium leucanthum

Parthenium lyratum

376. **Engelmann daisy**   *Engelmannia pinnatifida*   Sunflower family

Perennial herb, the stems hairy, to about 28 in. (70 cm) tall. *Leaves* alternate, deeply pinnately lobed, mostly 2–6 in. (5–15 cm) long. *Flower heads* solitary on slender stalks, conspicuous, with yellow disks and large yellow rays, the rays about ³/₈ in. (10 mm) long, the flower head bracts in about 3 series, the inner series with fringed margins. *Fruits* of flattened achenes, these broader toward the summit, with a single rib on each side, and crowned with minute, unequal teeth, or the crown absent.

Range and Habitat: Arkansas to Kansas, southward to Louisiana, Texas, New Mexico, and Arizona. Locally abundant on open hills or plains throughout New Mexico; 5,000–6,500 ft.

Key Characters: Engelmann daisy is distinguished by the pinnately lobed leaves, the daisylike yellow heads with conspicuous ray flowers, and the inner flower head bracts with fringed margins.

377. **Green eyes**   *Berlandiera lyrata*   Sunflower family

Woolly perennial herb, the stems marked with longitudinal lines, to 16 in. (40 cm) tall. *Leaves* alternate, simple, to about 5¹/₂ in. (14 cm) long, pinnately lobed with each lobe often toothed, on stalks sometimes nearly as long as the blades. *Flower heads* large, about ³/₄–1¹/₄ in. (20–30 mm) wide, daisylike, with red or yellowish red disks and showy yellow rays, the rays ³/₈–⁵/₈ in. (10–15 mm) long, with reddish veins, the flower head bracts in 3 series, the outer ones much smaller than the often rounded inner bracts. *Fruits* of flat, finely hairy achenes, each with a ridge on the inner surface.

Range and Habitat: Arkansas and Louisiana to Arizona and Mexico. Mostly found on dry, open plains and hills throughout New Mexico; 4,000–7,000 ft.

Key Characters: Green eyes is distinguished by the somewhat woolly stems and leaves, the pinnately lobed leaves, the large yellow rays with reddish veins, and the conspicuous inner flower head bracts.

378. **Rough ox-eye daisy**   *Heliopsis scabra*   Sunflower family

Coarse perennial, the stems to 3 ft. (1 m) tall, usually rough to the touch. *Leaves* opposite, triangular to lance-shaped, stalked, about 2¹/₂–4 in. (6–10 cm) long, usually rounded to somewhat notched at the base, conspicuously 3-veined, at least the lower ones coarsely toothed, both surfaces rough to the touch. *Flower heads* showy, 1–2 in. (25–50 mm) wide (including the rays), sunflowerlike, with yellowish disk and oblong yellow rays, the rays ⁵/₈–1¹/₄ in. (15–30 mm) long, the flower head bracts nearly equal but the outer ones spreading. *Fruits* of 4-angled achenes crowned at the flattish summit by 2–4 minute teeth.

Range and Habitat: New York to British Columbia, southward to Illinois, Kansas, and New Mexico. Mostly found in open meadows in the mountains of north-central, central, and south-central New Mexico; 7,000–9,000 ft.

Key Characters: Rough ox-eye daisy is distinguished by the coarse, upright habit, the opposite leaves, each with 3 conspicuous veins, and the large heads with both disk and ray flowers yellow.

Engelmannia pinnatifida

Berlandiera lyrata

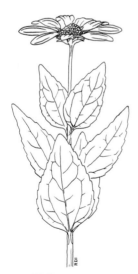

Heliopsis scabra

379. **Rocky Mountain zinnia** *Zinnia grandiflora* Sunflower family

Perennial herb, the stems branching, to about 8 in. (20 cm) tall. *Leaves* opposite, sessile, linear to narrowly lance-shaped or sometimes awl-shaped, to 1 in. (25 mm) long and ⅛ in. (3 mm) wide, the margins without teeth. *Flower heads* (including rays) 1–2 in. (25–50 mm) wide, with small orange disks and bright yellow rays ⅜–¾ in. (10–20 mm) long and about as wide, becoming papery and remaining attached for several months, the flower head bracts rounded at the apex. *Fruits* of compressed, angled achenes. This plant would be useful in desert landscape projects.

Range and Habitat: Texas to Colorado, New Mexico, and Arizona. Locally abundant on dry slopes and plains throughout New Mexico; 3,500–6,500 ft.

Key Characters: Rocky Mountain zinnia is distinguished by its low bushy shape, the bright yellow rays which become papery and persistent, and the dark yellow or orange flower head centers.

Related Species: The similar southern zinnia, *Z. acerosa*, differs in having 1-nerved leaves and white to pale yellow rays.

380. **Threadleaf** *Thelesperma filifolium* Sunflower family

Annual or biennial herb, the stems leafy, to 32 in. (80 cm) tall, smooth. *Leaves* opposite, repeatedly divided into narrowly linear or filiform segments, the segments about as wide as the leaf rachis. *Flower heads* showy, with brownish or purplish disks and yellow rays, the rays about ½ in. (12–15 mm) long, the flower head bracts in 2 series, the inner series united to about the middle or less, the lobes with whitish margins. *Fruits* of slender achenes covered with small bumps and crowned with a pair of short bristles.

Range and Habitat: Nebraska and Colorado to Texas and New Mexico. Mostly found on dry plains and slopes throughout New Mexico; 4,500–7,500 ft.

Key Characters: Threadleaf is distinguished by the slender stems, the narrowly linear or threadlike leaf segments, the flower heads with purplish disks and yellow rays, and the partially united inner flower head bracts.

Related Species: The closely related Hopi tea, *T. megapotamicum*, differs in having stiffish leaves, flower heads without rays but with yellowish disk flowers.

381. **Tickseed** *Coreopsis cardaminefolia* Sunflower family

Annual herb, the stems smooth, leafy, to about 20 in. (50 cm) tall. *Leaves* opposite, without hairs, once or twice pinnately lobed, the upper leaves narrower and sometimes not lobed. *Flower heads* conspicuous, about ¾ in. (20 mm) wide (including the rays), with brownish purple disk flowers and about 8 yellow rays, the inner series of the flower head bracts larger than the outer ones. *Fruits* of elliptic-oblong, broadly winged achenes, sometimes crowned with a pair of minute teeth.

Range and Habitat: Louisiana to Arizona and northern Mexico. Occasionally found on open plains or in meadows, sometimes in low ground, in northern New Mexico; 5,000–7,000 ft.

Key Characters: Tickseed is distinguished by the pinnately lobed leaves, the segments linear, the flower heads with brownish purple disks and yellow rays, and the fruits with broad marginal wings.

Related Species: A similar species, *C. grandiflora*, of southern areas, differs in having yellow disk flowers and orbicular fruits. A species of the northern part of the state, *C. lanceolata*, differs in having unlobed leaves, the leaves rarely with 1 or 2 lobes.

Zinnia grandiflora

Thelesperma filifolium

Coreopsis cardaminefolia

297

382. **Prairie coneflower**   *Ratibida columnifera*   Sunflower family

Erect perennial herb, the stems branched, to 32 in. (80 cm) tall, with stiff, often bristly hairs. *Leaves* alternate, pinnately divided into several narrow segments. *Flower heads* on elongate stalks, with yellowish, columnar disks $^3/_8$–$1^1/_4$ in. (10–35 mm) long and yellow or brownish purple rays $^3/_4$–$1^5/_8$ in. (20–40 mm) long, inserted at the base of the elongated disk, the flower head bracts in 2 series, linear, $^3/_{16}$–$^1/_2$ in. (5–12 mm) long. *Fruits* of compressed, winged achenes crowned by 1 or more small teeth.
Range and Habitat: Minnesota to British Columbia, southward to Tennessee, New Mexico, and Arizona. Sometimes locally abundant on plains and open slopes throughout New Mexico; 5,000–7,500 ft.
Key Characters: Prairie coneflower is distinguished by the pinnately lobed leaves with narrow segments, the elongate columnar disks of the flower heads, and the yellow or brownish purple rays.

383. **Cutleaf coneflower**   *Rudbeckia laciniata*   Sunflower family

Erect perennial herb, the stems smooth, to about 9 ft. (3 m) tall. *Leaves* alternate, smooth or rough to the touch, at least the lower ones long-stalked, the lower leaves usually pinnately compound, with lance-shaped, coarsely toothed segments, the upper leaves often without teeth or lobes. *Flower heads* large, showy, mostly solitary on long stalks, with greenish yellow, conical disks, these to $1^1/_4$ in. (30 mm) high, and yellow rays $1^1/_4$–2 in. (30–50 mm) long, the rays usually reflexed downward, the flower head bracts oblong to lance-shaped, becoming spreading or reflexed. *Fruits* of slender achenes, these about $^1/_4$ in. (5–6 mm) long and with a very short crown or border at the summit.
Range and Habitat: Maine to Saskatchewan, southward to Florida, Texas, and Arizona. Usually found along streams, often in shallow water throughout all but eastern New Mexico; 6,500–9,000 ft.
Key Characters: Cutleaf coneflower is distinguished by the deeply cut leaves, the tall, coarse stems, and the large heads with cone-shaped disks.
Related Species: Black-eyed Susan, *R. hirta,* occurring in the northern part of the state, differs in having roughly hairy stems and often toothed but never lobed leaves.

384. **Crownbeard**   *Verbesina encelioides*   Sunflower family

Weedy annual herb, the stems branching, grayish with appressed hairs, to 24 in. (60 cm) tall. *Leaves* mostly alternate, triangular to ovate, to about 4 in. (10 cm) long, on winged stalks, these usually with earlike appendages at the base, the blades with whitish hairs, especially beneath, the margins usually coarsely toothed. *Flower heads* large, with yellow disks $^5/_8$–$^3/_4$ in. (15–20 mm) wide and yellow rays $^3/_4$–1 in. (20–25 mm) long, the rays conspicuously 3-toothed at the apex, the flower head bracts usually spreading. *Fruits* of strongly compressed, broadly winged achenes crowned by a pair of slender teeth, these occasionally absent.
Range and Habitat: Montana to Texas, New Mexico, and Arizona. Usually found in waste ground, often along roadsides, throughout New Mexico; 3,500–8,000 ft.
Key Characters: Crownbeard is distinguished by large, toothed, often triangular leaves on winged stalks and conspicuous yellow heads with coarsely toothed rays.
Related Species: A very similar variety of this species, var. *exauriculata,* differs only in the absence of earlike appendages at the base of the leaf stalks. Another species, *V. rothrockii,* differs in having leaves without stalks (sessile) and clasping the stem.

298

Ratibida columnifera

Rudbeckia laciniata

Verbesina encelioides

299

385. **Rough mulesears**   *Wyethia scabra*   Sunflower family

Coarse perennial herb, the stems to 20 in. (50 cm) tall, both stems and leaves rough to the touch. *Leaves* alternate, linear to narrowly lance-shaped, to about 6 in. (15 cm) long and rarely to 3/4 in. (20 mm) wide, not stalked, the margins without teeth or else with minute ones. *Flower heads* large, yellow, sunflowerlike, with conspicuous rays, the flower head bracts in 3–5 strongly unequal series, the bracts covered with fine appressed hairs and with slender, spreading tips. *Fruits* of slender, 3- to 5-angled achenes crowned by a series of small teeth.
Range and Habitat: Colorado and Utah to New Mexico and Arizona. Mostly found on open or sometimes wooded slopes in northern New Mexico; 5,000–6,500 ft.
Key Characters: Rough mulesears is distinguished by the leaves and stems very rough to the touch, the linear or lance-shaped, mostly toothless leaves, and the large yellow flower heads.
Related Species: A similar species of higher elevations in the northern part of the state, *W. arizonica,* differs in having softly hairy leaves, the lower ones long-tapering and stalked at the base, and flower head bracts about equal in length.

386. **Parry wood-sunflower**   *Helianthella parryi*   Sunflower family

Perennial herb, the stems to 22 in. (55 cm) tall, covered with appressed hairs. *Leaves* mostly alternate, tapering from above the middle to the base or lance-shaped, to about 5 in. (12 cm) long, without teeth, the upper ones smaller. *Flower heads* solitary or few and stalked, sunflowerlike, with yellow disks and pale yellow rays 1/2–3/4 in. (12–20 mm) long, the flower head bracts narrowly lance-shaped and with a fringe of hairs on the margins. *Fruits* of compressed achenes about 1/4 in. (7 mm) long, covered with appressed hairs and crowned by 2 or more awns or scales.
Range and Habitat: Colorado to New Mexico and Arizona. Usually found in open meadows in the mountains of northern and central New Mexico; 8,000–10,000 ft.
Key Characters: Parry wood-sunflower is distinguished by the leaves mostly long-tapering to the base and the large, showy heads, resembling a small sunflower.
Related Species: The nodding wood-sunflower, *H. quinquenervis,* differs in having leaves mostly lance-shaped and fruits about 3/8 in. (9 mm) long and with a fringe of hairs on the margins.

387. **Annual sunflower**   *Helianthus annuus*   Sunflower family

Coarse, tall annual, the stems to about 9 ft. (3 m) tall, usually stiffly hairy and rough to the touch. *Leaves* mostly alternate, broadly lance-shaped or ovate, coarsely toothed, to 16 in. (40 cm) long, long-stalked, the lower ones somewhat heart-shaped. *Flower heads* large, with both disk and ray flowers, the disks usually 3/4–2 in. (2–5 cm) wide in wild forms (usually much wider in cultivated varieties), purplish brown, the rays yellow, 1–2 in. (25–50 mm) long, the flower head bracts lance-shaped, tapering at the apex, roughly hairy, usually with a fringe of hairs on the margins. *Fruits* of smooth, somewhat compressed achenes, usually crowned by a pair of scales, these often falling quickly. Varieties of this species are widely cultivated all over the world.
Range and Habitat: Scattered or locally abundant throughout much of North America. Typically found in waste ground of various types, often along roadsides or other disturbed areas throughout New Mexico; 3,500–9,000 ft.
Key Characters: Annual sunflower is distinguished by coarse, rough, often tall stems, the mostly ovate, coarsely toothed leaves, the large flower heads with purplish disks and conspicuous yellow rays, and the slender-tipped flower head bracts.
Related Species: A coarse, often tall perennial from large rootstocks, *H. rigidus,* is found in all but western New Mexico; it differs in having winged leaf stalks, much narrower leaf blades, and reddish purple disk flowers.

Wyethia scabra

Helianthella parryi

Helianthus annuus

388. **Prairie sunflower**   *Helianthus petiolaris*   Sunflower family

Annual herb, the stems to about 5 ft. (1.6 m) tall, branching, covered with appressed hairs. *Leaves* mostly alternate, lance-shaped to triangular-ovate, to 6 in. (15 cm) long and 3 in. (8 cm) wide, flattened at the base or often tapering to the elongate leaf stalk, sometimes shallowly toothed on the margins, covered with appressed hairs. *Flower heads* solitary on long stalks, the disks reddish purple, about 3/8–1 in. (10–25 mm) wide, the rays yellow, 5/8–1 in. (15–25 mm) long, the flower head bracts lance-shaped and covered with short stiff hairs. *Fruits* of sparsely hairy achenes.

Range and Habitat: Canada to Texas and New Mexico, also in California and midwestern and eastern states. Usually found on sandy plains or in sandy disturbed ground along roadsides in eastern and northern New Mexico; 4,000–6,500 ft. This plant is a characteristic sight in the Great Plains.

Key Characters: Prairie sunflower is distinguished by the leaves on long stalks, the much-branched stems, and the disks with a small whitish spot in the center.

Related Species: A widespread variety of the prairie sunflower, var. *fallax,* differs in having the stems with appressed and spreading hairs and the heads each subtended by a bract. Another species of sandy ground, *H. niveus,* is characterized by the densely whitish, hairy aspect of its leaves. Species which typically grow in alkaline soils include blueweed, *H. ciliaris,* from central and southern counties, characterized by the smooth bluish green stems and leaves, and rays about 3/8 in. (10 mm) long, and *H. laciniatus,* with pale green, smooth stems and often toothed or lobed leaves.

389. **Lobeleaf goldeneye**   *Viguiera stenoloba*   Sunflower family

Much-branched shrub, the stems leafy, mostly 24–36 in. (60–100 cm) tall. *Leaves* mostly alternate, to 2 3/8 in. (6 cm) long and 1 5/8 in. (4 cm) wide, these divided nearly to the midrib into 3 or more narrow segments, the upper ones often narrow and unlobed. *Flower heads* solitary at the ends of long stalks, with both disk and ray flowers, the disk yellow, 3/8–1/2 in. (8–12 mm) wide, the rays yellow, about 3/8–5/8 in. (8–14 mm) long, the flower head bracts 1/4–3/8 in. (6–9 mm) high, narrowly lance-shaped. *Fruits* of smooth achenes.

Range and Habitat: Western Texas to New Mexico and northern Mexico. Found mostly on rocky slopes in eastern and southern New Mexico; 4,000–6,500 ft.

Key Characters: Lobeleaf goldeneye is distinguished by the shrubby habit and deeply lobed leaves.

390. **Toothleaf goldeneye**   *Viguiera dentata*   Sunflower family

Perennial herb, the stems branched, to 6 ft. (2 m) tall, both stems and leaves with short hairs. *Leaves* opposite below, alternate above, usually ovate, to 6 in. (15 cm) long and 3 in. (8 cm) wide, stalked. *Flower heads* several in loose clusters, on slender, often elongate stalks, with both disk and ray flowers, the disks yellow, about 3/8 in. (10 mm) wide, the rays about 10–12, yellow, 3/8–5/8 in. (8–15 mm) long, the flower head bracts linear at the tip. *Fruits* of achenes covered with appressed hairs and crowned by a pair of slender awns or 4 fringed scales.

Range and Habitat: Western Texas to Arizona and Mexico. Usually found in canyons or on open, dry slopes, often in wooded areas in south-central and western New Mexico; 5,000–7,000 ft.

Key Characters: Toothleaf goldeneye is distinguished by the ovate, coarsely toothed leaves on stalks at least 3/8 in. (10 mm) long.

Related Species: Several other species of goldeneye flower in the summer months. These include *V. cordifolia,* differing in having leaves 3-nerved and rounded or heart-shaped at the base, the flower heads with only 6–8 rays, *V. multiflora,* differing in having lance-shaped leaves, and *V. annua,* differing in having linear to narrowly lance-shaped leaves, these strongly rolled under on the margins.

Helianthus petiolaris

Viguiera stenoloba

Viguiera dentata

Index

Index listings refer to entry numbers.
*Also shown in color section.

Aquilegia triternata, 56
Arenaria aculeata, 54
Arenaria obtusiloba, 54
Arenaria rubella, 54
*Argemone polyanthemos, 69
Argemone squarrosa, 69
Arizona blue-eyed grass, 23
Arizona kittentails, 291
Arizona honeysuckle, 313
Arizona lazy-daisy, 347
Arizona nightshade, 278
Arizona peavine, 144
Arizona poppy, 162
Arizona valerian, 314
Arnica, 356
Arnica chamissonis, 356
Arrowweed, 367
Asclepias asperula, 224
Asclepias brachystephana, 227
Asclepias macrotis, 224
Asclepias pumila, 226
Asclepias quinquedentata, 224
Ascelpias speciosa, 227
Asclepias subverticillata, 226
*Asclepias tuberosa, 225
Asclepias verticillata, 226
Aster, 352
Aster pauciflorus, 355
Aster spinosus, 355
Astragalus allochrous, 142
Astragalus brandegei, 137
Astragalus crassicarpus, 140
Astragalus flexuosus, 138
Astragalus giganteus, 138
Astragalus humistratus, 137
Astragalus lotiflorus, 139
Astragalus mollissimus, 141
Astragalus wootonii, 139
Avens, 107

Bahia, 373
Bahia absinthifoia, 373
Bahia woodhousei, 373
*Baileya multiradiata, 363
Baneberry, 57
Barberry, 68
Barberry family, 68
Barrel cactus, 188
Basketflower, 335
Bean, 126
Beardtongue, 284
Bedstraw, 305
Bee-plant, 83
Berberis fremontii, 68
Berlandiera lyrata, 377

Berula erecta, 204
Besseya alpina, 292
Besseya arizonica, 291
Besseya plantaginea, 291
Bigbract vervain, 259
Bigelow butterweed, 357
Bigelow leatherflower, 62
Big-flowered collomia, 240
Big golden-pea, 123
Bigleaf plantain, 304
Bindweed heliotrope, 245
Bistort, 36
Bittercress, 71
Bitterroot, 47
Bitterweed, 363
Blackbead elder, 309
Black-eyed susan, 383
Blackfoot, 374
Black indigobush, 128
Black nightshade, 279
Bladderpod, 81, 155
Bluebell family, 318
Bluebell lobelia, 318
Blue-eyed grass, 22
Blue-flowered wolfberry, 273
Blue toadflax, 282
Bluets, 307
Blueweed, 388
Boerhaavia coccinea, 46
Boerhaavia gracillima, 46
Bog orchid, 31
Bog primrose, 215
Borage family, 244
Brandegee alpine-clover, 133
Brook cinquefoil, 104
Brooklime, 289
Broomrape family, 302
Brownfoot, 331
Buckbrush, 166
Buckhorn plantain, 304
Buckthorn family, 166
Buckwheat family, 35
Buffalo bur, 276
Buffalo gourd, 317
Bundleflower, 116
Bush morning-glory, 230
Bushy fleabane, 351
Butter-and-eggs, 282
Buttercup, 67
Buttercup family, 55
Butterflyweed, 225
Butterweed, 357

Cactus family, 182
Caesalpinia gilliesii, 120

Corydalis, 70
Corydalis aurea, 70
Corydalis caseana, 70
Coryphantha vivipara, 189
Cottony everlasting, 337
Cowania stansburiana, 110
Cow-parsnip, 200
Coyote tobacco, 272
Crag lily, 14
Crandall's beardtongue, 284
Creeping vervain, 255
Creeping wintergreen, 207
Cress, 78
Crowfoot, 65
Crownbeard, 384
Cryptantha flavoculata, 252
Cryptantha jamesii, 252
Cucurbita digitata, 317
Cucurbita foetidissima, 168
Curled mallow, 168
Currant, 98
Cuscuta megalocarpa, 228
Cuscuta umbellata, 228
Cushion phlox, 238
Cutleaf coneflower, 383
Cutleaf germander, 265
Cutleaf globeberry, 315
Cutleaf gourd, 317
Cynoglossum officinale, 247
Cypripedium calceolus, 25

Daisy, 353
Dalea aurea, 130
Dalea formosa, 128
Dalea frutescens, 128
Dalea greggii, 128
Dalea jamesii, 130
Dalea lanata, 129
Dalea terminalis, 129
Dalmation toadflax, 282
Dandelion, 325
Dasylirion leiophyllum, 5
Dasylirion wheeleri, 5
Datura meteloides, 271
Datura stramonium, 271
Davidson sage, 263
Dayflower, 1
Death camas, 8
Deer brush, 166
Deer's ears, 219
Deervetch, 136
Delphinium nelsonii, 61
Delphinium novomexicanum, 61
Delphinium robustum, 60
Delphinium sapellonis, 60

Delphinium tenuisectum, 61
Desert cancerroot, 302
Desert crowfoot, 65
Desert dandelion, 330
Desert four-o'clock, 37, 39
Desert honeysuckle, 303
Desert innocence, 308
Desert phlox, 238
Desert marigold, 363
Desert plume, 73
Desert snowberry, 312
Desert tobacco, 272
Desert willow, 300
Desmanthus illinoensis, 116
Desmanthus obtusus, 116
Devil's claw, 112
Dithyrea wislizenii, 79
Dock, 35
Dodecatheon ellisiae, 213
Dodecatheon pulchellum, 213
Dogbane family, 222
Dogweed, 362
Dogwood family, 206
Draba aurea, 72
Draba streptocarpa, 72
Drummond clematis, 63
Dune broom, 152
Dwarf alpine-clover, 133
Dwarf alpine goldenrod, 344
Dwarf cornel, 206
Dwarf-dandelion, 329
Dwarf milkweed, 226
Dwarf rattlesnake plantain, 28
Dwarf Townsend's aster, 348
Dwarf yellow evening primrose, 195
Dyssodia acerosa, 362
Dyssodia pentachaeta, 362
Dyssodia thurberi, 362

Echinocactus horizonthalionus, 187
Echinocactus texensis, 187
Echinocereus enneacanthus, 185
Echinocereus fasciculatus, 185
Echinocereus fendleri, 186
Echinocereus reichenbachii, 186
Echinocereus triglochidiatus, 185
Echinocereus viridiflorus, 184
Echinopepon wrightii, 136
Elder, 300
Elephanthead, 294
Elk's lip, 58
Engelmann daisy, 376
Engelmannia pinnatifida, 376
Epilobium angustifolium, 194
Epipactis gigantea, 29